MEMORIES
Mostly True
Growing Up in the 40s & Fabulous 50s

DON FRIESEN

outskirtspress
DENVER, COLORADO

Contents

Foreword

AS A LIFELONG friend and public-school classmate of the author, I am delighted to have had the opportunity to read his manuscript before publication. My nostalgia about, and appreciation for, my childhood and youth (in my case from the female perspective) knows no bounds. I always jokingly say that the best decisions I ever made in my life were choosing to be born into my family, and choosing a family living in Thomas, Oklahoma, in the 1940s and '50s.

I have dabbled in publishing anecdotes that somewhat parallel the stories told in this book, but have never seriously worked at putting together a comprehensive, organized, thoughtful book such as this one. Nor is it likely I could do it as well.

What joy it is to have *Memories: Mostly True* supplement my collection of mostly one-page articles published in obscure magazines or in letters and booklets sent to my family members from time to time as I share with them my pursuit of our family genealogy. As a college professor, my published writing has been primarily focused on research relating to my field of study. I enjoyed that work. However, such writing cannot convey the warmth of human experience which involves both the heart and the head invoked in writing such as *Memories: Mostly True*.

I remember much that is related here. If you grew up in small-town Middle America at the same time, I think you, too, will find much to touch your heart and mind.

Karen McKellips, Ed.D
Professor Emerita
Cameron University
Lawton, Oklahoma

"The true meaning of life is to plant trees,
under whose shade you do not expect to sit."

Nelson Henderson

Introduction

"There is a history in all men's lives." – Shakespeare

ONCE UPON A time, someone said, "Sing your song, dance your dance, and tell your tale." I can't sing or dance, but the following is my attempt at telling my tale. My *once upon a time* is set in the '40s and fabulous '50s, a time when our world was being redefined by a post-war economic boom that was just starting to trickle into Custer County — a remarkable period in America's passage. I have written this memoir topically, not chronologically, hoping that C.S. Lewis was right when he said, "Who cannot bear such a story, will not see at once what they are in for."

This project started out as an effort to put some history down on paper for my family, especially my daughters and grandchildren (occasional references to this effect are made throughout the text). But as my writing progressed, my literary journey grew into something even larger in scope. It helped me to reconnect with old school friends who have aided my memory and provided additional information for the book. I have found Beatrix Potter to be correct when she said, "There is something delicious about writing those first few words of a story. You can never quite tell where they will take you."

For all my bluster, I have done my best to tell truthful stories, or at least a combination of fact and a tug of nostalgia, with the characters being completely non-fictitious. Or, to quote Huckleberry Finn, everything written in this document *is the truth, mainly*, even though there is a touch of embellishment periodically. However, Mark Twain also said, "The man has not yet been born who could write the truth about himself." But, like a piece of folklore, the details may change, but the core remains. No attempt has been made to protect the innocent or guilty, although I did disguise a person or two. I will attempt to share my luminous experiences as faithfully as I am able before the color fades any further. John Ford famously said, "When you had to choose between history and legend, print the legend." I have chosen mostly to write about the former. Lacking scholarly prose, I should have gone ahead and kissed the Blarney Stone while in Ireland for the gift of eloquence. I didn't (the local delinquents sneak up the castle at night and pee on it, and, furthermore, I am not superstitious), so as it says in the song "Kennesaw Line," "I can only tell you what I have seen and heard. Listen to the pictures forever etched in my mind."

Frank McCourt wrote in *Angela's Ashes* that "the popular thought seems to be that the happy childhood is a myth and that some childhoods are so pitiable you have to either laugh or cry. People everywhere brag and whimper about the woes of their early years." My life was not *Camelot*, but despite our austerities, life for me was innocent and safe. Most of our mothers were always home when school was dismissed, so we were never latchkey children. In fact, we had never even heard of the word. Plus, we did not even have a house key of which I ever knew. I was blissfully unaware of any sense of hardship, or any Dickensian *Oliver Twist* orphans, or a *Cratchit* family. I guess this was because everyone else was in the same economic boat, having just emerged from the Great Depression, and it wasn't a yacht. We were children of parents, very parochial, who lived under the continuing influence of the terrible Dust Bowl era, its attendant poverty, and memories of WWII. I'm sure there must have been poverty and welfare, but I don't recall any of it. I don't remember being bereft of anything, but there were lots of elbow and knee patches, homemade shirts, and rehemmed dresses, but at least we did not have to store acorns for the winter or endure home haircuts. But, Herodotus, father of history, did say, "Poverty is always a guest." I suppose people mostly just lived from paycheck to paycheck, and I don't remember anyone ever talking about investments or retirement. Thankfully, I think most of us were pretty much sheltered from the darker side of life.

There was little difference between those who had modest or low incomes; there was little sense of a class system during this time; no one, even the more opulent, could trace their genealogy back to the *Mayflower*; there were no patrician accents to be heard in town; and very few, if any, who could have made Scrooge McDuck look like a pauper. Even the most perfect-looking clan probably sailed through a rough patch on occasion. If there was a pecking order among the upper echelons it wasn't always clear, but it was fair to say that the local teachers, physicians, some landowners, and men of the cloth were somewhere at the top of the social ladder, but no *Croesus*. Perhaps we were blessed to have come from such modest beginnings because F. Scott Fitzgerald said, "The wealthy have problems that the poor know not of." Most adolescents and teenagers were no respecters of wealth, and up to a certain age kids are more or less pretty much egalitarian anyway. Karen Sweeney McKellips did tell me a sad story about spending the night with a classmate of ours. All they had for supper was a bowl of oatmeal and a glass of water. The next day she related this to her dad. He told her that her friend's father had only sporadic income as a laborer. Hamlet said, "Who would such a burden bear, but the dread of something worse." And I don't remember any turbulent family dramas that might have condemned them to a life curled up in the back ward of a mental institution. Perhaps one or two should have been. Almost all of us who were born and raised in the 1940s and '50s managed to bootstrap ourselves up a notch or two. "Nothing has more strength than dire necessity," said Euripides. There is an old Jewish saying that one is as wealthy as one is content. Thankfully, we were content or did not know that we were not content.

If you're writing a history of anything, it makes sense to start that history with the date the thing was first built, gestated, invented, born, or otherwise hurled into existence. I can't remember much of anything prior to age four or five, so this tale will begin with my entrance into the first grade and end at my high school graduation. Aldous Huxley said, "Every man's memory is his private literature." Oscar Wilde wrote, "Memory is the diary we all carry about us."

Even though these pages ache for more appropriate words, read on and enjoy my private literature as my diary has too long been without pen. As a story of images, memories, and emotions of childhood, this memoir does not grapple with family issues in a way readers find compelling. It is more or less a sort of haphazard chronicle in which only striking incidents and occurrences are brought out, and lengthy and wearisome details are avoided. It is just tales of an adventurous childhood — a childhood without electronic toys — a childhood that I remember in black and white — a book of memories.

For the most part, boyhood showed me a good time, and all the events depicted in this memoir certainly added spice and variety to my childhood. Life was simple, moved slowly, and was so mellow. I have many fond and cherished memories of life in a benevolent home, but the real fun and remembrances come from school days. The business of life is the acquisition of memories, and as I take you back to where my great store of memories remain, understand that it is not my intent to idealize the past and sentimentalize childhood, but to help you learn about many of my experiences and my voyage of discovery so that you will gain more of an understanding and appreciation for the culture and history of the 1940s and fabulous '50s. I have attempted to substantiate and bring to life some of this history as I resurrect distant memories to be commemorated for posterity.

Out of the hundreds of isolated events of my childhood, the stories here stand out in my mind, and memories continue to march through my consciousness, connecting me to parts of myself long buried but still alive. These stories will go a long way in letting you know who your father was. Most of the stories are obviously from my formative childhood years. Some of them are indirect experiences from other people's stories of which I knew. Shelley's poem "Ozymandias" implies that everyone and everything will ultimately be forgotten: "Nothing beside remains . . ." While visiting Eisenhower in North Africa during WWII, Churchill said to his physician, "We are only specks of dust that have settled in the night on the map of the world." This is why it is important to write it down so that it does not escape into the mist of history. As we get older, those treasured memories remain very important, but I think all of us know that they fade away and calcify as time goes on. Written records are more reliable than oral traditions. A. Whitney Brown said, "The past actually happened but history is only what someone wrote down." The passing of history by word of mouth peters out too quickly, and a story changes every time you say it out loud. Someone has said that the past disintegrates if you never mention it. Make it permanent like a birthmark because we are all just shadows on the wall of time. As Solomon said, "The wise man, like the fool, will not be long remembered." I was not privileged to have a written account of my parents' lives. However, I am grateful that they did leave me and my brothers a rich collection of family photos. This is a memoir and not a history book, although I have recorded a lot of history. People normally think of history as one catastrophe after another — war, outrage, and human pain. But history is also the narratives of grace, and recounting of moments when someone did something good, bestowed a gift, or gave something beyond what was required. I hope I have written more of the latter than the former. The theme of the poem "Ithaka" by C.P. Cavafy is that the journey is more important than the destination. This is the story of my journey.

I was born in 1939. The other big event of that year was the outbreak of the Second World War, but for the moment that did not affect me. In 1939, nylon shows promise as a more sheer and elegant material for women's hosiery than silk, Sigmund Freud dies, Enrico Fermi reports that atoms have been split to release 200 million volts of energy, *The Wonderful Wizard of Oz* premiers starring Judy Garland as Dorothy, *Gone with the Wind* opens in Atlanta, John Steinbeck's *The Grapes of Wrath* is published, and John Wayne gets his first big starring role in *Stagecoach*. The Supreme Court was 100 percent white and male, as was the United States Senate.

The time I am writing about was probably better than the present day in some ways and worse in some ways. As you read through this document you can decide for yourself. I hope this memoir will be like a good movie: a little spectacle, some laughs, a sense of reflection, and a modicum of literary merit. It is my expectation that I have succeeded in pleasantly telling you who I once was, and what strange, unusual, funny, bizarre, real-life golden-nugget anecdotes, and weird enterprises my friends and I sometimes engaged in. I will write about school legends . . . the way people know things about other people they weren't at school with, or if they were at school at some later time. *Memories: Mostly True,* covers an enormous and exuberant cast of characters. I will write stories about my siblings, classmates, friends, teachers, tricks played on teachers, naughtiness, and things that float down from generation to generation.

Here is Thomas, Oklahoma, *a town I loved so well*, and my colorful and unforgettable boyhood, written from memory that reflects both my memory's limitations and my imagination's proddings. A story of love reciprocated.

CHAPTER 1

Thomas

"No man," said one of the Greeks, *"loves his city because it is great, but because it is his."*

NAPOLEON SAID THAT geography is destiny. The Duke of Wellington said that timing is everything. Were these guys thinking of me and my world during the 1940s and '50s? The value of geography cannot be denied. The conclusion of where people live does make a difference. So, I guess I should be thankful that Daniel Boone made it through the Cumberland Gap, making him the first realtor through that region. My church-centered hometown of Thomas was the quintessential small American town, a lot like Garrison Keillor's fictional town of Lake Wobegon — "The town that time forgot, that the decades cannot improve." Thomas was located in rural West-central Oklahoma, where the land was punctuated by tidy little towns — a wide expanse of farmland that encompassed golden yellow wheat fields that rippled in the wind, sending waves as far as the eye could see, glistening pastures gently rolling and dipping over the bucolic hills of Custer County, where grain elevators dotted the horizon and with a landscape roaming with cows and horses. It was something like out of *Mayberry* or a serene Norman Rockwell painting when things were exactly as they seemed to be and all things appeared untarnished, uncomplicated, and wholesome. When you are born and raised in a place like this, you think you live at the epicenter of the solar system. As I would later learn, being raised in Thomas was an insulated, fun, and totally absorbing experience. Thomas was probably no different from any other small town; it is probably only my imagination that makes it seem different. "Old" Thomas started at the time the Cheyenne and Arapaho country was opened to white settlement, about April 19, 1892. The prominent chiefs around Thomas were Standing Turtle, Turkey Leg, Old Crow, Howling Crane, Yellow Bull, Brave Bear, Little Chief, and Mad Wolf. It wasn't until 1924 that American Indians became US citizens. The Cheyenne Arapaho Indians gave historical significance to my hometown.

A post office was established in 1894, and a blacksmith was the first business to start up. Thomas was much like any other small town. It had two main streets, one called Main and the other Broadway . . . no traffic lights. There were no architectural glories or towers in the town's mostly two-story buildings with their tall pressed tin ceilings, but they served their purpose. There was a large dip on Broadway (Hwy 33), one block west of Main, so that water would drain when it rained. People hated this dip because they had to slow down when crossing it. Strangers would always hit it too fast, and you could hear a loud metal-against-concrete sound all over town. Ray Cain reports that he once saw a Corvair, driven by a stranger of course, lose its transaxle and engine from hitting this dip too fast. He thinks maybe they had just had some repair or replacement work and just didn't get it properly secured. Your mother even remembers this dip from their family trips to Altus from Pioneer to visit her Grandmother Plew long before she ever knew me.

At the end of Main, north of town center, perched like the Parthenon on its hill, was the school on its hill presiding over the town. It was not a grand neo-Gothic building like Yale or Princeton that oozed knowledge, no dreaming spires like Oxford, nor did it have crenellated walls that dripped with history, but it was rife with ivy which gave it a certain scholarly appearance and looked like Westminster Abbey to me. Until it was razed for a new building, leaving an architectural void, it stirred nostalgia in the breasts of THS alumni. I am so glad that this edifice was not a hideous, characterless, anonymous, inartistic glass, and concrete monolith that would have had as much architectural appeal as an outhouse. It was proportionate, and with its hallowed portals it just had a beauty of order and charm about it. There was a time when architecture was as much about beauty as function. This two-story temple of learning contained grades one through twelve. In addition to the school building, the campus consisted of a band building, a lunch-room building, the stadium, Vo Ag building, and the bus shed. The main building was built in 1922. The landscaping was done by the father of one of my classmates who later became the longtime superintendent, Kenneth Sweeney. This building with the circle drive landscaping had an almost absurdly pretty aesthetic quality resting upon the prominence of this hill.

The 1950s was a time before Walmart wiped out most of the small downtowns. Our downtown that was a four-block (one block each direction from town center) stretch of retail tranquility. Thomas had two doctors, a dentist, a lawyer, Indian chief, two drugstores, two barbershops, three grocery stores, one hardware, two cafes, a blacksmith, lumberyard, two grain elevators with the largest grain storage capacity between Enid and Amarillo, TX, a Watkins variety store, and a TG&Y (five and dime). This store was often referred to as Turtles, Girdles, and Yo-yos. Also, Toys, Games and Yoyos and other irreverent monikers. Actually, the TG&Y name came from the initials of its founders—Rawdon Tomlinson, Enoch Gosselin, and Raymond Young. We also had a dry-goods store, one pool hall, a skating rink, and four gas stations (Texaco, Mobil, Sinclair, and Gulf). There were two shoe cobblers, a beer joint, an ice plant, Ford dealership, hatchery, John Deere dealership, a newspaper, two produces, a hatchery (chickens), hospital, a town drunk, our share of less cerebral eccentric misfits, a few who lived on the rusty razor's edge, a junkman, a few old coots, some idlers, a telephone office with a live operator, the Frisco and Santa Fe railroads. But no candlestick maker and no statues. There was no village idiot. We each took turns. We also had a bootlegger. They were like doctors and lawyers. Every town had one. We had lots of churches and a cemetery where people named Combs, Christensen, Roof, Hooper, Hutchinson, Jones, Sweeney, Schantz, Johnson, Ames, Ray, Perkins, Richardson, Ryan, Self, McNeil, Kippenberger, and others lay shoulder to shoulder.

There were no Confederate flags flying anywhere that I can remember. Although, we did have one of the Southern rites known as initialization with such names as J.E., K.O., L.G., J.H., P.L., R.L., K.D., J.C., H.L., C.L., R.E., C.R., G.L., and A.L. Girls were never known by their initials, but many were known by another Southern rite, middle names, i.e., Billie Sue, Mary Lee, Dorothy Sue, Velma Lee, Norma Gail, Norma Fay, Mary Lou, Vickie Jean, Ann Marie, Connie Jean, Jimmie Rae, Joy Carol, Mary Belle, Joi Dell, Millie Mae, Emma Ruth, Zeta Beth, Ila Lee, Etta Mae, Mabel Joy, Dorothy Dean, Linda Lou, Letha Gail, Janice Kay, and Norma Jean. Then there are the old-time names that no one uses anymore: Hester, Cleo, Bessie, Louise, Beulah, Mildred, Opal, Bernice, Arda, Oveta, Velma, Imogene, Cleta, Gladyce, Viola, Myrtle, Zella, Lucille, Alverta, Eunice, Alta, Anabele, Nellie, Maggie, Lillie, Ruby, Thelma, Fern, Maud, Maudine, Audine, Elsie, Mayme, Bertha, etc.

Oh, that lonesome and comforting sound of the old whistle of the Frisco Doodlebug passenger train trundling into town that resonated deeply within me. The whistle starts softly, like a lullaby, but crescendos as the train nears the depot. This is a sound that I will never forget on a lazy summer afternoon competing with the shrill choral sound of the locusts radiating similar feelings as they kept me company. Some referred to locust sound as summertime music. They were really cicadas. Karen Sweeney McKellips has written, "In the summer, locusts lived in the trees and made a marvelous noise that I still associate with homemade ice cream, swimming in the river and polio naps. Your mother wouldn't let you listen to the radio during your polio nap so the locusts' music had to do." I always thought that the cicadas sounded a lot like a rattlesnake's rattle. I would also include dove cooing, cricket serenading, and frog croaking as summertime music.

Jackie rode the Doodlebug to Enid with Jerry Mitchell on their way to Jerry's home in Tulsa. I don't remember ever riding it, but on occasion I would be at or near the depot when it would come to a hissing stop at the station. According to Andy Smith, he and some of his buddies used to hitch free rides on the Doodlebug to Clinton to go to the movies. Back to Jerry Mitchell. He had an older brother, Bobby, who died of polio or diphtheria at the age of 12. Jackie thinks it was polio, but I think it was diphtheria. This was the first and only friend I had during my adolescent and teenage years to die. I remember it being very sad and difficult. I had never seen that much sadness before. Death was new to me, an uncomfortable event that I did not understand.

The first time I ever saw images that were probably somewhat inappropriate for a prepubescent boy was at Harry Wanzer's blacksmith shop. I went in there once with Dad to get some plow shears built up with stoodite, a hardening alloy, and saw these somewhat prurient girlie pinup calendars prominently displayed wherever there was an available space on the wall. They were really lithographs, not photos. Nevertheless, I studied them surreptitiously as I gave them scrupulous examination as they burned into my retinas like neon. It was enough to stun me into silence. The three grocery stores were IGA, Farmers Union, and Brown's Grocery. There was a bench in front of Brown's Grocery for the "spit and whittle" club, of which my maternal Grandpa McCracken was a charter member, and we still had hitching posts just across the street west from the Farmers Union store for the Amish to use when they came to town on Saturday and my Grandpa McCracken, who always rode a horse. Grandpa told me he saw a hanging while driving a wagon hooked to a team of horses when he was sixteen. This would have been in 1896. He drove down into a draw and saw this man hanging from a tree. "It scared me and I got out of there fast," he said. This happened near Gainesville, Texas.

The gym in the Community Building was where we played most of our high school basketball games and was also used as a skating rink. There was a jail in the rear of the building that on rare occasions held a prisoner for a day or two and was never guarded by anyone that I ever knew. It was considered a real coup to sneak up and get a peek at a real crook through the window! However, we never smuggled any small comforts through the jail window to any occupants as Tom Sawyer did. The Community Building is on the National Register of Historic Places. It was built in 1939 by the Works Progress Administration.

At the ice plant, you could buy ice in just about any size chunk you wanted. The most popular sizes were 25, 50, 75, and 100 pounds. Ice was delivered to homes that had well-insulated wooden iceboxes once or twice a week. Most people didn't have the luxury of an electric refrigerator at this time. If the iceman did not have a block of ice already cut to the size you wanted, he would cut it in his white delivery pickup before bringing it into the house. He would stab the ice where it had been scored with his pick as expertly as a diamond cutter. He seemed to know exactly where to aim the ice pick to create a wholesale seizure of fractures and crystalline shrapnel. The ice would crack with a sound like breaking tree branches. It was beautiful to watch. Every home had an ice card that was placed in a front window. One would turn the card so that the amount you wanted was on top. The iceman wore a thick leather apron on his back so that he could carry the ice with his tongs in a way that kept him dry and to let his back carry most of the weight. The ice would be placed in the top compartment of the icebox and it would keep perishables from spoiling. The water from the melt would trickle down through a hole into a pan under the icebox, and woe unto those assigned the chore of keeping this pan empty who failed to do so. Ice cost one cent a pound at the ice house and two cents a pound if delivered to one's home. Ross Pickens was the last person to deliver ice in Thomas. Carl Halle and Frank Brundage were other deliverymen.

Richard, Jackie, and I were born on the McNeil farm six miles southeast of town. My tonsils were removed in the old hospital. I remember Dr. Ryan telling me to hold my arm up and to count backwards, beginning at 10, then the nurse put an ether mask over my face and I don't think I made it to zero.

CHAPTER 2

The Drugstore

"In its prime the drugstore was a warm, clean place where one could idle respectfully." – New Yorker

LIKE MOST AMERICAN towns, Thomas had a corner drugstore. Because of its familiarity, it was like the town's favorite uncle. As you will read later, the 1950s were considered the golden age of the car, pop music, and television. The 1950s are also considered the golden age of the corner drugstore. In the '50s the drugstores were identified with every small town across the nation — each town having one or more of these drugstores. They were a part of the American experience.

Regardless of the season, weather, or impending nuclear catastrophe, I would end up at the drugstore after dinner and completed homework each evening during my high school years, and more times than not, I would begin my evening with a chocolate milkshake or cherry root beer. These two treats tasted like a touchdown. And on rare occasions when an athletic practice was not scheduled, I would end up there after school. My head is dense with tender and affectionate memories of the festive corner drugstore with the marble countertops, the old brass cash register, metal malt cans, metal holders for the paper cone cups in which water was served, the plastic-covered round rotating stools at the counter, the booths and the small circular tables with those ice-cream chairs with curly wrought-iron legs and backs. I spent many evening hours at the soda fountain skewered to one of the counter stools flirting with the female soda jerks who served us cherry root beers (5 cents), milkshakes (20 cents), and malts (25 cents), nickel scoops of ice cream, phosphates, sundaes, and happiness that made life sweet and innocent. I drank more root beer, mostly cherry root beers, because it was cheaper than the higher-octane Coke. My evening-time nectar. A unique practice by the drugstore owner was to give all football players a malt every time we won a football game. If we lost, we had to mop the floor after the closing time of 10:00 p.m. I only had to serve on the mopping crew one time.

In the larger cities, soda fountains were to be found in not just drugstores, but the large department stores as well. I was always fascinated by the unique function of the lever action of the actual soda fountain. If the handle was pulled, a regular stream of soda water flowed out. Pushed into the reverse position, it would shoot forth a small thin forceful stream that was used to kind of break up the ice cream when making an ice-cream soda. I rarely ordered this dish. When soft-serve ice cream first came out, the drugstore had a contest to name the new product. Warnie Taylor, in Richard's class, won the contest with the name "Dairy Whip." His prize was a supply of free ice cream for a time. Once, the drugstore came out for a brief time with a new ice-cream drink called a Whing Ding. They sold them for 10 cents one Saturday, and with a binge mentality I drank about three strawberry Whing Dings and had to go out behind the drugstore and throw up. All that sugar must have choked up my pancreas. When I arrived home from this little episode, I started chugging Pepto-Bismol like a cherry root beer.

Back in the day before the digital age, the drugstore was where we dropped off our camera film to be sent off for developing. The drugstore would then send the film to Owl Photo in Weatherford, where it was processed. It usually took about three to five days to get our pictures — something that was always eagerly anticipated.

The drugstore sold comic books, or as most kids said, "a funny book." It was popular to sit on the floor and read them without buying. Comic books were produced in massive numbers in America in the 1950s. One billion were sold in 1953 alone. Along with the cowboy comics (my favorites), there were *Buster Brown, Mutt and Jeff, Blondie, Li'l Abner, Superman, Roy Rogers, Gene Autry, Zorro, Batman, Dick Tracy, Archie, Little Orphan Annie*, and *Rubber Man* to name a few. For the most part, comic-book writers developed heroes who fought for democracy and freedom to instill positive values in children. All these heroes of the day had particular specialties. Superman fought for truth, justice, and the American way. He could leap tall buildings in a single bound, change the course of mighty rivers, and bend steel with his bare hands without having to worry about FAA regulations, environmental impact studies, or union contracts, and he unfailingly saved the day. Roy Rogers went almost exclusively for communist agents who were scheming to poison the water supply or otherwise disrupt and insult the American way of life. Zorro tormented an oafish fellow named Sergeant Garcia for obscure but apparently sound reasons. Batman, the caped crusader, had no superhuman powers, but used his scientific knowledge, athletic prowess, and detective skills to catch bad guys. The Lone Ranger, the resourceful masked rider of the plains, and his faithful Indian companion Tonto, fought for law and order in the early West. I never understood the reason for the tiny mask. Who was he trying to fool? He was the good guy. He also had a catchphrase — "A fiery horse with the speed of light, a cloud of dust and a hearty, 'Hi-yo, Silver': the Lone Ranger" — that made no sense whatsoever. Generally, most movie cowboys would ride their horses across blazing deserts searching for their girlfriend and finally, after killing ten men, wearing out three mounts, surviving two avalanches, a prairie fire, a blizzard, and a passel of varmints, he finds her being held captive by the Comanches. Anyway, whoever invented comic books should have been awarded a Nobel Prize for literature. Some parents would not let their children read comic books. They were considered *a road map to the jailhouse*. I never understood that philosophy. The fact that they were forbidden by some added to their appeal. There was also a weight machine in the drugstore that for a penny, one could get their weight on a ticket and a Chinese fortune printed on the back. Some restaurants had those combination napkin dispensers and a Swami penny fortune device. The napkins were dispensed on each side with the fortune-telling matching in the center.

Dr. Young, the dentist, was a familiar sight in the drugstore. Indeed, they were synonymous. His and Dr. Ryan's offices were above the drugstore. He had a special chocolate ice-cream dish that the soda jerks fixed for him. Sometimes he would go behind the soda fountain and fix it himself. G.L. Alexander, who bought the drugstore from Millard Wright, Sr., told me that Dr. Young had a key to the drugstore and frequently would go down after closing and fix himself something to eat or drink. He lived in an apartment above the drugstore next to his office. Dr. Young once gave me five dollars for what he said was playing a good football game. Did that make me a professional? He was a strong supporter of the football team. He once bought the team 22 new Ridell helmets, and on another occasion bought new sideline warm-ups. He would, on occasion, call Lloyd Ray to come sweep his office and pay him from $2 to $5. Dr. Young had some neurotic tendencies such as constantly using mouthwash while working on you as well as some nervous speech patterns. I dreaded going to the dentist because Dr. Young used no anesthetic with his demonic dentist drill. Surely he used some Novocain, but I just don't remember it. High-speed drills were unheard of during my childhood. I think Dr. Young must have used a small grindstone powered by a foot pedal when I came in for a visit. The grinding seemed to go on ad nauseam. When I approached his office, it was done with great trepidation. His dental chair had to be the most glacial place in all of my known world. Time did not move forward. It just hung like Father Time in lead boots.

The drugstore was the temple to Thomas's history, at least to me, and was the centerpiece of the town. I spent so much time in there that they should have named a booth after me or at least a counter stool. The drugstore was a refuge, a haven, and a source of diversion.

The drugstore accepted strangers. If you needed company, and it seemed to you that there was no one left in the world, you would find it in the drugstore. It was the place where the solitary night owl could go when he did not know where else to go. The drugstore was the kind of place you want to head for as winter sets in, and hibernate. The drugstore was as snug as a badger's hole and so cozy and comfortable that once you were inside, you would never want to get out. At the time, to me, there was simply no "opiate" like a chocolate milkshake. The drugstore just made life more livable. If every town had a corner drugstore, *there would be peace in the valley.*

CHAPTER 3

The Pool Hall

"And that rhymes with P that stands for pool." – Meredith Wilson

ANOTHER LAIR OF mine was the pool hall — a place where I spent much of my time playing snooker in the back of Blackie's Barbershop when there was no one with whom to visit in the drugstore. Each game cost 15 cents. The winner paid five cents and the loser paid ten cents. We referred to this as nickel dime snooker. Snooker, with smaller pockets and more complicated rules, is a much more sophisticated game than straight pool. A player is said to be "snookered" if he cannot shoot in a straight line at a red ball because a numbered ball is in the way, or at a numbered ball because a red ball blocks the way. Alan Vaughn, who was in the class just ahead of me, was the town pool shark, played with a velvet touch, and was poetry-in-motion with that cue. I loved the symphony of those snooker balls smacking against one another as they rolled across the green felt and the clacking of the dominoes at the domino tables where the men played moon and 42. *What a beautiful noise*. While we played, we would get a cold glass bottle of Pepsi from the pop cooler, and pour a bag of Planters peanuts in the bottle to eat as we drank. There was a small snack bar in the northwest corner from which we could buy snacks. Other brands of pop that I remember were Nehi, Coke, Dr. Pepper, Double Cola, Grapette, Orange Crush, Hires Root Beer, and

Royal Crown Cola (RC). Grapettte was introduced in 1939, my birth year. Another drink and food combination was Royal Crown (RC) Cola and MoonPies. MoonPies were originally made as a snack for coal miners.

During the '50s pool halls were perceived as a social ill by many and carried the aura of tough-guy danger and dens of sin, even in Iowa. I know this is accurate because Professor Harold Hill said it was in *The Music Man* musical and movie. Laws were passed in many places to set age limits at pool halls and restrict gambling and the sale of alcohol. In many places they had curfews and were closed on Sunday. However, none of these vices were allowed in the Thomas pool hall. This was not one of those pool halls *spelled with a capital P that rhymes with B that stands for Bad*. The capital P that rhymes with B phrase came from the song *Trouble* in the 1957 hit musical *The Music Man*. This song lampooned the prejudice of the pool hall being a bad place. I never ever saw a payday drunk walk in the Thomas pool hall. Alcohol and gambling were not permitted in Blackie's Pool Hall. So, it was okay for minors to frequent the pool hall. However, there was an unwritten law that girls did not frequent the pool hall. A very young Mary Lee Norris once went in to get her dad from one of the domino tables and was quickly informed that girls did not go back into the pool and domino parlor. With mild exasperation she told me, "I would have burned my bra but I didn't need one yet." The older men played dominoes there, and there was not even any bad talk from the men. These men never called each other to set a time to play dominoes. There was no official time. There was never any planning. They all just seemed to meander together, seemingly by instinct, to the pool hall at a given hour that had magically planted itself in their collective noggins.

You could say that I majored in drugstore and minored in pool hall. I didn't go to the pool hall so much for the snooker tables as I did for the atmosphere and a place for engrossing conversations with friends. It was sort of like what J.R. Moehringer said in the prologue of his memoir, *The Tender Bar*. "We went there when we didn't know what we needed, hoping someone might tell us. We went there when looking for someone because eventually everyone turned up there. We went there to be found." I did not know this at the time and would not have been able to put all this into words, but I understood. The pool hall was one of my anchors. Most evenings I would drift down to this establishment with a reasonable amount of predictability, like snowmelt flowing downstream. There was probably no single person who was a central player in my childhood and adolescence, as I came to realize, but the town itself and the sturdy values it reflected. These adolescent years were very insular; there was athletics, hanging out with friends, the pool hall, the drugstore, the skating rink, and after that, the world didn't really exist for me. Everything else was beyond the pale. I don't ever remember the litany of, "What do you want to do tonight?" "I don't know." We knew what we were going to do — the drugstore, the pool hall, or the skating rink — this was our *modus operandi*. As the winter solstice grew nearer after football season and the nights grew longer, I spent more and more time at these places — enough time to read *War and Peace* several times. This experience was a romance between a boy, the drugstore, the pool hall, and the skating rink. The happy mood of these places kept the outside world away. These establishments were so cool that it was like finding Beethoven in Hoboken.

Slick's Barbershop

"There is only one thing in the world worse than being talked about, and that is not being talked about." – O. Wilde

SLICK SLAGLE OPERATED the other barbershop and was where I got my haircuts, amid the mixed scents of Wildroot, Brylcreem, and Vitalis hair tonics that were used to slick back our hair, giving us that Valentino-like appearance. Barbershops were revered places men went to for a haircut and to talk about politics, farming, commerce, fishing, celebrity, sports, and nostalgia. And, on occasion these topics could be debated with theological exuberance. The barbershop could keep us entertained for hours. There were more fish caught in Slick's than in the ponds and rivers. Birds had to fly. Fish had to swim. Men went to barbershops. A true barbershop announced itself to the world with a barber pole next to the front door. It featured a spiraling red stripe that snaked eternally upward. I think the red in the spiral came from the fact that medieval barbers were also surgeons that would let blood as a curative. After the haircut, out came the razor and lather as he trimmed up your sideburns, around your ears, and the nape of your neck. Finally, you were liberally doused with hair oil with a fragrant scent, announcing your arrival before you got to where you were going. I came along after the "Shave and a Haircut, Two Bits" era, but a haircut when I was a boy cost thirty-five cents. Most of the time, I wore my hair sheared off in a horizontal plane in the style known as a flattop.

Lloyd Ray shined shoes at Slick's. He could put a shine on your shoes as shiny as fire-engine chrome. His competition over at Blackie's was Merl Potter and Alan Vaughn. Truman Park took Lloyd's place when he quit. Truman was in Jackie's class. Slick's was a popular hangout for many people. Regulars there were Bill, Jackie, Darrell, Clyde, Don, Herb, and Jack, and Millard Wright would come over from his dad's drugstore next door. I have a picture of my Granddad McCracken sitting in Slick's extra barber chair with Slick cutting someone's hair. During football season, Slick always ran a football pool for local "big time" bettors. One might say that Slick was Thomas's number-one football fan.

One time Mother told me to get some money for a haircut out of the jar in the cabinet that contained the grocery money. I fingered more money than was needed for the haircut. When I gave Slick a five-dollar bill to pay for the haircut, he knew I wasn't supposed to have that much money and called my mother. I paid for that mistake with a spanking and an upset stomach for buying and eating two candy bars and a chocolate milkshake with some of the change. *It takes a village . . .*

In a flag dedication and memorial service honoring Slick at Sewell Park on Veterans Day, November 11, 1989, David Self read a letter written by Jackie that described the shop and the people.

Slick's Barber Shop was more than a place to get a haircut for a lot of people. I guess I was 12 or so when I first started going there on a regular basis and continued until last year — 35 years.

During those years I can't remember Slick ever being down or not in a jovial mood. If you couldn't take a kidding you wouldn't go into Slick's Barber Shop.

Whenever I have to list my educational resumé I probably should list Slick's Barber Shop, Thomas, Oklahoma. I am sure my eight to ten hours a week spent there increased my knowledge, as well as giving me a better appreciation for life. As a parent I am sorry my sons don't have a similar place to go and spend some free time.

There was always a fish or hunting story. One thing I never did understand was how Slick could leave the shop for an hour during lunch and get his limit of quail and I would go out all day and be lucky to get seven or eight. I guess Slick didn't tell me everything.

Do you remember the weekly football pool — seeing who could come up with the closest score on the Thomas football game each week?

Slick's Barber Shop! Yes, it was more than a place to get a haircut, it was a way of life for a lot of us. Slick, we miss you. Oh, I can find a place to get my hair cut, but that was such a small part of it. Lea Elma, Debbie and Sue, thanks for putting this flag pole here in the park. If anyone deserves this, Lue Warren "Slick" Slagle certainly does. Slick's Barber Shop is closed at this time, but will always be remembered as the place to rehash the ballgames and to hear a story or two.

The barbershop was an unassuming, friendly place I remember from other days. A place of social interaction to meet friends, share news, influential in helping to shape male identity and eventually leave feeling and looking like a new man. The barbershop provided a source of comfort. I remember coming out of the barbershop once with my hair all slicked down before my teenage flattop years and meeting my Uncle Floyd sitting on the front fender of his parked car. He remarked to me, "Hey Donnie Pop, where are you preaching?" He called me "Donnie Pop" because I liked strawberry pop.

The Skating Rink

"I'm gonna go on down to the roller rink and roll my blues away."
– Trooper

THE THOMAS ROLLER-SKATING rink, in the Community Building, was a good meeting place to hook up with friends to start one's evening activities or to skate with girls. Because of the inescapable burden of gravity, I decided not take up roller skating on a regular basis. When I reminisced with Karen Sweeney McKellips about the rink and all the life that flowed in and out of it, her memories of the rink proved fondly philosophical.

To this day she regards the rink as an important milestone in shaping the lives of Thomas children and adolescents for whom it was a site of entertainment and social interaction. It was a place where, especially after the town theater closed, young people gathered, and where there was enough supervision to prevent much bad behavior from occurring. Parents were rarely there so one had some freedom to discover how to negotiate the world outside home, school, and church. Karen credits Lew Baker, the nice man who ran the place, with being as positive an influence on her and her peers as any scoutmaster or Sunday School teacher; in fact, more than most adults in such roles. He also was a skilled archer, who sometimes demonstrated that skill at town events.

As Karen remembers it, skating talent varied greatly among the throng of skaters. There were a few excellent skaters who were also good-looking, athletically talented, nicely dressed middle-class kids from families considered "good." However, there were excellent skaters who didn't have all these characteristics; some had none of them. But when good skaters got on the rink floor and began to whirl and skate, individually and in couples, as if they were Olympic ice skaters or ballet dancers, their "popularity" among the rest of those present soared. It was a place where teenagers who were on the lower rung of Thomas's teenage social hierarchy, who didn't stand out for other reasons, could rise to the top, at least when on skates. Karen remembers herself as a very poor skater, barely able to make it around the rink without falling and certainly unable to skate backwards or twirl around. Very rarely did one of the really good skaters ask her to couple skate, but when he did it was the highlight of her week.

She remembers Clyde Threadgill, whom kids called "Pee Wee," who was an excellent skater and did sometimes ask her for a couple skate. The nickname was not because he was short; he was so tall he had to bend over to skate with her, and he was four years older than she was. To this day she isn't sure why he would skate with her, but she is grateful he did because it did great things for her self-confidence.

There was a brother-and-sister skating team who were also talented dancers who occasionally appeared at the rink dressed in appropriate costumes. Jana Lou had the only short, sequined "skating skirt" that Karen remembers seeing at the rink, although later she made one for her sister Linda but doesn't remember if she ever wore it. Jana and her brother Charles were outstanding skaters and Charles once or twice asked Karen to skate, but she doesn't count that as important because their parents were best friends with Karen's aunt and uncle and he probably had to ask her. Also, Charles was not from Thomas but went to school in a nearby town, so the triumph of skating with him didn't carry over into Karen's everyday life.

Another out-of-town couple who frequently appeared at the rink were two boys from Watonga whom the girls called "Baggy Pants and Belt Buckle." When they appeared to be approaching girls for a couple or triple skate, most girls skated as fast as possible into the women's restroom. They wore "un-cool" clothes, were physically un-attractive, and were terrible skaters. Even Karen raced to get where she couldn't be asked to skate with them.

Most of the time, people skated as individuals or couples or how-ever they chose. Sometimes one from a menu of skating events was announced over the public address system. There were couple skates, triple skates, ladies' choice (Sadie Hawkins) skates, and, for the boys, races. The couple skate required a boy and a girl, and the triple skate required two of one gender and one of the other.

Karen considers the music at the Thomas rink super to the organ music used at most rinks. She considers it the white people's "soul" music of the time, the oldest version of what today is called "clas-sic country/western." Hank Williams, Sr., Ernest Tubb, Kitty Wells, Wanda Jackson, and Carl Smith crooned the tunes to accompany Thomas skating. Karen still considers this her "soul" music. At closing time Lou always played, *Goodnight Sweetheart, Its Time to Go*.

CHAPTER **5**

The Croquet Courts

"Memories of childhood were the dreams that stayed with you after you woke." – Julian Barnes

THE GENTEEL SPORT of croquet in Thomas? Yes, we had two professional-quality, well-manicured courts with concrete, steel-lined courts, hard sand surface, and rigid steel wickets made from one-half-inch rebar. The steel-lined walls were really railroad rails laid on their side and set in concrete with the bottom of the rail facing the court allowing the balls to be banked off it. The pegs at the end of each court were anchored with a piece of railroad iron buried a foot deep. After each game played, the court would be dragged and swept with three- to four-foot devices that one would pull with a rope attached. The clearance between the ball and wicket was only the width of a dime. An annual tournament was held in Thomas that rivaled any. However, one would not ever see resplendent tennis whites on any elite players. One would more likely see Oshkosh and Tuf-Nut overalls — Arkansas tuxedos. All over town, you could hear the balls ricocheting off those walls. Because we did not have air conditioning and left our windows open at night, I was serenaded to sleep many a night to the harmony of those balls. Sort of like a nocturnal symphony. I listened to these sounds of the night and if there weren't any, I imagined them. Also, the sounds of yelps about a successfully entered wicket accompanied by the desolate groans of those who missed. The players had to keep plugging the electric meter with dimes to keep the lights on at night.

I never played much croquet, but Jackie and Richard did. The best croquet players were the older men — guys like Johnny Jones, Milt Herring, Harley Hamar, Tom Buchanan, Alphus McNeil, R.L. McNeil, Calvin Keller, Fred Foust, John D. Foster, Ed Sweeney, Don Roof, and Raymond Williams. Raymond had arthritis so bad that he had to play with a long-handled mallet. He played every day and was one of the best. Darrell Hamar and Jack Williams teamed up to win a state tournament once. Most of these guys were as smooth as a milkshake with that mallet in their hands. The Hockaday Hardware Store sold new and used mallets and balls. Some were made by Joe Ross. The mallets had rubber on one end and a hard fiber material on the other. Calipers were used to measure the balls before a tournament, and everyone had to play with new balls issued by the tournament officials. Mallets had different-length handles. Some employed one-handed, two-handed, and even a one-handed side stroke for their mallet swing. The term *roquet*, in the game of croquet, was putting your ball next to someone else's and knocking their ball into a bad position while knocking yours into a good position.

On the north side of the croquet courts was a horseshoe court area. Bud Cleveland and Frank Self won a national horseshoe pitching tournament one year. At least the locals referred to it as a national tournament. The courts were torn up and moved to the park in 1970.

I never knew of any girls ever playing croquet at the Thomas croquet courts. However, just today (9/3/2013) I had a forwarded e-mail from Keren Miller who had had an e-mail from Jana Lou Scott, who grew up in Fay, telling her that she and Louise Abercrombie used to play and many times beat some of the men. Also, Jana Lou mentioned that Fay had a croquet court. I never knew that.

If I ever wanted to find my grandpa while roaming the town as a kid on Saturday, I would go to either the bench in front of Brown's Grocery Store or the croquet courts, where there would always be several relaxed spectators sitting on the small bleachers on the west end of the courts. Grandpa stuck to these two places like bubble-gum on a shoe. He was always a good touch for at least a nickel. I would usually buy a scoop of salted Spanish peanuts with this money at Brown's Grocery Store. Mr. Brown would always give me a huge rounded scoopful. I'm sure everyone else only got a level scoopful. If I were broke and couldn't find Grandpa, I would go look for empty pop bottles lying around somewhere, occasionally find a few, and go sell them for two cents each at the grocery store. Sometimes if I had an extra nickel or dime I would go into the TG&Y store. Our five-and-dime had everything in the world in it — or so it seemed to a kid. That made deciding what to buy a big problem.

Every Thanksgiving, to start the holiday season, across the street west from the croquet courts, as a giveaway promotion, the merchants would throw live turkeys off the top of the buildings. If you could catch a turkey, you could keep it. I remember once seeing an adult male take one of these turkeys away from a kid who had caught it. This guy would probably steal Tiny Tim's crutch. My cousin, R.L. Cline, took it away from the guy and gave it back to the kid.

The croquet courts, barbershop, pool hall, drugstore, filling stations, and skating rink — academic centers all — disseminating the wisdom of the time — were places serving far greater purposes than their intended constructs could have ever dreamed of embodying. They were a source of weather reports, current events, and general gossip — delicious possibilities.

CHAPTER 6

The Shoe Cobbler

"Half past two is much too late. Get it done by half past eight."
– Mother Goose

THEY SAY THAT your shoes say a lot about you. However, this aphorism, as with most kids, never was a concern of mine, although I do remember Richard always being careful to wear newly shined shoes. It was also important to wear shined or polished shoes to go to church.

During the Great Depression there were over 120,000 shoe cobblers in the United States, and in Thomas there were two shoe shops: Charlie Buchanan's and Jack Clifton's. I don't remember too much about Mr. Buchanan's shop. Mr. Clifton's shoe shop, located just north of the movie theater with a vacant lot between, was an interesting place. Because we always repaired our shoes as many times as possible before buying a new pair, I had occasion to frequent his shop. There was always the aroma of leather, glue, shoe polish, and mink oil as you walked in. Rows of newly repaired shoes would be neatly lined up on the shelves behind the counter, waiting for the owners to pick them up. The counter was an old big mirrored saloon bar. Freshly repaired shoes always looked new to me after Mr. Clifton had shined them on a long horizontal, cylindrical whining, spinning machine that had several functions. This machine was known as a cobbler's arbor. There were several brushes and smoothing wheels for heels and soles. Afterwards, that fresh coat of sole dressing really put the finishing touch on them.

Charlie Buchanon's shoe shop was originally a shoe, harness, and secondhand store in the building that was Dr. Brundage's first office. Charlene Roof (Charlie's granddaughter) used to play house in his shop with her sister and saw her first Indian there. The Indians would come in and trade beaded work for other products or repairs. Eva Old Crow was one of the Indians who made and brought beadwork to the shoe shop. She could not speak English. Her granddaughter, Dorothy, translated for her.

Karen Sweeney McKellips related a hilarious shoe story to me. "Claire Hooper, Jean Dykes, and I think Paulette Steward, and I bought matching high heels to wear to church on Easter. They were black suede — totally inappropriate for that late in the season, but we didn't know any better. We couldn't walk in the things, but thought we could. On Easter morning, with an astonishing spirit, we trouped as a group into the Methodist church with the slanted hardwood floor sounding just like a herd of cattle. Everyone turned and stared at us, but I just thought they were admiring us." Now, I would give a pretty penny to see a reenactment of this rollicking event.

CHAPTER 7

The Telephone Office

"I can resist everything except temptation." – Oscar Wilde

THE TELEPHONE SYSTEM of the 1940s and early '50s had its frailties and frustrations, but it also had the virtues of friendliness and warmth. Thomas had a telephone office staffed by a live operator. When you rang her, she would answer with the word "central," and you would give her the number you were calling. One would also have to call the operator if one wanted to make a long-distance call. A lot of the time one would hang up after giving the operator the long-distance number, and she would call you back when she had been able to complete the connection. One would even call the operator for the time of day. In some towns the telephone switchboard was set up in private homes. The first telephones we had were hand-cranked phones.

If the operator chose, she could unashamedly listen in on your conversation. In 1950 75% of all lines in the US were still party lines. If one lived in the country, one had to share the same line with other parties, thus the term "party line." You could listen in on these conversations, also. Each party had their own ring identified with a sort of Morse Code; two longs and a short, for example. Your mother remembers their ring as a long and a short. I don't remember ours. So, every time anyone's phone rang, everybody's phone rang. You only picked it up if it was your ring and were encouraged by the phone company to limit your calls to five minutes. If it wasn't your ring, you just might pick it up and listen in, even though you weren't supposed to! Everyone listened in, as if there was nothing wrong with it. This type of snooping was called *piking* and was a source of entertainment and gossip. Don Richardson remembers one of the ladies on their line saying, "I heard you say on the phone yesterday when you were talking to somebody that you all were going to do this or that." In Jimmy Carter's memoirs, he described their operator in Plains, Georgia, as being omniscient. When one would ring for Roy Brannne, for example, she would say, "He left for Americus this morning at about nine thirty, but he plans to be back before dinner. He'll probably stop by the stable, and I'll try to catch him there." Alberta Ryan (my class) tells of her mother having the "Hello Girls" chase Dr. Ryan to ground in more than one medical emergency. "When you find him tell him to go to the hospital, or Grandma so-and-so's . . ." The operator knew every number from memory. They knew everything and everyone. Instead of the caller giving the operator a number, they would many times just say, "Ring Auntie for me!" If someone had an emergency, the operator would have to break into the conversations. The operator usually had the latest news on any sickness in the community, plus a lot more information that indicated there were maybe three listeners on most calls. In small communities this type of operator behavior was pretty much pro forma, and information and gossip could travel with the speed of a card dealer in Vegas.

One advantage to the party line was that when school needed to be dismissed because of bad weather, all Mr. Sweeney needed to do was call the operator and have her do a line ring announcing the intended message. What an epochal change we have had in this industry.

People would call the telephone operator to get a football score from an out-of-town game because someone at the game would usually call home right after the game from a public telephone.

School Street

"On The Street Where You Live." – Lerner & Lowe

SCHOOL STREET WAS Main Street, but everyone called it School Street because the school stood majestically on the hill at the north end of Main Street in a cul-de-sac just behind an attractive circle rock-wall garden designed by Mr. Sweeney, our superintendent. I am told that at one time this elegantly landscaped circle looked like something out of *Architectural Digest*. This design and arrangement gave the venerable ivy-covered building a distinguished manicured-campus appearance. This "school circle" was the frequent scene of parked cars where we would congregate at night to hang out. The most famous officially named School Street is in Boston, Massachusetts. It was so named for being the site of the first public school in the U.S. (the Boston Latin School).

School Street is probably remembered best because of all the kids who lived on this "thoroughfare." There was Bobby Johnson, Mary Lee Norris, Ronnie Ogden, Bruce and Bobby Thompson, Katrina Buchanan, Karen, Linda, and Mike Sweeney, Janice Potter, Claire and Sam Hooper, Jean Dykes, Don Herring, Meb and Gary Ray, Jackie Brundage, Richard, Alberta and Pat Ryan, Ethel and Max Simpson, Jo Jo Ross, Dorothy Sue Cornelius, Glenda Reiswig, Judy and Jeannie Perry, Paulette and Larry Steward, the Diel girls, Jan Sturgeon, Virgil and Patty Talbot, Millard, Mark, and Marian Wright, and yours truly (we lived there only two years). Mr. Ross also lived on School Street. I'm sure this list is not exhaustive.

This was an era when people used sidewalks and sat on their front porches, especially at night. There were no stop signs and cars frequently drove a little too fast, sometimes dragging. It was a common sight to see anywhere from two to six people walking up and down the street with no particular objective in mind. It was even a place to meet up with your girlfriend and to just walk and talk.

Karen McKellips tells of her and her School Street gang sleeping outside a lot during the summer on somebody's back lawn on pallets and engaging in all kinds of nocturnal activities, roaming the whole town, after their parents had long gone to bed. I can't believe that my circle of friends and I did not know about these nighttime adventures. My mind comes up with all kinds of scenarios of fun we boys could have had with this situation. I would like to have seen what effect a rumor about a tattooed scary man on the loose would have had on these girls. This group of Karen, Claire, Jeanette, Jean, and Paulette was affectionately referred to as the "Flirty Five." They even had a theme song that went something like, "We are the Flirty Five, and thank God we are alive." Another nocturnal girl story is told about some girls before our time. They were out one night sitting on the grass visiting when this guy comes along. He goes over to a pile of straw, takes out a bottle of whiskey, takes a drink, and replaces it. After he leaves, the girls get the bottle and pee in it.

School Street was point zero. This street was a compass, a way to know where you were.

CHAPTER 9

School Stories

"High school is closer to the core of the American experience than anything else." – Kurt Vonnegut

THE THOMAS SCHOOL building was a wonderful old building, enormous to a small child, like a castle made of red brick, two severe stories off the ground. Dedicated February 16, 1923, it stood at the top of Main Street. This school had an auditorium that was just like a real theater, with a stage, curtains, and a real projection booth in the rear, although I don't remember a movie ever being shown from there. Sunken below the first floor right below the auditorium was the gymnasium with real basketball goals and not five-gallon buckets with the bottoms cut out. The gym had echoing acoustics that made every bouncing ball sound seriously athletic. This is the place where we all ate lunch before we had a cafeteria, and the place where we gathered before school during the cold winter months. The one thing our school did not have that I really wanted was a sliding tunnel fire escape from the second story like the Custer City School had.

Except for one semester, Richard, Jackie, and I attended all twelve years of public schooling at Thomas. That much-needed stability allowed me to develop at least normal social skills. I made many good friends and remember those days fondly. This other semester was when we lived in the Arapaho district, with Jackie being in the first grade, me in the second, and Richard in sixth. I hated school at Arapaho. Not because of Arapaho itself, but because moving there took me away from my friends and the positive influences I was having at Thomas. At Thomas my teachers were Mrs. Cochran in first grade, Mrs. Brundage in second, Mrs. Herring in third, Mrs. McCrary in fourth, Mrs. Barrick in fifth, and Mrs. Rassmussen in sixth. Mrs. Harmon took Mrs. Barrick's place after she became pregnant. In junior high I had Miss Woods, Mrs. Barnard, Mr. Roof, and Mrs. Hutchison. Junior high is what the seventh, eighth, and ninth grades used to be called before society was vastly improved by some genius who thought of "middle school." In high school there was Mr. Roof, Mrs. Huffman, Mrs. Graft, Mr. Litsch, Mr. Ross, Mr. Hutchison, Mrs. Lundy, Mrs. Hayes, Mr. Westmorland and Mr. Smith, and a science teacher whose name I can't recall.

Stepping into the school building for the first time with its labyrinth of rooms was the scariest event of the first six years of my life. I just about never attended school. Just before school was to begin my first grade year — no kindergarten in those days — Richard told me that on the first day of school, the teacher would take all the boys into the girls' home economics room, take all our clothes off, strap us into a chair, and give us a shot with a big needle. When he said "big needle," the idea of a *sword* went through my mind. Well, slam, bam, alakazam, there was no way a girl was going to see me *au naturel*, so I immediately went to Jackie in tongue-tied fright, told him the story and my idea of how I thought we ought to run away to Sweden, Bulgaria, or Mexico. This growing boy did not need a full-time education of cultural and intellectual needs and resolved to hand in my resignation before it ever had a chance to germinate. Jackie readily agreed, realizing what lay ahead for him the following year. However, Mom and Dad had other plans for our future. When Mom got wind of this plan before we could get it off the ground, she gave Richard a good strapping for this ill-timed, if not clever, yarn. At least he did not tell us that they were going to cut our arm off like some rascals did in the book *A Tree Grows in Brooklyn*. I read where in England if little boys did not want to go to school they were told that they would be put into boxes, turned into rabbits, and get chopped up on Sunday.

There were obviously several conflicts among brothers during our elementary school years, and we would occasionally fight or wrestle one another. I think it important that you be aware of a couple of terms boys used when competing or fighting. The term "calf rope" was used to designate that you gave up or surrendered and called for immediate mercy. In extreme cases, however, the conquered was made to spell it out. At branding time new calves were chased, roped, trussed, and rendered helpless for branding, hence "calf rope." I probably hollered "calf rope" more than Jackie when we would scuffle, wrestle, or fight as kids. And, believe me, the view was much worse from below. Even though Jackie was 18 months younger than me, he could usually whip and outrun me. "King's X" was a term used to call a temporary truce or an exemption from being tagged. One would cross their fingers and say, "King's X," which was amnesty, meaning to wait a minute while we regrouped or to see if anyone was really hurt. "King's X" comes from England, with "King's excuse" being the base and "King's X" being a shortening of it. It is likely this term refers to the act of crossing the fingers, often as an essential part of claiming a truce or time-out. Also of note is the use of crossing one's index and middle finger to indicate that it was okay to tell a fib. Usually, one did this crossing behind their back and when found out one would say, "I had my fingers crossed." This made it okay since you were really not telling a lie. Similarly, when someone had had enough in a fight, they might be told to say, "Uncle!" This comes from the Irish, meaning "have mercy."

As one might suspect, I don't remember much about the first grade except that everything about my first year was easy, I could count to a hundred, write my name, and I liked school. I was the oldest kid in my class by virtue of my birthday and the November 1 cutoff date to enter the first grade. Today, I might be called a "red shirt." This boded well for me all through my school years. Mrs. Cochran was my first-grade teacher. With her hair braided loosely on top of her head, she resembled the actress Marjorie Main from the Ma and Pa movies. She was a hugger, and whenever you did something good in her class, it ended up with her pulling you close and telling you just how good you were and always offering a reassuring smile. I was in no hurry to leave her class. I do remember that our desks were the old-fashioned individual, combination desks and seats and had probably been there ever since the school had been constructed. Mrs. Cochran called on me once when we had a visitor to demonstrate the correct way to safely hand a pair of scissors to another person. We had a *Three Bears* play where Karen was Mama Bear, Don Waters was Papa Bear (he was the biggest kid in class), and Larry McKellips was Baby Bear. I am pretty sure our classrooms had the obligatory reprinted portraits of George Washington and Abraham Lincoln hanging on the front and back walls. Also, we probably had unsettling self-portraits posted around the room as part of some art project.

There are four memorable incidents from the second grade. Jackie was in the first grade and Mother made us wear short pants to school one day when we didn't want to wear "sissy" pants. Of all days, Jackie had an attack of the runs and poop ran all down his legs, and his teacher made me take him home. We never had to wear short pants again. One day Wanda Cox, who lived across the street from me, walked home with me for lunch at recess thinking it was lunchtime. Lanny, a neighbor, wanted to show me how he could shoot a bullet without the use of a gun. This I had to see! He took a .22-caliber bullet, laid it on a brick, hit it with a hammer, and promptly shot himself in the wrist. I took off running home like a scared jackrabbit. I have just recently learned that four-year-old Richard Ryan (Dr. Ryan's son) once put a .22 bullet into the cigarette lighter in his dad's car and it fired off. Another memorable moment is one day when Haze Park and I were walking home after school, and for some reason, we started throwing rocks at one another. Mother drove by and saw the rocks raging through the air like a hailstorm and thought we were in a fight, which we weren't. She told me to get in the car — that she was taking me back to school to be punished. Why would my own flesh and blood turn me in? How come Haze didn't get in trouble? A stinging injustice — sometimes life just isn't fair. The second grade was my first introduction to the hectograph, the forerunner to the mimeograph, which was the forerunner to the copy machine. The hectograph produced one copy per pressing of a sheet of paper on a purple gooey substance contained in a pan that looked like a cookie sheet. The mimeograph cranked out copies as fast as one could turn the crank, again producing images in purple.

In the third grade, I remember Mrs. Herring reading *Uncle Wiggly* to us during story time. I have a couple of these books in my library. Story time and recess were my favorite times of the day. Ah, recess, always occupying all my available brain space along with dreams studded with Oreos and Almond Joys. It always seemed to me that recess would never arrive as we sat "locked" in our desks. In fact, it seemed to me that it didn't come around any more frequently than Halley's Comet. In cinema terms, we are talking *From Here to Eternity*. Sitting at my desk with my chin resting on the back of my hand, I must have looked like a rusty version of Rodin's *Thinker*. I was giving my full 85% sustained attention to mediocrity watching the prisms in the windows bend the light into rainbows or the carvings on my desk, thinking about recess, the playground roaring like a rodeo, and what I would be doing in the world outside the classroom walls when the bell rang — the sound of music itself. These moments of bliss always ended with the sound of a teacher's voice rousing me from my stupor reminding me of my failures of the moment, reluctantly letting reality intrude. When recess did arrive and we charged outdoors, it was like a feeling and smelling of April and May even when it was not springtime. Like getting a present when it wasn't your birthday. The only other time I might have been more wired to get out of the classroom would have been the 3:15 dismissal bell. This was the best sound one heard in the school day. In seconds the exodus was in full bloom as another day's honest work had been completed.

We were taught to read from Dick and Jane books. They had short sentences in large type and many color illustrations showing a happy, prosperous, good-looking, and law-abiding family. Father is always called Father, never Dad or Daddy, and always wears a suit, even to drive to Grandfather and Grandmother's farm. Mother is always Mother. She is always on top of things and groomed in a clean frilly apron. They live in a pretty house with a picket fence, but they have no radio or TV. The children — Dick, Jane, and little Sally — have the simplest and most timeless of toys: a ball, a wagon, a kite, and a wooden sailboat. The sun always shines. The dog never poops on the lawn. Everyone is always clean, healthy, hard working, American, and white, and the kids are well behaved. Interestingly, the British had similar books. Here is what Bill Bryson wrote about the British Ladybird books in *Notes From a Small Island*: "They contained meticulously drafted, richly colored illustrations of a prosperous, contented, litter-free Britain in which the sun always shone, shop-keepers smiled, and children in freshly pressed clothes derived happiness and pleasure from innocent pastimes — riding a bus to the shops, floating a model boat on a park pond, chatting to a kindly policeman." We always had three little cozy reading groups called reading circles. The Bluebirds (the smart kids), the Redbirds (the average kids), and the euphemistic Busy Beavers (the not-so-good readers). Our little reading groups would always place our chairs in a circle and do round-robin reading during reading time. Sometime in the third grade I flunked an eye test and had to go to Dr. Winchester in Clinton to get fitted in wire-rim glasses. This brought an unwelcome dimension to my self-esteem. I wore them about two weeks and discarded them, seemingly with no difference in my ability to read.

Events from the fourth grade that I most vividly remember are my favorite teacher, Mrs. McCrary, and getting my *Weekly Reader* each week. A story in one of my *Weekly Readers* was the telling of a WWII story in which Gen. Douglas MacArthur was rescued from the approaching Japs on the island of Corregidor in the Philippines by a PT boat that took him, his wife, and son to Australia. Another *Weekly Reader* story that my mind has stored is about a Great Lakes freighter named the *Wilkes Barre*. I remember my mother making a pin cushion in the shape of a heart that I gave Mrs. McCrary for Valentine's Day. My classmate Karen has undoubtedly forgotten, if she ever knew, that she received the largest valentine that I gave any girl in the fourth grade. In the fourth grade, Mrs. McCrary read the *Bobbsey Twins* books to us during story time — Bert & Nan and Freddy & Flossy. It was in the fourth grade that I developed a love of geography. I liked to peruse the cartography and photos of the world with its profusion of mysterious names, manner of dress, and interesting cuisines.

Usually, my buddies and I were just vapor trails in school plays. I think the teachers thought that the only way we knew how to act was naughty. In elementary school I was always the spear carrier and never the king. I have a memory, mercifully dim, of performing in a play as a Christmas tree costumed in crinkly green crepe paper. I did not have a speaking part but was just one of many trees who sang group songs. I didn't even get to say — *"and God bless us, everyone!"* The only part less prestigious than being a Christmas tree was pulling the stage curtain ropes. However, the next year I advanced to play the mailman in a Valentine program. I can barely recall, but at one time we had a rhythm band. I had to play the sticks. Stick players were the bottom level of instruments one would have been given. The triangle would have been my instrument of choice. In high school, I had thespian roles in the junior and senior plays. The junior play was *Bandits for Breakfast*, and I played the character of Tom. I acted the character Clem in a hillbilly senior production called *A-Feuding Over Yonder*. I was never too excited about school plays. I participated just because everyone else was doing it, but as Shakespeare said, "The play's the thing."

There were special assemblies called "Lyceum" programs. A 10-cent charge was usually assessed, and there were always a few in each class who could not afford this fee. I have since learned that after the lights went down, Mr. Sweeney would go around collecting all these kids and let them sit in the back of the auditorium. Hooray for Mr. Sweeney! He was our "Mr. Chips." The performances were usually ventriloquists, magicians, hypnotists, etc. In one show, I was called up on the stage to participate. "William Tell" shot an apple off my head with a bow and arrow. I did not know until my blindfold had been removed that the archer had shot it off from very close range.

It was during a recess on the east side of the building, so I was in at least the third grade or maybe fourth when I discovered that my kneecap was a movable object. This startled me. *My knee is broken* was my first thought. I ran over to the merry-go-round where Gary Hooper was playing and asked him about it because he knew everything about life. He laughed loudly and said, "It is supposed to move."

In the sixth grade, I had a real setback. For some reason, Norma Jean Eyster and I ran a 50-yard dash during the noon recess and she beat me. This cheered me up to no end. It was devastating to be outrun by a girl in front of everyone! I couldn't understand how this could happen. After all, I was one of the fastest runners in the class. In desperation I flew for refuge to Gary Hooper, who knew all about girls, the birds and bees, naughty schoolboy functions, and the female anatomy. Apparently his older brother had given him the scoop, and he was only too eager to pass it on to me as the need arose. Also, he had just been studying adolescence in seventh-grade health and tried to explain it to me. Gary was a mine of information. This didn't help my understanding very much and was of little consolation. At this point this was one of life's enduring mysteries. A most unpleasant experience.

I came back to school in the sixth grade after a family trip to California in our 1949 Chevy Fleetline. I was the only kid in class to have seen the Painted Desert, Hoover Dam, the Petrified Forest, Indian teepees along Route 66 that were motel rooms, the Pacific Ocean, mountains with snow on them in the summertime, and the giant redwood trees — all wonders of the world, at least to me. This was amazing information that we had written with our #2 pencils in our Big Red Indian Chief tablets, so that we could tell everyone when we read our class reports of "What did you do this summer?" This was an enormous status event for me.

I can't remember in which grade, probably somewhere between the third and sixth, when we were trusted with the responsibility of taking the chalkboard erasers down to the boiler room at the end of the week for cleaning. This was a reward for good behavior or for being the teacher's pet. Jackie and his buddies were able to sign up on Monday to clean them on Friday so that they could get out of school for a few minutes. None of my teachers ever let us do this. There was this amazing machine with a big hand crank. A huge circular brush turned inside a metal case while you held each eraser against it to remove the chalk dust. Billy Wilmeth remembers needing to be careful not to hold the eraser too far down or the brush would scrape the ends of your fingers. Before getting the fancy crank machine, we simply pounded them together or beat them on the sidewalk or against the north wall of the school. Jackie remembers being able to get the erasers cleaner by beating them against the wall of the building. It is a big wonder we don't all have chalk dust lung cancer.

A funny fifth-grade story about Jackie and Don Ealy happened during the Christmas season. They arrived at school a little early one morning and their teacher asked them if they would go find a Christmas tree for the classroom. They were only too eager to take on this task and took off for the first canyon about one mile east of the school. They did not show up with the tree until fifteen minutes before dismissal time that afternoon. They had spent all the school day horsing around in the canyon. The teacher said nothing to them about this tardiness. How lucky could these dudes get? This equated to a free day playing hooky, but I guess the teacher considered this behavior *pro bono publico* — for the good of the public. Back in the 1940s and '50s, being absent from school without a valid excuse was known as playing hooky. One time Haze Park (my class) and Kay Foulk played hooky and hiked out to Sugar Loaf Mound, a rather large hump of earth, about three miles south of town. Their dads found out about it, went out, and got them, whipping those chaps over and over all the way back to town.

Lloyd Ray, Larry Steward, and some other guys were out driving one noon recess and just kept driving out north of the trash dump and ended up at the river. Not a lot of people knew that if you went on past Twin Bridges, you would end up at the river. They ended up missing biology class. Mr. Ross sorted the situation out quite simply. These perps were given the option of expulsion or swats. All took swats. This little jaunt became known as the "river trip."

One dressing-room anecdote ranks up there with the Fourth of July cherry bomb story (see story in Cars chapter). Gordon and Don Richardson were in typing lab. They never did type much on their Royals anyway with their fingers click-clacking in every direction except where they were supposed to. So, as their intellectual curiosity waned, they decided to go to the dressing room and dress out for basketball practice and be ahead of everyone else. Don had to go to his locker to put up a book, and, as he turned around, Mr. Ross was turning the corner coming out of his office. Gordon had already gone back to the dressing room. Mr. Ross saw Don with a menacing look, so Don coolly picked up another book from his locker and waltzed back to typing lab without ever looking over his shoulder, wisely deciding that discretion was the better part of valor. Don was sitting at his desk, as if carved in stone, when Gordon walked into the lab a couple of minutes later. He was shaken with absolutely no color in his face and as blank as an empty canvas. Don said that he would never forget the countenance on Gordon's face when his first words, in *sotto voce*, were, "Where in the hell did you go?" Gordon said he had hidden behind the door of the dressing room, and, as the door opened, Gordon jumped out, acting the court jester, and gave a cataclysmic yell that would have registered 6.6 on the Richter scale right in Mr. Ross's dispassionate face, thinking it was Don. Mr. Ross, with his commanding presence, loomed like a giant from a children's fairy tale of evil in a midnight forest. Gordon was not expecting this depth charge and looked like he had just seen Jacob Marley's ghost. Time stopped for one fat, floating second as his facial muscles became paralyzed. His face was as pale as a daytime moon as he looked into the strong-featured face of Mr. Ross that could wake up *Rip van Winkle*. He was as unruffled as a serene lake on a dead-calm day. Mr. Ross's somber gaze would have given Edgar Allan Poe nightmares. There was an immediate funereal silence after this outburst as Gordon, with a look of amazement, stood as rigid as a cigar-store Indian as he uttered to Mr. Ross, in less than an animated voice, "Where is Richardson?" Mr. Ross stared down at Gordon with a mixture of curiosity and confusion and told him, with the force of one of King Arthur's knights, that he was in class where he was supposed to be, and "you had better get your butt there right now." Don says he still thinks about the non-rapturous look on Gordon's face and laughs and yet feels so thankful it wasn't him. Don said that Gordon looked like he had been asked to say grace at Buckingham Palace. Don and Gordon had just a little too much mustard for lunch.

One Halloween night some guys from the class of 1954 were prowling around the school looking for some mischief in which they might engage. One of the more cerebral guys in the group decided that it would be a fun action to cut the utility line running from the school building to the Vocational Agriculture Building. From somewhere a ladder magically appeared, and as Warnie, the "chosen one," was climbing the ladder with a pair of wire cutters in his hand, Mr. Ross tranquilly walked out from around a secluded corner of the school building with a flashlight and starter's pistol and calmly said to Warnie, "Warnie, don't cut that wire." Warnie was so startled that he fell off the ladder.

Some of Jackie's friends were going to the County Livestock Show, and Jackie wanted to go with them to get out of school for a day. To do this, he had to get some kind of an animal to show. JoAnn Deck was sweet on Jackie and let him take one of their turkeys. Anyway, while in Clinton for the show, they went to Pop Hicks Restaurant to eat a meal. Uncle Corny had this radio show where he went around to the booths talking to his customers. Mr. Ross always listened to this show in shop class. Uncle Corny asked Junior Garner, Larry Crowdis, and Jackie — or better known as Moe, Larry, and Curly — what they were doing in town. Responding like they were wearing shining armor, they replied that they were showing animals at the fair and my switched-at-birth brother responded that he was showing a turkey just to get out of school. Uncle Corny asked them if they would smoke a cigar if he gave them one. They replied, "Sure." When they arrived back to school for football practice, Mr. Ross was waiting for them at the dressing room door. "Just wanted to get out of school, huh, and smoking on top of that?" Mr. Ross rearranged some of their molecules after practice by making them run several laps as punishment. Jackie swears that they didn't smoke the cigars. These guys' intellectual compass was a bit out of line with magnetic north and sorely in need of being recalibrated. I think they had been sacked one time too many while playing football without a helmet. These guys were permanently one yard short of a first down. It was like football *Hamlet* . . . to rehab or not to rehab; *that is the question.*

David Stratton, a graduate of Clinton High School, passed along the following information to me about Uncle Corny. Uncle Corny was actually Lew Preston, who owned and operated the KWOE 1,000-watt radio station at Clinton. The station was located across the road from the county fairground. This station was pretty much a one-man operation, signing on at 5:00 a.m. and signing off at 10:00 p.m. The show was popular with high school kids because the early morning and afternoon shows had requests and dedications. It was a big deal to hear your name on the radio and listen to who else was dedicating a love song, gag song, or whatever to his or her sweetheart. A line from a poem recited often on the show was, "I've heard it said, and it's true I'm sure, that too much bathin' weakens ya." The theme song was "Life Gets Teejus, Don't It?"

For some reason Maynard Book and some associates decided, in their wisdom, to steal and break Mr. Ross's and Mr. Roof's paddles and throw them away — *mischief afoot.* They thought they had pulled off this escapade without being caught. However, one of the "Mata Hari" office girls had seen and ratted on them. With this inside information, Mr. Ross was after them like Crassus after Spartacus. They were told to retrieve the pieces from on top of the school, where they had thrown them, and get new ones made in very short order or face the wrath of Mr. Ross. I wondered if Mister Christian had offered similar comforting words as he cast Captain Bligh adrift. It seems like some guys are always pulling the Devil by his tail. Did these non-angelic guys evolve from the same species as the rest of us? Oh well, as Thornton Wilder said in *Our Town*, "Wherever you come near the human race there's layers and layers of nonsense."

CHAPTER 10

Other School Stories

"You ain't heard nothin yet." – Al Jolson

RUSSELL WAS A poor, speech-impaired Dickensian urchin that many picked on and teased. I was walking down the hall once and saw Richard buy Russell a coke from the pop machine located in the hall just outside the school offices. This really impressed me. I guess it shouldn't have because Richard bought me and Jackie a $60 Schwinn Deluxe Streamliner bicycle with a cantilever tank from his first wheat harvest check. This was an act of purest generosity even though I am sure he found his little brothers annoying at times. This stylish bike had a horn, light, and everything — the best bike in town. A neat thing most boys did with their bikes was to use a clothespin to clip small cardboard strips to the rear fender brace to whap against the spokes to make a clacking engine sound, transforming your bike into a "motorcycle." Jackie and I did a lot of pumping on the bicycle. Pumping was giving a ride to a second person with this person sitting on the handlebars with his feet hanging free or placed on the front wheel axle. Getting the bike was really great because as a younger kid, I had always wanted a red Radio Flyer wagon and a pedal car, but never was lucky enough to have either.

When marble season began, we would rush out of the building at recess time, find a fairly flat piece of ground that contained just the right degree of moisture for one to carefully take a stick and draw a ring, and date'em up. That meant to put your marbles in the ring to get ready to play. The teachers would not allow us to play "keeps." *Keeps* meant you could keep all the other guys' marbles that you could knock out of the ring, but we usually did play "keeps." *Peaks* meant you could build up a small dirt mound on which to place the marbles in the ring. This made it easier to hit and knock out of the ring. Some other marble terms were "bull fudging" (having your thumb with your shooting taw over the line), shooting taw (your best shooting marble), and "steely" (a steel ball bearing). The best and somewhat rare taws were the agates (aggies). They were harder and less likely to chip. It was a form of quartz with variously colored stripes or clouded colors. Steelies were sometimes prohibited because they would chip the glass marbles. Of course, chippies were not allowed. No one wanted to win a chipped glass marble. Every now and then, some rogue would try to slip one in the ring. "Glassy" or "Clearies" were marbles that were transparent. Of course, there were those small "peewees." "Boulders" were very large marbles, and "Cat-Eyes" were the most common. There was also a game called Cat-Eyes. You would shoot your shooting taw and shoot your next shot from where your taw stopped on the previous shot. "Grab dates and run." That's what you said when you were tired of playing or a teacher was approaching and you were playing "keeps." At this command, everyone would quickly grab all the marbles they could and run because we did not want the teacher addressing the matter of provenance of our marbles. We carried our marbles in an old Bull Durham pouch or Prince Albert tobacco tin. Your tin had better be full or the marbles would really jingle, making a lot of noise as you walked with the tin in your pocket. I remember Prince Albert advertising on the *Grand Ole Opry* WSM radio broadcast. I think everyone lettered in marbles.

A couple of other recess sports were top spinning and yo-yoing. Some of the more skillful kids could make their yo-yos do things like looping-the-loop and walking-the-dog. No one really knew when marble season ended and yo-yoing season began. One just knew it.

Top-spinning kids were basically of two kinds: the regular spinners and the "spikers." The spikers' tops had sharp metal spikes on the ends of the tops, and the regular tops had a round knob on the ends. A spiker's objective was to spike another person's top, splitting it to pieces. This was against school rules. It was like playing "keeps" with marbles, so one had to always be on the lookout for teachers. I do not know what girls did when the boys were playing marbles, yo-yoing, or spinning tops. Probably playing "jacks."

Another competitive thing we did during recess was seeing who could bail out of a high-flying swing and land the farthest in linear distance. We had no sand or grass so we landed hard and solidly on a dirt and gravel surface. I can't remember who the champion "flyers" were. In our younger elementary school years, we spent a lot of time cutting sharp arcs with the swings in the spring air. The pendulum seemed to calm our overactive minds. I guess we should have done more swinging in junior and senior high. Jackie says that I dislocated my shoulder doing this in the park one evening, but I don't remember it. There was a tall slide that we would use with wax paper under our bottoms to make the slide slicker and increase our speed to something like 40 miles per hour. We got our waxed paper from the little "school" store just east of the playground. We would go to the store and buy fresh doughnuts (served on waxed paper) timed to come out of the piping hot grease right at recess time. These doughnuts made my mouth water just thinking about them. Kids who chewed gum while doing turns on the monkey bars would stick their gum on the bars thinking that they might choke to death if they swallowed their gum while doing flips. Once while playing on the bars, Karen chewed Frankie's already chewed gum on a dare. Another recess game we played a lot when the football season was over was kick-over. You divided up into teams and tried to push the opposing team back by way of kicking or punting the football. There were two methods of pushing them back: just by kicking the ball further each time than the opponents or by catching a kick or punt and getting bonus steps — five for catching a punt and 15 for catching a place-kick or drop-kick.

Bonus steps meant that you could take free steps toward their goal; otherwise you had to kick from where you caught the ball. When you thought you were close enough to place-kick or drop-kick the ball over the opponents' goal, you made the effort and, if successful, won the game. If you did not make it, the opposing team would more than likely catch your kick for 15 bonus steps. Burt Currell did not play on the football team, but was one of the better punters in kick-over. I can still see that unorthodox style of his as he took his punting steps.

The three greatest sins one could commit at school were breaking a window, losing your report card, and stepping on the gym floor in street shoes. I always wondered why after hitting or throwing a baseball, it would, by design, search for the nearest window. Walking on the gym floor with street shoes was next to the sanctity of taking communion. I saw Richard get a strapping from Mr. Ross with his own belt for being on the gym floor illegally one noon recess. I think these rules must have been written in blood and kept in secret files in the principal's office.

One of the neatest of the older guy tricks was the cadaver episode at Southwestern State College during one of our high school day visits. Some college science students removed the cadaver from its table in the anatomy lab and replaced it with one of the more daring conspirators crawling under the sheet. When some high school students came through on their guided tour, the cadaver rose up. One girl fainted and all screamed. Thomas was only seventeen miles from Weatherford, the home of Southwestern State College. It was not uncommon for college fraternity initiates to come straggling into town at night after having been blindfolded, disoriented, tied up in some fashion, and turned loose. I thought these "old guy" tricks were really cool and one big reason why I wanted to attend college.

A humorous story that was a little before my time in high school involved Gene "Sally" McCall, Herb Taylor, Kenny Self, and Tommy Threadgill (Pee Wee's older brother) and others. One Halloween these guys wanted to sneak in the school and write something funny on one of the chalkboards. They crawled through an unlocked window in the gym, dropped down on the floor, and were getting ready to rumble when Mr. Ross shot his track-starting pistol that fired blanks. These guys thought they were really being shot at. Herb fainted, and Tommy hollered, "You killed him." Pandemonium (*pandemonium* is always a good word to use, because it can mean almost anything) broke out, their slapdash maneuverings exploded into frantic agitation, and they scattered like cockroaches. This would have made Wile E. Coyote proud. They were approaching Mach 1 when, in panic mode, they tried to climb, jump, and grab the windowsill to pull themselves up off the gym floor to get out. They were running pell-mell, falling and stumbling all over themselves in this effort when the lights came on. It was like a bedlam scene from the bungling Keystone Cops tumbling out of some paddy wagon or the running of the bulls at Pamplona. Some were nabbed with the finality of a guillotine while some managed to escape the mayhem of these proceedings.

CHAPTER 11

Boys/Girls State

"Friendship is love without its wings." – Lord Byron

SOMETIME DURING THE spring of my junior year, Alberta and I were selected by our high school teachers to represent our school at the annual Boys State and Girls State conferences. Boys and Girls State is a summer leadership and citizenship program first held in 1937, sponsored by the American Legion and the Legion Auxiliary for high school juniors. Girls State was held at Oklahoma College for Women in Chickasha. The boys were housed in the old WWII barracks on the old naval base at the Norman airport. We were very much regimented in a military style for ceremonies, marching from one activity to another, classes, the dining hall, and a lot of whistle blowing by our counselors. Elections were held for mock legislative offices so that we could learn more about this process. Each attendee was randomly assigned to the Boomer and Sooner political parties. I do not remember to which party I was assigned. On Friday night all the boys were bused to Chickasha for a dance with the Girls State gals. After Alberta and I returned home, we gave an oral report to the Thomas Service Club. I met a lot of neat and interesting guys who I would later run into at high school athletic events and college.

CHAPTER 12

Literature Class

"How many a man has dated a new era in his life from the reading of a book." – Thoreau

G. K. CHESTERTON said, "Literature is a luxury; fiction is a necessity," but being a rather pedestrian student, there were many things I would have rather been doing than sitting in my rather featureless high school literature classroom. A slow root canal ranked high on the list, along with Roman Numerals. I think it might have been called diminished enthusiasm. I would rather have been in science class with a Bunsen burner than be tormented with *Beowulf*. Simply put, *Beowulf* was a danger to my equilibrium, but most efficient at inducing sleep. In retrospect, I would probably have done better with *Beowulf* if I had not turned the pages two or three at a time, wandering through my own thoughts — mostly of the 3:15 athletic time barging into my mind. My idea of literature was looking at pictures of half-naked female natives in *National Geographic Magazine*, of exotic places — Switzerland, the Serengeti, India — places I never expected to see, not studying *Silas Marner* or archaic Victorian boy novels (the sign of a superficial mind, obviously). This type of literature and Poe were as dark as India ink to me. I agree with Theodore Roosevelt when he said that the Badlands of South Dakota look like Poe sounds. However, I did like Poe's poem "Annabel Lee." *Wuthering Heights* is rather bleak and was my limit when it came to literature darkness. However, nothing excites our sympathy like a Cathy and a Heathcliff. Some of this stuff would turn one against life in general and God in particular. Ironically, it was Poe who wrote, "Never to suffer would never to have been blessed." I had not been raised in a home that emphasized reading or provided many magazines or books, and at the time I probably did not know the difference between Plato and Pluto. At the time, I thought literature was the last refuge of the tragically uncool. The benefits of studying literature simply eluded me. Yet in spite of all this, Mrs. Huffman battered our oafish wits with rudiments of knowledge, hoping that at some point it would sink into our brains.

In addition to studying the great writers and their works, we were required to read six books each year and make a report on them. I was never negligent in completing this requirement and enjoyed the books I read, but, for some reason, I never burned any brain cells reading a book or exploring new ideas unless there was something mandatory about it. I just never got too intellectually excited about investing too much time and passion in reading books or had my mind roused to any exertion or to anything resembling active thought. It was just not what boys did. No chance of me suffering from a terminal case of pedantry, becoming a member of the Thomas Literary Society, the next Gertrude Stein or Ernest Hemingway. When it came to literature, it was like I was on a different continent. I might have connected to better literature if there had been comic books of the Brontë sisters or Jane Austen. It seemed that Mrs. Huffman was throwing me literature curve balls and I wasn't hitting many of them. I used to have bad dreams of trying to fake my way through a discussion or test of Shakespeare because of not having read the assignment.

However, more of my literature instruction took hold than I ever realized, and Mrs. Huffman did try to instill in all of us that literature itself was a form of holy orders and that reading could shape and exalt anyone. A big "thank you" to all teachers who introduced their students to the power of literature and learning to feed the soul and the power to visualize an oak when they saw an acorn. For the most part

I found that my teachers were idealistic, really did serve learning all their lives, and really were admirable with a steady wisdom. Little did we know that our teachers were conspiring in a noble enterprise that would lead us to the next level — college. They unlocked possibilities of so many people's lives. *Well done, thou good and faithful servants.* And I later learned how to plant myself in a college library chair. I would have been a good candidate for Mrs. Huffman to make me her own "Donnie *Doolittle*," but I probably would not have turned out as successful as Eliza.

I wish I had been as smart as Karen, Alberta, Billy, and Dorothy Dean. They were well read and knew the grammar rules better than a Talmudic scholar knows the Torah. They dwelt on a plane of sophistication kind of rare for our class. I lacked all their qualities and saw no prospect of ever achieving them, but this didn't really present any discouragement to me at the time. I remember Billy and Alberta having a poetic articulacy that none of the rest of us had. At least I remember them occasionally writing poetry. Mrs. Huffman's tenure as our English teacher was not without significance, and to be honest, most of the time she was, to quote Shakespeare, "Naught but a cooing dove" as she extolled the virtues of literature. I just did not yet know that there could be beauty in literature, writing, music, and art. I am grateful that Mrs. Huffman was able to open, even if I did not know it at the moment, the doors to a dreamer like me who had no clear vocation at the time. As I look back on Mrs. Huffman, I now kind of feel sorry for her. She was willing to give so much more than I was willing to take. I wish I could or would have appreciated her gifts at the time.

Because of Mrs. Huffman's polite insistency, I find that I can still recall passages she dispensed in the form of required memorization. "Let us then be up and doing with a heart for any fate. Still achieving, still pursuing. Learn to labor and to wait." — Longfellow. "Of all sad words of tongue and pen, the saddest are these, it might have been." — Whittier. "The evil that men do lives after them. The good is oft interred with their bones." — Shakespeare, Mark Antony from *Julius*

Caesar; and "Out, damn'd spot! out, I say!" — Shakespeare, *Macbeth*. "To thine own self be true. Thou canst not then to any man be false." — Shakespeare, *Hamlet*. "In Flanders Fields the poppies blow. Between the crosses row on row…" — John McCrae. "Parting is such sweet sorrow, that I shall say good night till it be morrow." — Shakespeare, *Romeo & Juliet*. However, if asked to quote Shakespeare, a majority of people would choose one of the following of Shakespeare's two most celebrated quotes: "To be or not to be" and "O Romeo! wherefore art thou, Romeo?" "Home is the sailor, home from the sea and the hunter from the hill." — Robert Louis Stevenson, *Requiem*. My favorite quote would be from Thoreau's *Walden*: "If a man does not keep pace with his companions, perhaps it is because he hears a different drummer. Let him step to the music which he hears, however measured or far away." This list is exhaustive of my memory, but she peppered us generously with quotes from many of the literary greats. So, I guess I did catch a few pearls of wisdom with my intermittent attention that slipped from her mouth without even knowing. Because of our attitudes, at times, I wonder why Mrs. Huffman did not make us memorize "The fault, dear Brutus, is not in our stars, but in ourselves." Roger Rosenblatt did say that: "Literature gets on your nerves, but you can't shake it." Mrs. Huffman should have been given some kind of a prize or obscure title for her intellectual contributions to Thomas.

Alberta remembers laughing when Mrs. Huffman tried to get Don Herring to put some Elizabethan expression into his voice when he read the line, "Thou cream-faced loon," in *Macbeth*. Alberta also said that Mrs. Huffman offered her a peek into the world beyond Custer County and that she was a gift none of us recognized and few appreciated until much later. And I am sure Mrs. Huffman was as unreserved in her encouragement of me as she was of Alberta, but my attitude at the time just did not allow me to fully appreciate it. With Mrs. Huffman's love of all things written, I really do think she was trying to unlock and elucidate jeweled literary cabinets for us. Billy Wilmeth remembers Mrs. Huffman's perplexed look when we seemed disinterested or made light of those classic literary works she so wanted us to appreciate! It was sort of a combination of concern, disbelief, and amusement, all at the same time.

Finding consolation in a library was something I never managed to do until I was in graduate school when my professors gave me an "epiphany." As an adult, I have read many of the old classics and enjoyed most of them regardless of what Mark Twain said about a classic being a book which people praise and don't read. To name just some of the classics I have enjoyed, *Two Years Before the Mast*, *Les Misérables*, *A Tale of Two Cities*, *The Alhambra*, *Ivanhoe*, *The Mayor of Casterbridge*, *Jane Eyre*, *Oliver Twist*, *Anna Karenina*, *The Scarlet Letter*, *The Prince*, *Robinson Crusoe*, *The Talisman*, *The Canterbury Tales*, *Walden Pond*, *Life on the Mississippi*, *Sea Wolf*, *Hard Times*, *Cape Cod*, *Pride and Prejudice*, *Sense and Sensibility*, etc. I have read that Thoreau found no book so bad it couldn't be used in some fashion. I wonder if he ever read *Paradise Lost*? *Tom Sawyer*, *Huck Finn*, *Robin Hood*, and *White Fang* were my favorite adolescent books. I am no literary expert, but I believe Earnest Hemingway was on to something when he said, *"Huck Finn* was the beginning of American literature. No book written before or after was ever as good. Mark Twain used the way Americans talked and turned it into literature." In high school I also remember reading *They Were Expendable* and *30 Seconds over Tokyo*. These were WWII stories about PT boats in the Pacific and Doolittle's raid on Tokyo. Charles Sumner, an early American, wrote, "To be unable to read was the ultimate measure of wretchedness."

Today, I find myself "cabined or confined" by my ignorance of literature. However, literature has touched my mind, untutored as it is, like a beautiful piece of music. In the world of books and reading, I was a late bloomer. There is so much I haven't read — *so many books, so little time*. I have twinges of guilt and this constant gnawing feeling that I am missing out on something from not reading more books. I like what Samuel Clemens said about reading when he was working in a bookstore in his younger days: "The customers bothered me so much I could not read with any comfort." "This is the beauty of literature," F. Scott Fitzgerald said. "You discover that your longings are universal longings, that you're not lonely and isolated from anyone. You belong." Frank McCourt said that storytelling is a source of deliverance. Thomas Cahill, writing in *How the Irish Saved Civilization*, said, "Whoever has grammar —whoever can read — possesses magic inexplicable." Walter Myers has said about reading, "I was like an archaeologist, in a state of constant discovery." The most famous and rare book I have ever seen is the Book of Kells, containing the four gospels of the New Testament. Now, that was exciting when I got to cast my eyes on that beautiful 800 AD manuscript in the library at Trinity College in Dublin, described by some as *the most precious object in the Western world*. In the twelfth century, Giraldus Cambrensis concluded that the *Book of Kells* was "the work of an angel, not of a man." How ironic it was that I got a little excited when I cast my eyes on the original manuscript of *Beowulf* in the British Library. I have always enjoyed the physical presence of seeing my books lined up on my shelves. I guess it is part of the only redeeming feature of my limited background in good classical literature. Additionally, I have most of Stephen Ambrose's WWII books. Ambrose and Ernie Pyle are like mashed potatoes. You can never get enough of them.

Not acquiring an appreciation for Shakespeare and Greek plays is my greatest regret from literature class. I would have been a greater admirer of Shakespeare and willing to forget about all the nonsense of 1776 if he would have put asterisks with notations at the bottom of the page to explain all those *forsooths*, *quoths*, and *methinks*. Think Tower of Babel. A kind of literature *Rosetta stone* to translate Shakespearian English into English would have been helpful. These aids would really have helped because Mrs. Huffman spent a lot of time asking us what we thought Shakespeare meant. I never knew and still don't. I could no more understand Shakespeare than I could sing *La Traviata*. I never knew why he didn't just come right out with it, but I guess that is just the way they talked in sixteenth-century England. To me, this Shakespeare stuff was more complicated than a mitral valve replacement. Shakespeare was just too cryptic for me.

Shakespeare's words, to me, were entangled like the vines of a briar patch. At the time, I thought studying Shakespeare was *Much Ado about Nothing*. Get it? Shakespeare must have been really good because even the Irish, who don't love anything English, love him, and I know in the right hands, Shakespeare is eternal. I am not the only one who had difficulty with Shakespeare. Walter Dean Myers, writing in his memoirs wrote, "She took us from the sonnets of Browning to the sonnets of Shakespeare, which I found difficult. Where Browning was straightforward and usually clear, Shakespeare was devious, never being quite where you wanted him to be." Also, I have recently read that Victor Hugo knew little or nothing about Shakespeare. This makes me feel not so bad and puts me in good company.

As you girls know, Jean Valjean, the main character in *Les Misérables*, is my all-time favorite literary character. People have been attracted to Victor Hugo's book for more than 150 years. A 1,200-page book of suffering, vulgarity, pity, fury, revolution, worship, and self-sacrifice. He was Roy Rogers, Abraham Lincoln, and Mohandas Gandhi all rolled into one person . . . a great story of redemption for the most heroic character in literature, in my opinion.

Some of the most notable children's books that came out in the 1950s were: *The Door in the Wall, Secret of the Andes, ...And Now Miguel, The Wheel on the School,* and *Rifles for Watie.*

Books and reading have, to a large extent, defined my adult life: I read to escape the prison of my own mind, to expand, and experience vicariously. Books have been my essential solace, my consolation. They take me to exotic places full of adventure and intrigue. The world is just waiting for us in books. Today, I am like Stephen King. "I take a book almost everywhere. Books are the perfect entertainment: no commercials, no batteries, hours of enjoyment for each dollar spent. What I wonder is why everybody doesn't carry a book around for those inevitable dead spots in life."

CHAPTER 13

The Lunch Room

"Ask not what you can do for your country. Ask what's for lunch."
– Orson Wells

UNTIL WE HAD a lunchroom, everyone took a lunch to school and ate it on the bleacher seats in the gym. My favorite lunch was a cheese sandwich with Kraft sandwich spread and a banana. I took this lunch to school in a small tan grocery sack with my sandwich carefully wrapped in waxed paper with the corners tightly tucked, looking almost like a gift. Today, I occasionally have a fit of nostalgia and buy a jar of this cholesterol-laden spread.

An old rural one-room school was moved on campus when I was in the third grade and remodeled for a lunch room. Maynard Book's mother was the head cook and the culinary spread was very good. This was just the balm I needed every day around noon for my insatiate hunger, especially the scents of their marvelous homemade bread. Food could ease problems from heartache to broken bones. We ate like starved kids. Actually, we were starved kids after three and a half hours in the classroom. My stomach always started growling just before lunch as if I had been hibernating all winter. The food was really good because this was before frozen prepared foods were available and all the food was cooked from scratch. I did court gastric disaster one day when I ate two bowls of beans when I was in junior high. Frankie didn't want his beans, so he gave them to me. I guess two bowls was one too many. I liked to watch George analyze the eating of a chicken breast on the rare days that we had fried chicken, as he decided on an angle of attack after he had stuffed extra rolls in his pockets going through the line.

The most remarkable thing I remember about the lunch room was the spring-loaded pell-mell stampede by the older guys to be up near the front of the line when the noon bell rang to be among the first to begin putting food down our gullets. I guess we were always desperate with the hunger at this orgy of communal gluttony, in which everyone took pains to eat more than his money's worth. If one did not get out there quickly, it would be like standing in line at the post office. The slow and timid really had to be careful. Some of the high-schoolers could get down a flight of stairs in about three leaps. Tim Cagg jumped over the banister once and broke his leg. Once Alberta Ryan took a tumble on the playground and was on crutches for a few weeks. She remembers Jerry Vickers and Pee Wee Threadgill gallantly trying to get her to ask for help getting to the lunch room. Was this duty before nourishment or were they just trying to get out of class early to be first in the lunch line?

Before we had the lunch room, there was a little "school store" owned and operated by the Bus family just off the school grounds to the southeast. They were famous for their delicious fresh-cooked doughnuts.

CHAPTER 14

Shop Class

"Respect was invented to take the place of love." – Tolstoy

ONE STARTED TAKING shop in the eighth grade, and this class was conducted down in the dungeon basement, which looked like a room borrowed from a Dickens novel. There were two large rooms down there. One was the boiler room and the other was used for shop class. These two dreary rooms reminded me of the grim buildings in *Bleak House*, but the atmosphere was more friendly because we could talk during shop class and get a brief break from intellectual inquiry. The boiler room was somewhat sinister to me, being so cavernous with its pipes, boilers, electrical conduits, big fuse boxes, and other equipment that created a maze bewildering to one as young as me. There are three main things I remember most about shop class. Number one, it was taught by the sternest of teachers, Mr. Ross. He was very stern, but not Machiavellian, and very good at his craft. Number two, you did not chew gum unless you had enough for everyone. If you were caught and did not have enough to go around, Mr. Ross made each class member give you one swat with the paddle. If you gave too light a swing, Mr. Ross would give you a swat. One time Maynard Book was first in line to give a swat to a fellow class member, and he gave a "brother-in-law" tap and Mr. Ross promptly took the paddle from him and gave Maynard two swats. Number three, the first assignment as an eighth-grader was to square a block of wood using a hand planer. Very few were able to accomplish this in less than two weeks. Some of us felt like the proverbial Sisyphean boulder in trying to square our blocks. That's how much chance we had. In this project I was lacking in confidence as profoundly as Uriah Heep. Ronnie Ogdon was the best block squarer in our class. If we would have been smart, we would have just handed in the block without doing anything to it, but Mr. Ross would probably have figured it out. Anyway, after starting this project we had committed ourselves to a course as irreversible as the one that Columbus had taken when he weighed anchor in 1492. When my block squaring had finally passed inspection, I felt like I had swum the English Channel. Mr. Ross looked at me like I had just explained the Mystery of Life.

After this initial project the most popular items made in class were ashtrays, small chest-type boxes, and lamps. My major project that year was the building of a bookcase that is still in use today. The number-one item for the high-schoolers was the ubiquitous cedar chest. This was the in-thing to give your girlfriend. Richard was good at shop and made a lot of furniture, including cedar chests. Mr. Ross was very strict about having your project well sanded before the finish was applied. His rule was sand it until you think it will pass my inspection and then sand it some more. Lloyd Ray recently reminded me of the steps to finishing a project after it was assembled. Sand, shellac, steel wool, varnish, sand, varnish, sand, and wax. Mr. Ross made his own glue that we used in our projects. It was hide (cow hide) glue. It was made and kept in a kind of crock-pot container that kept it warm. I was definitely happy to exit this course with all my fingers and a passing grade.

There is a humorous story about Edward Blagg and Pee Wee Threadgill, class of 1954, incinerating Mr. Ross's trash box. At the end of a class, students were to sweep the floor, pick up the little pieces of wood, put them in the box, and take it to the incinerator outside. Edward and Pee Wee took out the trash one day and came back empty handed. Mr. Ross asked about the box. Now, they knew they had made a big mistake and hated telling Mr. Ross as much, as if they had lost his favorite rifle or put a fender-bender in his car. Edward said, "We burned it up," in a voice that was as doom laden as the creak of a dungeon door in Poe. Mr. Ross thought they were kidding, but they had to admit they didn't know the box was to come back in. Mr. Ross was not a happy camper and mentioned this incident several times.

CHAPTER 15

Farm Life

"I think that I shall never see a poem lovely as a tree.
Poems are made by fools like me, But only God can make a tree."
— Joyce Kilmer

THE 1950S HAVE often been called the last golden age of the family farm in America. This land was originally distributed in 1896 with each homesteader getting 160 acres. We lived on a farm during my second- and third-grade years. When I was in the second grade we lived on a farm in the Arapaho school district for one semester and then moved to a farm five miles southwest of Thomas near the Murray and Frymire farms. This was a time of no indoor plumbing (an indoor toilet was the ultimate mark of rural sophistication), a party-line telephone, a coal-burning potbellied stove, kerosene lamps, lanterns, and no rural electricity. The coal-burning stove in the middle of the living room did provide a cozy comfort with its roaring fire, but was the house's sole source of heat. We had to use what was called kindling wood to get the coal fire started. Kindling was small thin scraps of wood. We would start the small kindling fire and by the time it was going out, the coal had started to burn. Some families did have wind chargers that produced electricity. Clifford and Bea Murray had the first wind charger that I remember. They lived one half of a mile north of our place. One of the greatest challenges of living in a house without running water was taking a bath. We bathed in a small round galvanized wash tub with water heated on top of the cooking stove and then poured into the tub. We also used water heated on the stove to wash dishes. We washed dishes in a dishpan and wiped them dry with cotton-drying cloths, or as we sometimes called them — tea towels.

Rural farm life was a place where nature ruled and humanity kept a low profile. Much of my time was spent at the creek swimming, skipping smooth rocks on the mirrored surface of the water, digging caves (we knew that we could always hide in our caves if the North Koreans ever invaded), climbing cliffs, building bridges and swings, playing Tarzan, Robin Hood swordplay, war, spies, detectives, or maybe just wandering aimlessly. We slew a lot of creatures playing Robin Hood. Yes, the protagonist of this memoir grew up playing and dressing up in the masks and capes of the heroes of movie serials, as they were a decisive influence in my early life. I remember having a Lone Ranger cap pistol and always wanted a Red Ryder BB carbine. We did have a Daisy BB gun when I was in the second grade. I enjoyed these happy outings because, for their duration, I could pretend I was tough and smart. Every day I spent on the creek was an adventure, something different at every turn. I loved the creek; its gentleness, its gurgling sound, birds greeting us with an assortment of sounds, bees buzzing, the sound of the breeze gently rustling through the tops of the cottonwood trees. In the fall the cottonwoods would shed their yellow and gold leaves, drifting all over the place, and the cedar trees giving out the scent of Christmas every day. I did not know it at the time, but I was experiencing the peace, beauty, and tranquility of rural life. Little did we know that our lives were free of crowded highways, urban sprawl, and hectic schedules. The creeks on the two different farms on which we lived were not stately like a river, but were soothing and serene and where one could easily pass a day. This was about as *Walden Pond* as it gets — the free green world all around me. This was my uncluttered world with its simple pleasures. As I roamed these meadows, creeks, and hills as a young boy,

I had nothing to concern me except my next breath and what might lie beyond the next bend. I don't remember ever worrying about any varmints bothering us like rangy coyotes, snakes, or wild dogs. Not even any nasty trolls under any of the bridges we played under. The creeks and meadows were my Mecca and sacred ground. As I think back on this as an adult, it was like a piece of music as water rippled over stones in the sunlight. Jane Austin must have had similar feelings when she wrote in *Mansfield Park*, "To sit in the shade on a fine day and look upon verdure is the most perfect refreshment."

I don't remember my parents ever bothering to set any limitations on our explorations around the farm or even the creeks. They expected me to perform my chores and know basic safety rules, but otherwise, I was completely free to explore as free as the birds. And we took this freedom to the extremes. As Bob Seger wrote in one of his songs, "Fields of green tumbling through our summer days." Jackie, my fearless playmate, and I lost ourselves in gallant fantasies. We had much autonomy and often played games and engaged in activities that would send shivers down the spines of parents today, not to mention our parents. You might say that we were "free-range kids." We were allowed a free and unencumbered childhood. We walked, biked, and rode our horse everywhere. We rode in the sun, snow, and rain. Roy Rogers and Trigger would have been proud of us. Jackie would have written that Gene Autry and Champion would have been proud of us. We were sort of on the loose — in a community that held us in balance. I dove into this life like a pirate seeking treasure. I was comfortable and at home in this environment — alive, awake.

I guess everyone has a special place of shelter or protection, where their mind is freer, where they feel closer to whatever it is they revere or respect. My special place was the sheltering arms of the creeks and pastures, the barn and meadows where the sorrows of the world seldom intruded. It was not uncommon to leave the house after a meal and not return until the next meal. If we were not around near mealtime, Mother would go out into the yard and wave a white towel hoping that wherever we might be we would be looking toward the house. The white towel was our prearranged signal that lunch was ready. Our world had no fence around it. This rural experience reminds me of some words from Wordsworth's "Splendor in the Grass."

There was a time when meadow, grove, and stream,
The earth, and every common sight,
To me did seem
Appareled in celestial light,
The glory and the freshness of a dream.

One of our chores was to go get the cattle each evening for milking. It was great fun to grab a cow's tail when going up a creek bank to keep from having to climb it, and the steeper the gradient, the more fun it was. However, we were careful to not let Dad catch us doing this, because it caused the cows to run and this was bad for giving milk. Normally, the cows walked in an unhurried gait. Bringing in the cows could be a very calming experience — walking through the pasture, creeks, and trees as if I were in a landscape painting. Even the cows, with their mixed-paint hides, looked like painted china.

When the cows were herded into the barn, they would walk docilely and obediently into their regular time-smoothed oak stanchions as they had done so many times previously. Their grain and hay had already been placed in the eating trough, and as they began to eat, they were locked in by two upright two-by-fours, which were held firmly into position with a locking block, through which the cows stuck their heads so that the animals would stand still for the milking except when they shifted their weight quietly from one set of legs to another. We then picked up our one-legged stools and milk buckets to begin milking. For the most part, the cows would stand patiently, immobile, eating, chewing their cud, and flicking away flies that buzzed around them with a swish of the tail steady as a metronome. This flicking could be hypnotizing, but at other times their ropey bovine tails would irritably hit me in the face like a slap. Occasionally, I would also get stepped on from a failed dancing lesson with a cow. However, it seemed that we always had at least one ornery cow that had to have "kickers" placed on its hind legs to prevent her from kicking over a bucket of milk.

I liked the sound the milk made as it hit the metal pail and the rhythm established by the alternating streams of milk bouncing off the bucket. In the wintertime, the warmth of the cow, her teats and the milk, were welcomed by my cold and stiff fingers. The milking barn obviously had its distinctive smells. The animals had a warm smell with a sweet quality. The tang of cow manure was more tolerable than horse or pig. The sweet smell of newly mown hay was a fragrance that I liked, as well as the earthy scent of freshly plowed soil, the fresh smell of incoming rain, and the welcoming aroma of a cool breeze coming off of an alfalfa field or a blossoming meadow and other sum-mer scents. During winter it could get quite cold in the barn when an exceptionally below average cold spell would come through. The wind would blow through barn wall cracks like a straight razor. It would cut your gizzard out. This would cause me to snuggle up closer to the warm skin of the cow. Those long winter nights required us to carry those indispensable kerosene lanterns to the barn with us to provide lighting to do the milking.

Richard and I had to milk two cows each, twice a day. I once poured a bucket of milk on Richard's head because he kept squirting me from one of his cow's teats. Dad spanked both of us. That milk was a valuable commodity and not to be wasted. We had a cream separator in the kitchen. Dad, Richard, and I would each carry two buckets of milk from the barn to the house. The whole milk would be poured into a large metal bowl on top of the separator. We would then turn the crank, creating centrifugal force to separate the cream from the milk, each pouring out of a different spout. The milk, less the cream, was called "skimmed milk." This was what we would call "fat free milk" today. The cream and whole milk that we would take to the produce on Saturday would be stored in a little spring house just out-side the kitchen door, close to the cistern. There was a two-by-six-foot concrete tank in this little shed that was filled with water to keep the cream and milk from getting rancid before we could get it to town.

Other chores for which we stable hands were responsible included slopping (feeding) the hogs, feeding all other animals, cleaning old straw out of the barn, weeding and harvesting the garden, taking the trash out and burning it in an old 55-gallon oil barrel, and breaking ice on the cow tank when necessary in the winter. Hog slop was mainly any leftover food or grains mixed with either water or skim milk and soaked overnight. Skim milk would have been kind of a luxury for the hogs. Sometimes we might have had some grain to mix in with the slop. Every spring we would buy baby chickens at the hatchery to raise. In addition to feeding them, Jackie and I, as wardens of the baby chickens, had the disagreeable task of discarding any chicks that might have died. I usually managed to somehow con Jackie into performing this chore. We called the shed where we kept the chickens the "chicken house" or "hen house." However, most people referred to it in more accurate terminology as the "chicken coop." Inside the coop were individual boxes for egg laying and perches on which the birds could sleep. We would put straw in the floor of the boxes for easy cleaning. Our inside-the-house chores were drying the dishes, washing woodwork, and cleaning the cream separator discs.

We spent quite a bit of time over at Ernest and Dwaine Switzer's farm, where we would make a warren of tunnels, mazes, caves, and hiding places with hay bales up in the hay loft — or "haymow," as some called it. Ernest and Dwaine were adept at making their own toys that I always liked to play with. These toys were made mostly of wood, unlike store-bought toys that were made of materials and paint that contained lead so that children could poison themselves. We also had our own rodeos in their corrals. We would ride yearling calves. I never did ride one for more than three or four seconds. When I was in the third grade, I broke my arm trying to act like a cowboyesque hero, when I was bucked off a steer shortly after leaving the gate. Man, I dropped like a canary in a coal mine when I left that steer. I ran up to Richard and said, "I can't bend my arm. I think it is broken." He said, "Naw, it's not broken." He then pulled on it and it snapped back into place (elbow). "See, I told you it wasn't broken." I was really relieved, but later in the day, while picking corn with Dad and my brothers, it started hurting, turning purple, and stiffening like a strap of wet rawhide in the sun. I was really hesitant to tell Dad because we were not supposed to be riding the calves. He took me to the doctor and he set it without any anesthetic. This was not done as punishment. That was just the way they did it then. The doctor was my dad's Uncle Jake Schlicting at Corn. He was a bone setter, not an M.D., osteopath, or chiropractor. As he told me much later, "The manipulating, feeling, and setting was a gift of God passed on by my father." This was my second broken arm, and these were the most significant injuries I had as a boy.

Summertime food on the farm consisted of fresh fryers (chickens), real cream, fresh fruit, and garden vegetables, especially the fresh tomatoes eaten warm right off the vine with the juice running down our chins as we sucked up this warm nectar. At least one of the thighs was always reserved for me when we had fried chicken, and the pulley bone was always a fun thing to pull with any two of us. Mother made homemade cottage cheese. She would put the clabbered milk in a dish towel, fold it, and hang it on the clothesline to let all the whey drain out. On a sunny breezy day, I liked to see the weekly wash hanging on the clotheslines. The big white sheets flapping in the wind reminded me of sails on a storybook boat as I caught the scent of wind-dried laundry.

When Mom wanted a chicken for a meal, we would go catch one, wring its neck, pulling the body free from the astonished head, and take it to the house for cleaning and dressing when it had stopped flopping and bleeding. Before cleaning, we would dip the chicken into boiling water to make it easier to pluck off the feathers. My favorite meal to eat on the kitchen table, covered with an oilcloth, was beans, homemade bread, and cinnamon rolls. Mother's cinnamon rolls were a cataclysm of deliciousness — a miracle of nature. The smell of her bread was better than breath itself and meant good times at home — heaven on earth. I just hope that we adequately showed our appreciation for this labor-intensive dough-kneading process. I could die happy if my last meal ended with Mother's cinnamon rolls.

Today, when I catch a scent of cinnamon rolls, it gives me a stab of homesickness. I also liked her butterscotch pie with cherry-pie filling on top, homemade syrup, lemonade, and hot chocolate. We always had globs of real whipping cream for our pumpkin pies and fresh in-season peaches and berries. When in season, we would go pick wild sand plums, currants, and blackberries from which Mother would make jellies and jams. Mother would frequently have to reprimand me and my brothers for putting handfuls of squashed berries in our mouths instead of the collection bucket. Blackberry Johnson was one orchard near Oakwood where we would pick berries. "Licking the pan" was a treat we boys always looked forward to when Mother would bake a cake and cook the icing. "Licking the pan" was a term used to describe taking a spoon and scraping what was left of the icing in the pan after Mother used all she needed to ice the cake. How can mothers can know from another room that you are about to dip a finger into the icing of a freshly baked cake?

Even though the Rural Electrical Administration (REA) was enacted in 1938, only the most conveniently located farms were the first to get it, and our farm was a mile off the main section line. So, we listened to our grandest amenity, a battery-powered tube radio, the night's center of attraction, by the light of coal oil (kerosene) lamps. Radio was our prime means of communication with the rest of the world, and we listened to *Burns and Allen*, *Fibber McGee and Molly*, *Lum and Abner*, *G-men*, the *Inner Sanctum Mysteries* (the source of some of my radio-induced nightmares with that creaky door sound), *Jack Armstrong, the All American Boy*, *The Shadow*, *Melody Ranch* (Gene Autry), *King of the Cowboys* (Roy Rogers), *The Lone Ranger*, *Your Hit Parade*, The Nashville *Grand Ole Opry*, *Jack Benny*, *Amos 'n' Andy*, and *The Aldrich Family*. Sponsors of these shows encouraged you to send for all kinds of gadgets to promote their products. Box tops or other proofs of purchase could be exchanged for toys such as a silver bullet from the *Lone Ranger*, interplanetary maps from *Buck Rogers*, magic tricks, a correspondence course in jiu-jitsu, and decoder rings from *Little Orphan Annie*, which glowed in the dark if you held them under a light first and then wore them into the closet. A small magnifying glass could be ordered so that you could become a spy. One could also collect cereal box tops and send them in for an eagerly anticipated prize. One I remember would be the X-Ray glasses from the back of *Superman* comics that could "see" through clothing. For a dime one could order a pamphlet about telegraphy that would teach you Morse code. During these hours that we listened to the radio, the world outside withdrew while we shared something that brought pleasure to each of us. We probably did not understand it at the time, but with comics, problems remained contained. Life was something you could laugh at.

Our first basketball goal was an old barrel-stave hoop nailed up on the granary wall, sort of like the peach baskets Dr. James Naismith salvaged from the janitor when he invented basketball in 1891 in Springfield, Massachusetts. Later, we advanced to a five-gallon bucket, with the bottom cut out, nailed up on the garage, and then to a bucket attached to the makings of a real goal post. Until the third goal, when we got our first real goal, we used a stuffed sock for a basketball. I played many H-O-R-S-E games on these goals. Near the completion of the last goal, we received a real basketball for Christmas. Even with winter's icy roots coming on, we were so excited with this ball that we braved the freezing weather shooting baskets until we played ourselves into exhaustion and were made to come into the house. Sometimes, if snow was on the ground, we would stay out so long that our jeans would get wet and freeze as stiff as lumber. We would have to lie down on the kitchen linoleum floor and pull one another's britches off. Not only was this fun, but it helped escape the doldrums of winter. Actually, life for us didn't change much when snow came. Snow meant snowmen, forts, snowball fights, and snow ice cream! Everything looks so clean after a snow. It covers the brown grass, bare ground, old weeds, cow patties, and everything ugly.

Some of my more vivid merriment and gaiety of my Christmas memories, other than getting presents and the traditional family Christmas foods, were getting sacks of treats from various sources.

The church always gave sacks of treats that included an apple, orange, assorted hard-shelled nuts, peanuts, soft and hard candy. There was a one-room country school near where we lived that always had a Christmas function that gave all the kids sacks of fruit and candy treats. My two favorite candy treats were those soft gummy orange slices and soft chocolate candy pieces with a white filling. We went to a Christmas program once out in the Amish community and they gave a sack of treats that contained all homemade candy. The town also gave kids a sack of treats from out of the back of the fire engine. Our bus driver would always give us a candy bar on the last day of school before the Christmas holidays.

There were two creeks separating our farm from a friend's farm that was located in the Custer School District, so I didn't go to school with him. He had a hobby of making model airplanes, and I really enjoyed walking over to his place to visit and admire his planes that included a Piper Cub, a Spitfire, a P-51 Mustang, a Jap Zero, and other WWII planes. We played football mostly in a plowed field, but we had a "real" track-and-field running track. Dad would take a carryall earth mover and smooth out a surface around one of the little fields. We used empty oil drums for hurdles. I used Mother's quilting poles to pole vault. I guess all this is where I picked up my love for athletics, plus having an older brother who excelled on the school athletic teams. Jackie and I had watched enough war movies to know that jumping out of an airplane was a fairly easy thing to do. You jumped, your parachute opened, and you floated down. So, we thought we would do the same thing by getting a quilt and jumping off the barn roof. Well, fortunately for us, we just happened to jump into a haystack. No major damage.

I was always glad I wasn't a girl for many reasons, but the main one is because they couldn't have peeing contests, pee their initials in the snow, or pee on a dying campfire. Jackie and I used to see who could pee the farthest and highest. We would aim for the stars, but hit only a few feet up on the barn wall. For some reason, Jackie used to always win these "athletic" events. An event that brings back painful memories for some was when older guys would get lucky and talk some younger naive boy into grabbing hold of an electric fence to receive a shocking shock, or worse yet to pee on an electric fence. Jackie remembers Sam Hooper peeing on an electric fence once, and that was talked about for a long time by his friends and dad. This happened at some night gathering of Sam and a few of his friends. Jackie was not there and does not remember any details about the event. There were other ploys one would use to shock an unsuspecting neophyte. One might say, "Here, touch the fence with these pliers to see if it is working," for instance. On a double dare challenge, Gene McCall had a similar experience when he was fourteen-years-old. An electric fence was a temporary fence farmers put up once a year when they put cattle out on wheat pasture. It was quick, easy, and economical to put up for the short wheat pasture season.

Our aunts, uncles, cousins, and neighbors lived close by and would come over a lot at night. The adults would play cards and gossip while we kids would usually go to the creek, even if it was a cold crisp winter night when the trees were naked with snow on the ground. We would tromp all over with only the moon to light the way. We would always look in the sky for the few constellations that we could recognize, for shooting stars, the Big Dipper, the immensity of the Milky Way, the North Star — the same North Star that guided Columbus and all the great explorers. In the summertime we would lie on our backs to look at the stars. I remember Huck Finn saying, "The sky looks ever so deep when you lay down on your back in the moonshine." I used to wonder what the sky would be like if I could look at it through a telescope. Talk about a Great Beyond. If someone would have told me then that man would someday walk on the moon, I would have laughed at them. Today, everytime I look at Ursa Major (the Big Dipper), I feel my boyhood's presence. For a kid like me, the only thing that could improve a week in paradise was to have a cast of cousins with which to play.

In the summertime listening to hoot owls, turtle doves, and the rhythmic measured cadence of the clattering cricket sounds, we would play games such as hide-'n'-go-seek, cops and robbers, cow-boys, Indians, and rogue pirates. However, we were not real pirates because we did not have a spyglass. I loved shooting my cap pis-tol terrorizing the Indians and bad guys. "Oly-Oly-Oxen-free, all out come in free" was a phrase we would recite when we had been play-ing hide-'n'-seek awhile and most had been found. However, there were always a few really good hiders who would still not be caught. What this really meant was that we had given up, and they were the winners. We would also spend hours chasing lightning bugs, some-times called fireflies. We would catch these fiery specks in the sky, put them in a jar, and eventually let them go. These bugs would use their bioluminescence to attract mates or prey. Annie Over was a game we played by throwing a ball over the house. We would shout, "Annie Over" and throw the ball over the house. If someone on the other side caught the ball, they would get a point. They never knew for sure just which part of the roof it would come over on, and this is what made the game interesting. We would spin our bodies around and around, getting dizzy and falling down, which was cause for giggles. Other games we played were blind man's bluff, tag, capture the flag, and kick the can. When we would stay in the house with company, we would play Old Maid, Books, Slap Jack, and I Doubt It. Most of these games were played at night when our parents were visiting with rela-tives or neighbors — games that the night demanded.

The scariest thing I remember about living on the farm was when a guy by the name of Billy Cook murdered six people on a 22-day rampage hitchhiking and kidnapping people between Missouri and California in 1950–51. Like the *Scarlet Pimpernel* he was reported to have been seen here, there, and everywhere. He killed a family and their dog in Joplin, Missouri, dumping their bodies down a mine shaft. He killed another person in California. One frighteningly dark night, we three boys were home alone and saw this car driving down our dead-end lane. We turned out all the lights, grabbed cast-iron cook-ing skillets, and hid behind doors and under furniture just waiting for Billy Cook to break in. This made us feel *crawly*, as Huck Finn would say. When the car turned around and left we were very relieved. We never did find out any details about that mystery car.

I remember one snowy day after we had eaten our Malt-O-Meal and donned our four-buckle overshoes, we took our homemade sled down to the creek bank. An earthen dam that Dad had built with his tractor and carryall had washed out, leaving a huge gap right in the center. This gap was in direct alignment with our sled path so we needed to avoid it. We pushed off from the top of the bank into the whiteness flowing to the creek with a mixture of adrenaline and speed. All three of us were on the sled having a good run at a faster speed than we had anticipated. Too late, we noticed we weren't going to negotiate the turn down to the creek bottom and avoid going over the embankment created by the washout. There was just no way to "bail out" of this situation. This can only be described as one seismic crash. We went slithering down that washout, catapulting and flying all over one another. I can't remember who, but one of us was knocked unconscious for a minute after the heavy sled landed on top of us. We had all been more or less concussed, but we knew that part of the fun of sledding was the risk of soaring off a jump. The only guy that I remember who ever had a store-bought sled was Gary Jones. He had a Flexible Flyer. We also would pull our sled with our horse. When we were older and living in town, we would always hook up with someone who was pulling a sled with a vehicle, and this could get very centrifugal when turning corners.

As we were trying to force a living out of this small farm, Richard would plow in the field while Dad was at his day job. On one hot summer day, I took Richard a drink of water in a jar wrapped in a soaking wet burlap sack to help keep it cool. When he finished drinking he asked if I wanted to drive the tractor. What biddable third-grader wouldn't want this opportunity? Richard went to the house and fell asleep under a shade tree with a slow summer breeze blowing over him. Granddad Friesen showed up at this time and thought Richard was shirking his duties and made him get back on the tractor, much to my disappointment. It wasn't too long after this, however, that this novelty wore off. Once, when I had taken some water to Richard in the field on our horse, I was galloping in perfect rhythm on the horse back to the barn with the wind whipping against my face yelling "whoopitiyiyo" when the cinch on the saddle came loose, causing the saddle to slide almost under the belly of the horse. Naturally, I took quite a tumble to the ground. However, the ground had just been freshly plowed and prevented me from seeing twinkling stars and Tweety Birds. I always liked the dusty warm pony sweat and the fresh air on my face as I rode our horse in the fields, pastures, and creeks. Our horse was never enthusiastic about much of a gallop when moving away from the barn, and I clucked my tongue in an attempt to quicken her pace. However, when we would eventually turn around to go back to the barn, she would immediately transition from a sedate cantering to a quickened pace on autopilot, doing her best to show me who was really in charge. Horses have that homing instinct.

I can recall, when I was quite young, riding the harrow with Granddad Friesen on his farm. We were pulled by a team of draft horses smelling of healthy horseflesh. I was in awe of how horses could defecate while walking or trotting. The horse lifts his tail and great lumps of steaming yellow manure drop from his behind. I wanted Grandpa to stop, but he said no, let them keep going. They always defecate on the go. Also, I remember hog butchering, lard rendering, making lye soap in a large black iron kettle, and swinging on large corral gates at Granddad Friesen's farm. The hog(s) to be slaughtered were herded into a small pen, and either Daddy or Granddaddy would go among them with a .22-caliber rifle and shoot one or more of them. Then they cut the throat and let the blood drain. The carcass was hung up by its heel tendons on sharp hooks, slit open with a knife, and the internal organs were lowered into a large washtub. The carcass was then skinned, cut into the different meat cuts and Grandma would be boiling the fat into lard and cracklings in a large black iron pot, cleaning the small intestines for sausage casings. Most of the lean-meat scraps were cut into small pieces and fed into a hand-cranked grinder to be made into sausage.

At a Friesen family reunion in Custer at Granddad's house, Jackie, cousin Bobby Friesen, and I couldn't resist the call of the bullfrog's deep bass croaking. We caught a frog in a ditch of rainwater and put the frog down the back of one of our citified cousins from California. He went ballistic running into the house. Mother and Aunt Leona came through the back door like a train out of a tunnel and let it be known to our fathers that we needed punishing. Lectures, lectures, lectures. I suppose that is what mothers and aunts are for, but they did put a crimp in one's style sometimes. Our dads spanked us, but their hearts weren't in it. It was mostly symbolic. I could tell they thought it was a clever trick but just couldn't let on like they did, lest we would be encouraged to do even wilder things. Actually, it was big brother Richard and cousin Junior who put the idea in our heads. I had to chuckle later in life when Bobby Gentry came out with a song titled "Ode to Billy Joe." There are lyrics in the song about some boys putting a frog down the back of a girl at the Carroll County picture show.

It was the last spring that we lived on the farm when a storm brewed up out of the west. It looked like it could be bad, so we quickly drove up to the Hooper place because they had a cellar and we didn't. We went down in their cellar prepared to spend the night. A tornado did come through and blew away the Hoopers' barn and several of their livestock. Most of the livestock were found a few miles away the next morning, but old Blue, Gary Hooper's prize coon-hunting hound, who took shelter in the barn, was killed. Many roads were clogged with debris and the school buses could not get through to many rural homes. Consequently, we missed the last day of school that year.

CHAPTER 16

Swimming

"Oh! The old 'swimmin' hole! When I last saw the place, the scenes were all changed."

– James Whitcomb Riley

THE PHRASE "LET'S go swimming" has magical connotations in my childhood memories. When we lived on the farm, we always had a creek and cow tank in which to swim. Those were the days before there were many upstream flood-control dams. This enabled there to be more and cleaner swimming water, so that we could make like Johnny Weissmuller (Tarzan). Not one of us knew when he had learned to swim any more than he could remember when he had learned to walk. I guess that I can attribute my learning how to swim to Richard. He would throw Jackie and me into deep water and attempt to teach us to dog paddle or at least how not to drown. We would thrash around hopelessly trying to look like swimmers. After mastering the dog paddle we learned the Australian Crawl — or "freestyle" as it is now known.

At a church picnic that was both sacred and secular, I have two photos of a group of us skinny dipping in Patton's Creek, which is the secular part. If this picture was in color, it would look like it had escaped from a Renoir painting. The nude dudes included Jr. Hart (cousin), Charles and Lyle Combs, Richard, Garland and Alvin Patton, and Billy Hart (cousin). Maynard Book, Jackie, and I were around the bend and not in the photo. There are a couple of bare behinds showing in the photo. One of the mothers slipped up on us and took the pictures. We had no prudish Victorian attitudes toward nudity. Swimming in the altogether was considered a healthy, manly outdoor activity. I don't remember ever being concerned about turtles, snakes, or other aquatic creatures.

On Sunday we usually went to Clinton, Weatherford, or picturesque Roman Nose State Park near Watonga to swim in public pools. The pristine setting of the Roman Nose pool was notable because of the frigid spring water. The pool was filled with water from a nearby spring and creek. Our parents would take us to one of these places almost every Sunday afternoon. Clinton had a large diving wheel that one would lie on and dive into the water as it slowly turned. After swimming, we would always stop at an ice-cream place because one is always hungry after swimming. Plunging your face into ice cream after swimming is the finest feeling a human being can have. While driving home from swimming, we would frequently hold our bathing suits out the car window to dry them and position our hands into the wind to test the aerodynamics of different hand formations. At other times during the week, a gang of us would often go to the river where there was a deep hole under the north side of the South Canadian River Bridge, where this languid river, for some reason, deposited a nice deep swimming hole for youngsters like me. I remember Richard and his buddies swimming in this hole with a thin sheet of ice one Easter. Mary Lee Norris Darter told me that her father bolted a plank on a part of the under-bridge structure that was used as a diving board. I do not remember this. It must have been put up after I graduated. This was a really neat place where there was no graffiti or empty beer cans.

One year, after school was out for the summer, Richard, Jackie, and I drained the cow tank to clean it for summer swimming. After cleaning, we turned on the windmill to refill it. As fate would have it, there was no wind. Dad came home and was very upset. We had to carry buckets of water from the cistern at the house to the tank for the livestock. A cistern was a small underground reservoir that stored rainwater for drinking, bathing, and dishwashing. It was lined with concrete to keep out underground water. It was about 10′ deep and 7′ in diameter. The cover was concrete, topped with a galvanized metal crank housing. A crank mechanism turned a chain of water cups that dipped into the water, brought the water up to the well spout, and dumped the water out into the spout on which the water bucket hung. For cisterns without a water-cup system, one would use a bucket tied to a rope, whereby it would be lowered and raised by a pulley arrangement. The bucket of drinking water was then taken into the kitchen and placed on the counter. A long-handled white enameled dipper was kept nearby from which we all drank. There was nothing more tasty and refreshing than a drink of cool rainwater from the cistern. Richard, Jackie, and I would periodically have to clean the cistern when the water level ran low. One of us would be lowered down into the well with a rope, broom, and bucket. The source of water was rain runoff from the roof of the house. The water would funnel into the cistern through drain spouts and through a filter just before dumping into the well. During a rain, we would let the water drain onto the ground until the roof had sufficiently been cleared of dirt and other grit before we would turn the valve letting water into the well.

Another thing we did on the river that was great fun was the climbing of young saplings until they bent to the ground. One would then, while hanging on, jump up. With the spring in the tree and your jump, you could fling yourself high in the air while still holding onto the sapling. The height depended on how much one weighed and the size of the sapling. With equal grace and dexterity, I succumbed to gravity and took a fall to the ground once when one broke as I started to descend. Fortunately, the ground was sand. We mostly played this activity with Jr. and Billy Hart. Read Robert Frost's poem "Birches." "When I see birches bend left to right across the lines of straighter darker trees, I like to think some boy's been swinging them . . ." Larry

Foster, from Alex, told me they used to do the same thing on the Washita River and called it "riding the willows down."

On the south riverbank were high cliffs where a long steep dirt slide had been created. One would climb to the top and glissade down at a steep angle on one's bottom. All went well unless you lost control of your speed and direction. All too frequently, one would end up tumbling and falling more than sliding. None of us had the sense to get a strong stick to use as a break and guide similar to how a mountain climber controls a glissade with an ice axe. Virgil Talbot learned a quick lesson in physics when he took a nasty fall on this slide, losing a battle with the tenacious grip of gravity. Oh well, what are cliffs for? I remember him having to be carried out. On the highway near this slide, there was also a steep highway grade that Richard and the more daring older guys would go down on roller skates. Like the slide, speed was hard to control, but when they wanted to stop they would roll off to the side of the road into sand.

One day Mike Smith, Jackie, and I and our wayfaring minds decided to go on an expedition out to the South Canadian River swimming hole on a day that would have one singing "Zip-a-Dee-Doo-Dah." I left the swimming hole that day a happy boy. This wide river was not a substantial artery, but more of an ambitious stream, except after a big rain. This little swimming hole was no sleepy lagoon, but it served our purpose and we had lots of fun swimming there. When heading for home after our swim, we decided to take a shortcut because we were short on drinking water. So, tally ho! *Over the river and through the woods* as our internal drought was at this time on par with the drier reaches of the Sahara. Well, bushwhacking across the wide sandy, dry, and tree-infested riverbed didn't turn out to be much of a shortcut. Our inherent navigational inabilities emerged and we got lost and folded in among the riverbank hills with our throats getting even more parched. I don't remember which one of us decided that he was captain orienteering himself and suggesting the shortcut as he sorted out his flawed mental coordinates. We finally traipsed straight south, figuring we would eventually hit the highway and could hitchhike from there to put a stop to this attack of wanderlust. We knew which way was south because I knew that lichen grew on the north side of a tree. I learned that in the Boy Scouts. Unlike today, hitchhiking was then a common and safe mode of transportation. My dad hopped a freight train to California before he was married. Maybe that is where I got part of my need for adventure. With stoic fortitude we did find the highway. Waving our thumbs like they were calling out for heavenly deliverance, we caught a ride with Good Samaritan Dr. Ryan, who was on his way home from fishing at Canton Lake. Bedraggled, we must have looked like we had been ridden hard and put up wet or like refugees I had seen in *Life Magazine*, because we found getting over this heavy ground as lightly as possible was very difficult. This was a penance for which we did not bargain. Dr. Ryan gave us a hydration sermon on taking plenty of water with us next time. I am glad that Dr. Ryan came by because with our dying-man-in-desert-sees-mirage image, no one else would probably have picked us up.

It was around this time that I joined the Boy Scouts looking for adventure, to learn how to build a fire without a fire (usually, I only had to bandage one finger after chopping firewood), to tie knots, to prepare and pitch a pup tent that would not leak during a rainstorm (mine always leaked), to dig a shallow trench around the tent to drain the water away, to do good deeds, to learn first aid, to "always be prepared" and all those other Boy Scout words, and to do the three-fingered salute and handshake. I got to wear a cool uniform with a neat hat and all kinds of bright-colored patches sewn on my shirt. We learned how to go to the bathroom in the woods in an environmentally sound manner. Oh, and I liked the smell of calamine lotion. We bathed by jumping into the creek. Also, I liked receiving my subscription to *Boys' Life Magazine* with its frequent Norman Rockwell covers, which came with one's membership. Every month it featured news, stories, jokes, and practical how-to instructions invaluable to all scouts. We had a nice scout cabin out on Clarence Patton's creek to which we frequently hiked on scout night. We employed the scout pace where you would alternately walk so many paces and then jog so many paces. This eventually got you to where you were going without having to stop and rest. My campfire cooking was not all that successful. The camp menu usually ended up being pork and beans with Vienna sausages and roasting wieners on a clothes hanger. However, campfire wood smoke was my favorite smell. Even today when I drive through outdoor smoke it brings on a nostalgic smell. And, I always enjoyed the flicker of a small smoking fire just before we would wiggle our way into our sleeping bags at night. On one weekend camping trip we had a serious rainstorm. My tent was the only one that held up and did not collapse. There must have been six guys who dove into my two-man tent. Obviously, my tent could not withstand this onslaught. It collapsed causing us to have to sleep in an open-air dormitory. We ended up building a large fire to dry out everyone's clothes and bedding. This was an inglorious start to the weekend. One year when I was a scout, I went to church camp near Ponca City. There were so many campers that a few of us had to pitch and live in pup tents. This was not a problem for me because I was a Boy Scout. What a miserable week that was. The camaraderie of scouting and camping was a positive experience for me.

Butch Self bought a leviathan eight-man military surplus rubber life raft. I am not sure why he bought this boat, but I guess he was thinking of floating the South Canadian River when the next big rain came along. Anyway, one night several of us decided to take the raft out to City Lake on the Clyde Jones farm for a little nautical nocturnal fun as if we were headed for a regatta. After we had pushed away from shore, bobbing about enjoying ourselves and listening to the swish and lap of the water in the middle of the lake and before Butch even had a chance to prove his navigational skills, the boat suddenly began to deflate. I can't remember whether someone pulled a plug or there was a mechanical failure of some kind. Or, we could have over-inflated the ancient craft and created a leak in a seam. As we were all thrashing about trying to untangle ourselves from the deflating boat, one of the comics in our yachting fraternity started yelling "Dive! Dive! Dive!" trying to emulate some line he had heard in a submarine war movie. Anyway, we ended up in the water and had to swim back to shore. Thankfully, the lake had a glassy calmness on a moonlit night, which gave the water a nice luminescence. We thought we were immortal as far as water was concerned. Sons of Poseidon! Unsinkable! I am glad there were no girls with us on this little, *I must go down to the sea again* adventure. As I think back on this exciting experience as an adult, I think we were just fulfilling an innate need for adventure. As one of Mark Twain's characters in *Life on the Mississippi* said, "It was only to get a ride on a raft. All boys does it."

Dripping Springs south of Custer was another good place to swim. However, we seldom went there, except for Boy Scout activities. The quiet pastoral simplicity of this place had a small lake, swimming pool, and a large shelter for picnics and other activities. I always enjoyed scout campouts. It seemed that food tasted different in the open air. Its flavor changed. Sitting around a campfire staring into the yellow, blue, red, and orange flames sending pins of embers skittering into the air was kind of magical. Watching the log surfaces smoke, shrivel, crack, glow, and collapse into dusty ash was almost hypnotizing.

One year the Boy Scouts entered a competitive regional swim meet at the Clinton pool. We won several ribbons in individual and relay events. Our 60-yard medley relay team won first, I placed second in the breast stroke, second in the side-stroke events, and third in the walking race in shallow water.

CHAPTER 17

The War

"Never in the field of human conflict was so much owed by so many to so few." – W. Churchill

I WAS TWO years old when America declared war on Japan in 1941 and almost six when World WarII ended. These were the "war years" as most liked to call them, or what Studs Terkel called *The Good War*, an oral history of WWII. It was not like other wars. Our enemy was the Holocaust maker. It was supported enthusiastically and was considered a "just war," if there is such an animal. WWII was underway by 1939 and ended in 1945. This war involved most of the world's nations — including all the great powers — eventually forming two opposing military alliances: the Allies (the good guys) and the Axis (the bad guys). It was the most widespread war in history, with more than 100 million people serving in military units. It resulted in over 50 million fatalities. These deaths make World WarII by far the deadliest conflict in all of human history. There aren't many earlier events in my life that are as vivid as the war. I knew about war; my dad, uncles, and one cousin were in it. My dad and cousin Roy Hart served in the army during the war. Uncles Arnold and Wesley Friesen served in the Pacific Theater in the navy. I remember visiting my dad when he was stationed at Fort Lewis, Washington. We stayed in guest quarters on the base sleeping on army cots. The green canvas on the cots was stretched tautly over their foldable wooden frames, and we slept on and covered up with army green itchy wool blankets. There were German POWs sweeping the streets under the watchful eyes of armed guards. I remember Richard telling me that there were real bullets in those guns. This was big stuff for a five-year-old.

My cousin, Roy Hart, was a .50-caliber machine gunner, and his picture came out in the paper showing him cleaning his gun in a fox-hole during a lull while fighting in France. From a distant hill, he was a witness to the Malmédy Massacre where the Germans machine-gunned over a hundred American prisoners of war near this Belgian town during the Battle of the Bulge in December of 1944. We used to play war a lot. Whoever played the Germans would periodically give the Nazi salute — the obligatory salutation in Germany during the war. When our parents realized we were doing this, we were promptly disciplined and that put a stop to that nonsense. After all, German immigrants did not want to appear unpatriotic because many German Americans and German aliens were interned during the war in locations throughout the country, including military bases and local jails. There were more than 26 million people of German descent in the U.S. at this time. It was later determined that there was no rational basis for these internments. Most German Americans were fervent patriots. Even though it came from WWI, we used to recite a popular slogan lampooning Kaiser Wilhelm II when playing war that went something like the following:

Kaiser Bill went up the hill to take a peek at France,
Kaiser Bill came down the hill with bullets in his pants.

After the war, a few of us were hiking — actually, we were walking, but any time there was a slight incline I called it hiking — out in the country and came upon an old abandoned house. We went in looking for anything interesting. We found a German helmet, Nazi flag, and other Teutonica. This scared us and we ran lickety-split out of there like we had just seen the Headless Horseman even though these items were souvenirs of some veteran.

Our local beer joint catered to an assorted cast of characters in their clientele whose intellects on their communal best days would make the inmates of the old bedlam asylums look like a collection of professors from Oklahoma University. The casual observer could easily conclude that one was witnessing the decline of civilization. I always wished that the owner would have named this establishment something like The Lazy Dollar, Gringo Gulch, The Purple Sage, Galoot's Rest, The Dirty Dog, Last Chance, or The Dry Gulch Saloon. One of the more colorful characters was a guy who went by the moniker of "Tarzan." Tarzan who had more rough edges than a piece of Precambrian rock and, as one of the local eccentrics, came home from the Pacific Theater of the war with tattoos of a dragon, snake, and mermaid and was considered a war hero by some. Although Tarzan had not personally taken credit for sinking the *Bismark*, he did have a lot of war stories he liked to tell. He was invited to speak at an all-school assembly about his war experiences. Someone at school should have checked with Tarzan's buddies at the beer joint about his suitability to be speaking to young people on any topic. Public speaking was not one of his more admirable qualities. In fact, some would have questioned his ability to communicate on the level of a functioning primate. Most of his adjectives were not to be found in the Webster's abridged or unabridged dictionary. It seems strange to me that no one on the faculty knew that he was rhetorically challenged and was not a paragon of virtue. He told stories using a lot of gore and rough language. One story was about how he cut the ear off of a dead Jap and brought it home with him. Shortly after he began speaking, it was no mystery to the faculty why Tarzan had never risen to the rank of Admiral of the Ocean Sea. History has not recorded what followed Tarzan's appearance as a public speaker. I may have been in the first grade but don't remember the event. Lloyd Ray (three years older than me) remembers being there. Having known Tarzan and hearing this story of his speaking before students sends shivers up my spine. The only work I ever remember Tarzan doing was as a plough hand for local farmers. He used to brag to me about how he could plough a really good dead furrow when finishing a field. This was always difficult for me, so he would try to tell me how to do it. "Just put the front end of the plough in deep and pull the back end out shallow and you will not leave a deep furrow to wash when it rains." Sounds easy, but I guess I just didn't have enough experience. I was only 16 years old. I think he acquired his nickname from having a muscular frame similar to Popeye and having vise-grip hands the size of his thighs. I guess every community needs a few eccentrics. However, to know him was to love him.

I used to dream a lot about being in the war fighting the Japs. When they would charge at me, my gun would never fire. I still remember these dreams being vivid and detailed — went to too many John Wayne war movies. The terms *Jap* and *Kraut* (for Germans) were derogatory terminology used by most Americans during WWII. I wonder what they called us? Most homes in town had either a blue or gold-star flag in a window. A blue star indicated that a member of your family was serving in the military. A gold star was a sad indicator of the death of a family member in the war. I have a picture of Richard, Jackie, and me standing in front of the door with our blue-star flag displayed in the window. Also, the Hockaday Hardware Store had stars painted on one of their outside walls — one for every local person serving in the military.

I remember a few of the old war posters: "I Want You," with Uncle Sam's picture, and also "Buy War Bonds," "Rosey the Riveter," and "Loose Lips Sink Ships." The government introduced rationing because certain things were scarce during the war and rationing was the only way to make sure everyone got their fair share. I recall rationing stamps, but don't remember anything about specific rationing or shortages, which were a very real thing that affected everyone. Older people tell me that there were never enough ration stamps. Gasoline, sugar, tires, silk, shoes, and meat were other commodities that were rationed. Sugar and coffee were the first two items to be rationed. Desserts were sweetened with honey or molasses. Tires were scarce and nylon hose was nonexistent. Rubber was the first nonfood item rationed. The Japs had seized the rubber plantations in the Dutch East

Indies that produced 90% of Americans' raw rubber. To help ease the burden of rationing, people were told to "Use it up, wear it out, make do, or do without." Many people raised what were known as "victory gardens" to lessen the effects of rationing and to show their true patriotism. I don't recall us ever referring to our gardens as victory gardens, and I doubt any farmers did because they had always raised gardens. In the larger cities, especially those with factories making war material, renting out spare rooms in one's house was considered patriotic. Rationing began in 1942 and ended before the end of 1945. Rationing was even more severe in England and did not end until 1954, nine years after the end of the war. My world, at the time, was relatively untouched by the privations of the war. While visiting the 1944 State Fair, in Oklahoma City I had the opportunity to walk through a B-17 bomber.

During a drive to collect scrap metal for the war effort, Dorothy Norris gave her dad's golf clubs to the cause. It was a long time before she heard the last of that from her dad. There was a slogan used during the war to encourage people to donate scrap: "All this scrap to lick the Jap." The ending of the war triggered national jubilation with the local residents building a huge bonfire in the intersection of Main and Broadway to celebrate the victory. At one point all the men began throwing their hats into the fire. This was an act of patriotic celebration repeated all over America and Europe in public squares and village greens. A terrible curse had been lifted from the world. After VE Day (Victory in Europe) the soldiers came home to a hero's welcome — Lowell Law came home with one leg. That was impressionable to a young boy who had seen movies where soldiers had their legs amputated without anesthesia, not that his had been done that way. Germany surrendered on May 7, 1945. Japan surrendered on August 15, 1945.

A few songs from the war era were: "The White Cliffs of Dover," "I Left My Heart at the Stage Door Canteen," "I'll Be Seeing You," "Don't Sit Under the Apple Tree," "G.I. Jive," "I'll Never Smile Again," "When the Lights Go On Again," "A Nightingale Sang in Berkeley Square," and "I'll Be with You in Apple Blossom Time." The Glenn Miller Band was probably the most famous big band during the war years. His most popular songs were "In the Mood," "A String of Pearls," "Tuxedo Junction," "Chattanooga Choo Choo," "Pennsylvania 6-5000," and the band's sentimental theme song, "Moonlight Serenade."

A belated WWII experience came my way when, in 2002, while sitting in the Welk Theater in Branson, Missouri, I had the opportunity to visit with Gen. Paul Tibbits, the *Enola Gay* B-29 pilot who dropped the atom bomb on Hiroshima. He just happened to be sitting in the seat directly in front of me.

While playing Capture the Flag as a kid during the war, little did I know that other little kids in Europe were being loaded into boxcars and hauled to concentration camps like Birkenau, Auschwitz, Dachau, Buchenwald, Treblinka, and Mauthausen, to be gassed just because they were Jews.

CHAPTER **18**

Smoking

"Avoid taverns, drinkers, smokers, idlers, and dissipated persons generally." – T. Jefferson

GRAPEVINES AND DRIFTWOOD were the smokes of choice among most farm boys, and were they ever strong. Grapevines were slightly superior to driftwood, but they were difficult to light. Smoking these things was a way for kids to imagine they were on the brink of adulthood, making one feel like a big shot. It may seem silly now, but it remains a nostalgic moment for people raised in rural areas. One friend told me that they would sometimes get old dried leaves, crush, and grind them, and roll them into a paper cigarette. Others tried smoking coffee grounds rolled up in a piece of paper. I heard of one guy smoking a rolled-up piece of paper with nothing in it. When he puffed on it he sucked the flame down his throat. He said he never smoked again.

It was thought to be a cool thing to get a used empty Bull Durham (we pronounced it "derm") brand tobacco pouch with a picture of a big, red-and-white snorting bull on it, fill it with dirt, put it in your pocket, and let the yellow drawstring hang out. The idea was an attempt not only to impress your friends that you were a smoker, but also that you hand-rolled your own cigarettes from loose tobacco and rolling paper. I learned much later that Bull Durham was a fourth-rate tobacco. A Bull Durham tobacco pouch should be placed in the

Smithsonian Institute, if it hasn't already. The older guys would stuff a pack up in the upper reaches of their "T-shirt" sleeve by the shoulder. Some would tuck a cigarette alongside their ear. I was told of a guy who once smoked a cigarette made out of Nestle's Quik rolled up in tissue paper. It burnt his tongue so bad that it blistered.

One of our friends, Gary Hooper, lived two miles north of us. While playing at his house one day, he suggested we (he, Jackie, and me) go down to the bridge and smoke some Lucky Strikes, Old Golds, Chesterfields, Camels, or whatever. I am not sure where Gary got his cigarettes; however, both his parents smoked and his uncle operated the local Sinclair filling station. I will let the reader draw his own conclusions. Chesterfield used to sponsor a popular TV show in the '50s — Ted Mack's *Original Amateur Hour*. Camel's commercial catchphrase was, *I'd walk a mile for a camel*, so we were literally walking a mile to smoke a Camel. Well, it wasn't really a mile from the house to the bridge. Winston cigarettes had an advertising phrase that said, "Winston tastes good like a cigarette should." Of course, Gary had to give us smoking lessons and that caused me to think of my possible punishment in hell. He later taught me how to spit and whistle. I will never forget the feeling I had when I first achieved that real whistling sound by blowing into my cupped hands. I felt like an astronomer feels who has discovered a new planet.

Gary was a confirmed and enthusiastic chain smoker, as if it were his job. He smoked unfiltered cigarettes down to the point that the calluses on his fingers were glowing red. He had the skills that marked him as a Grand Master of smoking before he was fourteen. He was almost as good as the charismatic macho of Humphrey Bogart with his smoking style. With Gary's smoking skills, one would have thought he was born smoking. He would reach into his shirt pocket and pull out a new pack of cigarettes, strip off the cellophane from a fresh pack of Camels, tap out a cigarette, plant it between his lips, and with a smooth hand casually strike the match. The fire from the match illuminated his face like Renaissance saints as his lips hugged the cigarette. The match was sometimes referred to as a "lucifer." Gary would hold it at the end of the cigarette as he studiously sucked the yellow flame into the tobacco until the cigarette glowed a hot orange and a distinctive smoky smell rose out of it as the cigarette smoke stripped the air. He would do this with an elegant flourish as he tossed his head like a thoroughbred, and then bent his arm and wrist just right and relaxed the fingers, holding the coffin nail reverently between the first and second fingers as if it were a magic wand, taking a deep contemplative drag, sighing with contentment, and then waving out the lighted match with its acrid sulphur smell. If a breeze was blowing, Gary would curl his hand protectively around the cigarette as he lit it, carefully cradling the match and let the smoke trickle out his mouth and draw it up his nose. He could keep one going in the teeth of a gale. I thought this was a pretty cool skill. Without any fanfare he would let the chalky gray wisp of smoke drift out through his nostrils in a long curl of gray nicotine fog. His squinted eyes would have cleared the first two lines of enemy trenches in World WarI, as the smoke swirled up past his half-closed eyes and veiled his face. I don't remember Gary ever graduating from his lucifers to a Zippo. Zippo lighters were cool. They had a *clink* sound when opening and a *clank* sound when closing.

Gary could even talk with the smoldering cigarette dangling from his lips, rising and falling in accent as he spoke without ever losing an ash. Gary could, with great self-satisfaction, blow smoke rings as easily as I could blow kisses. A veil of smoke exhaled out of his nose and mouth in such continuous volume that I would not have been much taken aback to see jets of it shoot out of his ears. He never ceased to amaze me with his professional smoking skills. One night we were playing on the creek, and I remember Gary came running down a trail practically invisible except for the tiny flow of a cigarette that zigzagged like a firefly.

Jackie and I lit off Gary's glowing cigarette and inhaled. It burned terribly! "Breathe it out, stupid," Gary says. We did and noticed a lightheadedness and nausea. We were quickly enveloped in an ominous cloud of tobacco smoke. Plumes of smoke were flattening against the bridge plank flooring, our ceiling, and billowing out the edge and through the cracks like an Indian smoke signal. Man, this was almost like Huck Finn teaching Tom Sawyer to smoke a corncob pipe. A few minutes later Gary took his cigarette from his mouth and turned it this way and that in his fingers, gazing at it as if its wrapper might be hiding a great philosophical answer. He blew out a breath, and said, "Man, this is the life." When we returned to the house, our mothers greeted us with frosty glares, asking us why we were smoking, having seen the smoke coming up through the bridge floor like a chimney. Unlike Tom Sawyer, we had no plan B for our mischievous deed, and lying through our teeth, we said that we had not been smoking. This attempted cover-up only compounded the crime. They knew better, of course, and spanked us with a switch from a nearby bush. I received my switching first and as Jackie waited in the on-deck circle as our common law punishment was administered. It provided the "rod" that the Bible taught my parents "not to spare." After the spanking was the threat of what was going to happen when Dad got home. Mother's threat of homicide would flat dampen down your spirits. And that is what nearly happened. There was little anger involved in a spanking, just a lecture explaining why you were getting one and why it was good for you. I guess the effects of those two spankings lasted as long as an ill-advised tattoo because that was the denouement of my smoking.

Just a few hundred feet west of this bridge where we were caught smoking was where we were once playing Tarzan, swinging across the dry creek bed when the rope broke. I landed on my chest, knocking the wind out of me. This was the first time I had ever had this experience, and I thought I was going to die. Gary grabbed my arm, taking long hard strides as he hauled me to the house, rattling off a litany of life-affirming promises that I would be okay and waving his arms like a semaphoring sailor to get the attention of our mothers. I was breathing before we arrived. The crisis was over. I had to choke back a chorus of Alleluias when my chest started rising and falling.

Mostly, only men smoked, at least in public. I remember the first time I ever saw a woman smoking. It was downtown in a cafe. Adah Isaacs Menken, from the bohemian subculture, shocked people in Virginia City, Nevada, in 1863 by smoking cigarettes while standing up. Women began smoking in earnest during WWII when they started working in war production plants by the millions. Chesterfield cigarettes were promoted as the "women's cigarette" after the war, as opposed to manly Camels. In the 1940s and '50s smoking was totally socially acceptable. The smells of the restaurants, the pool hall, and gas stations were threaded with cigarette smoke, and if you did not live through those times, you would need some imagination to understand how people tolerated this habit back in those days.

I recall a smoking story from school involving Haze and Larry. They were in the restroom with cigarette smoke wafting in the air like incense when Mr. Ross, unpretentiously, walked in and caught them. Smoke was coming out the top of the shower stall like a chimney in wintertime. Haze swallowed his lit cigarette and Larry tried to hide his behind his back quicker than you could say LSMFT (Lucky Strike Means Fine Tobacco), but he was doomed. Loyd, Don, and Gordon used to go up to feed the vocational agriculture hogs during class time and smoke their Chesterfields while lingering out at the school pigsty on the east side of town near Indian Hill. I am glad that my parents never smoked. I preferred the smell of the barnyard or garage.

CHAPTER 19

The Bus

"Go down to Kew in lilac time and you shall wander hand in hand with love in summer's wonderland." – Alfred Noyes

WE LIVED ON two different farms during our farm days, and at each place on school-day mornings, fall, winter, and spring, we had to walk a mile down an old rough-hewn country dirt road to meet the school bus. However, contrary to what some would tell you, we did not have to walk uphill both ways — that was for the generation before ours. I really enjoyed this safe meandering walk in the spring and fall. The most dangerous thing we had to deal with was occasionally dodging a skunk or opossum, and they weren't really dangerous. Nothing is sweeter than inhaling gallons of the fresh clean springtime air, viewing the fresh foliage of trees coming into full leaf, the smell of new growth everywhere, the budding trees no longer bare and skeletal with all their new chlorophyll (the principal industry of spring), their branches sprinkled with the bright fresh green back on earth in May, birds chirping, bees pollinating the flowers, and crocuses plunging up through the ground. It is nice to know that nature goes along just as planned with a particular rhythm, sound, and beauty. As it says in the song "If I Ruled the World," "Every day would be the first day of spring." I never cease to marvel at the profound observations of people to the first signs of spring turned green. It was kind of like this springtime spiritual renewal had never before happened. "Did you notice the redbud blooms?" "Can you believe that the wheat is starting to head out?" We know it is going to happen like clockwork, yet we speak about the first blooms as if it were some mysterious genesis. Some people refer to this time as "blossom time." I will never forget the breeze that carried the enchanting scent of those gloriously abundant lilacs which perfumed the air as we walked by these bushes twice each day in springtime to and from the bus. To me this was the aroma of spring itself. Some things you don't forget. There is something so comforting, so homelike, about lilac shrubs. It was days like those about which poets write. Every subsequent spring, even to this day, this aroma brings back irresistible memories of childhood summers and small adventures. In addition to the appealing bouquet of the purple lilacs, this great perfume bears testament to the fact that school was about to cease for the summer. Why wouldn't they be my favorite flower? There is even a song titled "Jeannine, I Dream of Lilac Time." The sweet smell of honeysuckle and clover weren't bad, either. Hollyhocks and gladiolas also proliferated in people's gardens. Spring, with its soft blue sky, could make one forget about the cold hostility of winter and all of its inconveniences.

We associated summertime with freedom. There was freedom from school and freedom to roam, and nothing is more American than freedom. Summertime was swimming, fireworks, hot dogs, cold watermelon, fried okra, and corn on the cob. Our summers were filled with awe and wonder. F. LaGard Smith and Mark Twain shed light and express my sentiments about summer in the following quotes respectively: "Summer reaches out to touch you. Not like winter, which stands off coldly. Nor even spring, which is exciting yet merely flirtatious." "All the summer world was bright and fresh and the sun rose upon a tranquil world and beamed down like a benediction."

There is one negative story about lilacs, however, that I should mention. The school bully would frequently ambush Lloyd Ray at the lilac bushes on the southwest corner of the school grounds and take his lunch money. Surprisingly, I never faced any teasing or bullying at school. Maybe it was because I had a big brother. These lilac bushes had tunnels in them, and we would play in them during the first- and second-grade years during recess. Maybe this is why the lilac fragrance is my favorite aroma.

A springtime story your mother tells is about Easter and the prediction of a wheat crop. If their wheat was tall enough in which to hide Easter eggs, they would usually have a good wheat crop.

As we crossed the railroad tracks on the way to the bus, we always put our ears to the tracks to see if we could hear a train approaching from miles away. We saw this old Indian practice in the movies of determining when buffalo or cavalry were approaching. Sometimes we would put a penny on the track on the way to the bus and look for the flattened penny after school when getting off the bus. Occasionally, we found it successfully smashed to smithereens.

Walking to and waiting for the bus in wintertime was a different matter. Once when the bus was late, our feet got so cold that we plodded back home through the snow, just sure that frostbite was imminent — and missed the bus. Dad was not a happy camper, having to take us to school. It is a wonder that we did not get hypothermia because it was cold enough to incapacitate an Eskimo. The only thing between us and the North Pole was a barbed-wire fence. This happened when I was in the second grade for one semester at Arapaho. The nearest friends we had at this farm were the Fisher brothers who lived one mile northeast of us. Anyway, a part of the walk to the bus at this farm was particularly nice. This old country road was almost arbored by the overhanging tree limbs and foliage through which we walked. It kind of reminded me of what I thought Robin Hood's Sherwood Forest probably looked like. I loved those Robin Hood movies with Errol Flynn and other actors who played Robin Hood. Robin Hood was the noblest man that ever was and he could lick any man in England. I would cheer when Robin and his merry men defended the poor Saxon serfs by jumping out of trees, foiling the sheriff of Nottingham's men as they rode out to collect taxes from the poor people, or when Robin would best the nefarious Prince John and his Norman lords in archery contests and other adventures while his brother, King Richard the Lionheart was out of the country fighting in the Crusades. While doing all this Robin still had time to woo the lovely Maid Marian and rescue maidens from wicked trolls or evil stepmothers.

CHAPTER 20

Your Hit Parade

"So Long for a While." – Theme song from *Your Hit Parade*

YOUR HIT PARADE was a popular TV show where singers would sing the current pop tunes of the country. One reason for its popularity was because it was viewed by people of all ages. One could hardly wait for Saturday night to find out what the top ten most popular and bestselling songs of the week would be. This ranking was based mainly on radio requests, sheet music sales, and jukebox tabulations. This show was broadcast from 1935 to 1955 on radio and seen from 1950 to 1959 on television. It was sponsored by American Tobacco's Lucky Strike cigarettes. Although the show had many different singers and groups in its 24-year run, I mainly remember the ones who appeared on the show during the peak years of the '50s. They would be Snooky Lanson, Dorothy Collins, and Gisele Mackenzie.

One time I told Jackie that I had just heard a song that was going to be a hit. He asked which one it was, and I replied, "The Little Drummer Boy." Perhaps I missed my calling by not becoming a musical critic. Jackie is the one who remembered this story.

CHAPTER 21

Polio

"Apart from the atomic bomb, America's greatest fear was polio."
— PBS documentary

THE THING I remember people worrying about more than anything else in the 1950s was polio, also known as "infantile paralysis." Polio had been a periodic feature of American life since the late 1800s, but it became particularly virulent in the early 1940s and remained at epidemic proportions well into the following decade, with between thirty thousand and forty thousand cases reported nationally every year.

Nobody knew where polio came from or how it spread. Epidemics mostly happened in the summer, so people associated polio with summer activities like picnics, crowds, heat, county fairs, and swimming. That was why you weren't supposed to sit around in wet clothes or swallow pool water. In fact, polio was spread through contaminated food and water, but swimming-pool water, being chlorinated, was one of the safer environments. Polio disproportionately affected young people, with symptoms that were vague and variable and always a worry to interpret. The best doctor in the world couldn't tell in the initial stages whether a child had polio or just the flu or a summer cold. For those who did get polio, the outcome was frighteningly unpredictable. Two-thirds of victims recovered fully after three or four days with no permanent ill effects at all. Others were partly or wholly paralyzed. Some couldn't even breathe unaided and had to be put in an iron lung. In the US roughly 3 percent of victims died. Your Grandmother Vanderwork thought the polio virus was contained in the tips of bananas and made your mother cut off the tips before eating. To this day, she still eats bananas in this manner. Also, it was thought that a nap in the hottest part of the day was a remedy for the prevention of polio. Karen McKellips relates a story about some mothers wanting to take their kids to Roman Nose to go swimming, but some didn't think they should go because of the possibility of getting polio. Lois Self called Dr. Ryan and asked him. He said, "Take the kids swimming." Dr. Jonas Salk developed a vaccine for polio in 1955. He first tested it on himself, his wife, and his children. Dr. Salk's parents came to the United States in 1914 as Russian Jewish immigrants and settled in East Harlem, New York City.

Alberta, a classmate whose father was a doctor, related the following about her remembrances of polio.

The memories I have of the "Polio years" include pictures of children and adults in iron lungs, braces, and bedridden.

As soon as the Salk vaccine was available Dad gave it to every child patient available. It was like penicillin, a medical miracle. Sometimes the vaccine was in short supply; then the research folks suggested children receive it first. Dad read, and talked to the doctors in the city and research hospitals. One of the things he took as a personal responsibility was the care of the community children. The Thomas teens knew they never outgrew his feeling of that responsibility.

We were kept in during the hottest part of the day to keep from getting too tired, bedtimes were pretty strict, meals and exercise were routine. All of the things that "might" contribute to catching the virus. At that time viruses were still pretty much in the "black box," so good health practices were wise. Contaminated water and food could be avoided and the Roman Nose pool was not contaminated, so if the kids were cared for routinely there was not much danger there.

The only polio patient I knew personally was Patty Talbot. If you remember she wore a brace for some time. I don't know if Patty ever knew where or how she contracted polio. It seems that there was a long recovery time with surgeries and the brace.

I have a vague memory of several "scares" when symptoms were present in different patients. There is a possibility that those were the ones who recovered.

Thomas School - *circa* 1940s

The water tower

My parents, Helen and Bert, Jackie, Donnie, Richard

Donnie

Richard, Donnie and Jackie

Donnie and Jackie

L to R: Jackie, Donald Waters, Donnie, Virgil Talbot,
Donald Schantz, Maynard Book

L to R: Jackie, Donnie,
Maynard Book, Richard

Donnie and Jackie

Donnie, Jackie and Richard

Swimming in Patton's creek

Norma Jean Eyster, Judy Robinson, "Butch" Self, K.O. Kippenberger, Donnie

Donnie

Donnie, 7th grade

L to R: Donnie (8th Grade),
Haze Park, Virgil Talbot,
Gary Hooper - 1953

Jackie #6, Donnie #9

L to R: Rusty Kraybill, Rodney Jump, Jackie, Donnie - May, 1958

. Jackie, Richard, Donnie - May, 1956

Donnie #23, Jackie #35 - December, 1957

L to R: Jackie Friesen, Fred "Butch" Self, Don Herring, and Donnie

CHAPTER 22

Cars

"See the USA, in your Chevrolet." – Dinah Shore TV commercial

CAR RUMBA! ONLY one thing exceeded America's infatuation with television, and that was its love of the automobile. In 1947 Studebaker came out with the first new car design since before the war. The rest of the automotive world would soon follow, creating some of the most distinctive car designs in history. It was indeed a "golden age" for the car industry and has had an enduring influence on the culture of the United States.

Having a car was the ultimate expression of freedom and of self. When a boy first received his driver's license, his playground just got a whole lot larger. Never has a country gone more car-giddy than we did in the 1950s. The '50s marked the golden age of the car culture and was a memorable time in America for cars. A decade of style with those killer swooping decorative tailfins, fender skirts, continental kits, steering knobs (also known as "suicide knobs" and "necker's knobs"), curb feelers, running boards, dimmer switches, gas-guzzling engines and starters that were on the floor, foot feed (accelerator) and all those sparkling abundant chrome accessories, not to mention those backseat romances. Some guys would put artificial white sidewalls — "falsies" — on their tires if they had not purchased factory-made whitewalls. Cars, in the words of one observer of '50s cars, wrote that they looked as if they should light up and play. These steering knobs could also be termed the early version of power-assisted steering. These cars were not built to be eco-friendly and economic. They were meant to grace the road with style and luxury. This was the era when bigger was better. Many of them looked like they might even fly because of their graceful curves and their sweeps of an aerodynamic masterpiece. Those large stop lights on those tailfins could make a whole city block glow red.

Pontiacs came with Strato-Streak V-8 engines and Strato-Flight Hydra-Matic transmissions. Chryslers offered PowerFlite Range Selector and Torsion-Aire Suspension while the Chevrolet Bel-Air had a hold-on-to-your-hat feature called Triple Turbine TurboGlide. By the end of the decade, there were no fewer than forty-six different Chevrolet models available. In 1958 Ford produced a Lincoln that was over nineteen feet long, and this was the year that the Chevrolet Impala was introduced. The 1959 Cadillac Eldorado Biarritz was longer than a sailboat and with tailfins nearly as tall as the roof. This was a time when a '57 Chevy was everyone's dream car. In addition to the Big Three — GM, Ford, and Chrysler — other car manufacturers were the Independents — Hudson, Nash, Rambler, Studebaker, Kaiser, Frazer, Willys, and Packard. In earlier decades Packards were the choice of Hollywood stars, and the mobsters preferred Cadillacs. During the Depression it was the Ford Model T that hauled migrants across the dust bowls.

This was a time when the local filling station was staffed by people eager to wash your windshield, check the oil, fill your tank, check your tires, and even whisk the car floor — for free. There were even a few filling stations using the old hand pumps that would lift the gas up into a glass container and then let gravity do the work of filling your tank. The filling station was also more than just a place to get your car serviced. It was a hangout, especially late on a Saturday night. Most males still remember the various big oil companies by their free road maps and snappy promotional images: Mobil's red-winged Pegasus, Amoco's flaming torch, Shell's orange scallop shell, Sinclair's emerald brontosauruses, and so on. I have wistful memories of people sitting around at family reunions or at the service station launching into long and very detailed stories about the cars that they owned, how well they ran, trade deals, prices paid, and/or describing repairs they might have performed.

I suppose every male has nostalgic memories of unique cars or the unique personalities of those who owned them. Cars could reflect the owner's character by the way they were driven, kept looking nice or not clean. Some would even use a chamois instead of a towel to wipe their newly washed car so that no water stains were left. Al Cagg drove a pickup and was always gunning it up and down School Street in second gear to make it sound like a Civil War cannon; the sound of his rumbling muffler caroming through the streets would herald his arrival. His pickup rivaled the chariot of Apollo. Hence, the nickname of "Second Gear." He would also, at times, cross any two spark plug wires to make it sound louder. Some guys would cut off their muffler and replace it with a straight pipe to make it sound loud. This was known as a "straight." Put it in first gear, pop the clutch, and it would backfire every time.

Gary Helzer, class of '59, told me the following story about his car.

I bought my first car in the summer of 1957. Before that I drove my folks' car, which was a 1952 DeSoto. It was a monster of a car. It had a Hydra-Glide transmission. I was never sure what that was. Those cars had trouble with their starters. When the starter would not work, you would have to crawl under the car, and with a screwdriver, short across the two posts on the starter, coming from the battery. My first car was a 1950 Chevy Deluxe Coupe. I purchased it from someone that lived in Thomas, and paid $500 for it. I borrowed the money from Charlie Johnson at the First National Bank and paid it off in about six months. I worked at the Mobil Station at the time, and from them bought new second tires, fake white walls, and rear-view mirrors that I placed on the front fenders. I ran two exhaust pipes out of the muffler so that I could have duel exhausts. I had dice hanging *from the mirror, new seat covers, a steering wheel knob, full rim hub-caps, and fender skirts. I drove this car until I graduated from college.*

Billy Wilmeth had a four-door 1948 spinach-green Plymouth that had a speedometer with a color-coded backlit warning light which was really cool. It glowed amber when driving between 0 and 25 mph, green between 25 and 50 mph, and all red for any speed over 50. It seemed like Chrysler cars were always the avant-garde company when it came to new gadgets.

Lloyd Ray had an old 1951 Ford that had a repaired engine with a metal pin fixing a cracked block. Even so, it got him through three and a half years of college. It did run kind of hot, but if he did not drive it any further than Weatherford and Clinton it did okay.

Darrell Hamar had a cool car. It was a 1950 Ford with a Mercury engine. It had chrome fender skirts that made it look low slung in the rear. To me, it looked so low slung that it would have trouble making it over freshly painted lines. In 1952 Darrell Hamar and Donny McDonald were the only seniors to have their own cars. Don Roof drove a 1936 four-door DeSoto that was passed down from his brother Ed. Some of the teachers didn't even have cars at this time. Rodney Jump had a turquoise and white two-door Chevy. K.O. Kippenberger had a blue 1957 pickup with fender skirts.

Jack Keller had a good-looking car, a '56 Chevy hardtop, dark green bottom with a cream-colored top. This car was so beautiful, the car should have remained under flattering spotlights, as though it were an art object in the Louvre. My teenage eyes thought Jack's car was the most glamorous mechanical creation in the history of manufacturing. Jack always drove too fast. One night he ran two tires off the rims taking a corner faster than you could say "Jack Robinson." We all talked about that for a long time. Jack tore out three transmissions from drag racing this jewel of a car. He once had a 1948 Ford that he thought was really hot. He was out on Highway 47 for a drag race, and when he popped the clutch, the transmission went through the bottom of the case. I would have loved to have seen the look on Jack's face. He had to be towed back to town. After it was parked, they went back out and got the parts and piled them under his car. Jack was driving his '46 Chevy to Tishomingo to see his dad once during a driving rain. He made his little brother, Richard, lie on the floorboard and operate a dysfunctional wiper by hand all the way to Tishomingo.

Maynard Book drove a 1947 or 1948 Dodge, and one night there was a gang of us riding around after Wednesday night church. We pulled up to a stop sign just east of the Crowdis home. A car was coming toward us and should have either turned west on the curve just in front of us or continued going straight north on the east side of the road. For some reason, that car just drove head on into us as if we were in a demolition derby or riding bumper cars at Springlake Amusement Park. It knocked Butch Self from the back to the front. Claire Hooper and Jean Dykes were in with us, also.

Eddie Beck, a local carburetor cowboy, had a 1952 two-door Chevy and was considered to be Jupiter on Olympus for lust of speed. He was a regular Sterling Moss — fearless, focused, fast. Eddie's most famous or infamous car event was on a Fourth of July evening when he, Larry Steward, and Lloyd Ray were dragging Main. What started out as a ripple quickly grew into a tsunami when they started throwing cherry bombs out of the car window. The first thing they did before the bombing started was to spotlight the photoelectric cell, turning off the street lights to get the night watchman on the run as part of their cat-and-mouse game with him. Not a difficult thing to do because Thomas did not have Pentagon security. Lloyd was in the front seat, and Larry was in the backseat throwing out the bombs. They had one bomb left. Larry said, "Let's make one more run." Eddie made a U-turn and headed for town center. For some reason, Lloyd rolled up the right front window so the bomb hit the window and fell on the floorboard. Lloyd panicked and curled up tight under the dashboard, while Larry bailed out with the car going a little too fast. Momentum caused Larry to take two to three extra-large giant steps and pirouette on his axis a couple of times before crashing face down on the pavement and bouncing around like a cue ball on a pool table. Eddie realized that the cherry bomb fuse had lit a three-shot repeater rocket that would have gone 175′ in the air if properly aimed. He managed, somehow, to grab it and throw it out. It went off aimlessly, of course, whistling, sizzling, ricocheting off the pavement, hissing like a snake, and firing at Larry lying on the ground. The cherry bomb went off and caused other fireworks to go off in the car, creating more havoc and smoke. This whole scene must have looked like a low-budget war film. These guys were in serious disarray at this point.

Eddie drove around the block, pulling into a hiding place. Pretty soon he and Lloyd decided they'd better go back and check on Larry. They couldn't find him. He had disappeared. It took an extended search, but they found him at his house on the lam sitting in a chair all skinned and bruised up with holes in his jeans and new shirt looking like an overdone Hollywood makeup job. The explosions in the car blew a pretty good hole in the backseat cover and burned a spot on the upholstery under the seat cover. However, the biggest problem was getting the burnt powder smell out of the car. One has to listen to Lloyd and Eddie tell of this event to have any hope of conveying the full humor of this wild happening. I just don't have the adjectives to do this story justice. I suspect that some of the other wild tales I had heard about Eddie's exploits were not entirely exaggerated. At times, Eddie could be calculatingly reckless. Eddie would have been a good character in *The Dukes of Hazzard* TV show. I think this escapade guaranteed these guys immortality. Stay tuned.

Another Fourth of July story worthy of note is the one about the Trent boys. They had a fireworks stand near where the present Sewell Park is located. These two guys got into a Roman candle fight and caught the stand on fire. It flamed up like the wreck of the *Hindenburg*, creating a pyrotechnic illumination event the likes of which Thomas had never before seen. It sounded like Thor, Scandinavian god of thunder, wielding his hammer. However, it was not well attended. In quick order, it blew from here to kingdom come, sounding like Vesuvius erupting and filling the air with acrid smoke. It was a Fourth of July "show" gone wrong. Lloyd Ray was a semi-witness to this event, also. He and Millard Wright quickly got on their bicycles and rode down there after hearing the explosion from Millard's house. If there would have been 24/7 news coverage as there is today, this event would have been a media carnival. These teenage hand grenades were not the von Trapp children, and if asked to name their 10 most admired people, they would have listed Jack Daniels among them. This family was like a Picasso painting. At the very least, they were a rough draft for a riotous cartoon.

Don Herring (my class) had a Jeep when he was in the sixth grade. I have a picture of Don, Butch Self, Jackie, and me in that Jeep on our way to the river swimming hole. This would have been at least four years before any of us could have had a driver's license. Don would sometimes use this Jeep to work his dad's ground with a spring-tooth implement. Virgil Talbot had an old '46 or '47 cream-colored Plymouth coup. The heater and defroster did not work, and he had to keep the windows rolled down in the winter to keep the windows from fogging over.

Archie Ames's nephew, Leslie Ames, from Oklahoma City, came to town every summer to work in the wheat harvest. He had one of the first cars with those huge tail fins and all the bells and whistles. That car had bulk and geometry. It was "souped up." He used to use aviation fuel, thinking it would enable him to go faster. He later became owner of a successful firm called "Mr. Pickup," which manu-factured special components like fancy running boards, tail gates, bumpers, etc. I once heard of a kid injecting pure oxygen into his carburetor so that he could really smoke the wheels on his car. It blew the head off and caught the rest of the engine on fire. Larry Steward had a prehistoric chariot — a '33 Chevy coupe with a rumble seat. It was black with the top painted pink. The old steering gear box, the crux of this story, was like stirring a stick in a porridge bowl. Here is his story.

This car had a chicken-wire, thin fabric-covered top, dual side-mount spare tires, wire wheels, rumble seat, and one of the most dangerous options ever put in a car — "freewheeling." When you pulled the freewheeling knob out, the car would coast as if you had the clutch engaged. So when you let off the accelerator pedal the car would go into "coast" mode. If you happened to be going down a steep hill your life was in peril as there was no engine compression to slow the car down. It also had mechanical and not hydraulic brakes, so this added to the danger factor. I soon learned to not use freewheeling if I wanted to live a long life. This car's steering was so stiff that no matter where the steering wheel was turned, it stayed there and wouldn't move. Our favorite game was to load a bunch of girls in the rumble seat, start going in a large circle, then jump out of the car. This of course freaked them out. We could catch up and jump back in and no one was hurt — pretty stupid of course. I'm sure Dad would have killed me if he knew what we were up to. The old Chevy finally broke a piston and went to the scrap yard. We were paid $15 for it. If I still had the car and it was restored, the value would be over $100,000. It was a very rare car with very few being built.

Here is another car story by Larry.

I had a '39 Ford Deluxe coupe that had an enormous trunk area behind the front and only seat in the car. It always smelled of gasoline and burned motor oil as the floors had rust holes and let exhaust and gas fumes into the car. We used to pile in and go to the movie in Weatherford. Some rode in the front seat, and when there was no room they would lie in the trunk on some old blankets. There was no divider between the seat and trunk, so we could communicate with the trunk passengers as we drove along. It is amazing that no one was asphyxiated from the fumes. I was too poor to buy fender skirts for it, so on the suggestion from someone I made a pair out of tempered Masonite in shop class. Dad helped me paint the car a deep red color. Lloyd's dad, Fred Ray, helped me rig up dual exhaust pipes for it. We used some old mufflers that I bought from Lloyd Ruddell's dad. It looked really cool and served me well.

Gordon Crowdis had a '46 Chevy with hot shocks. He never drove it over 35 mph. One night, his younger brother, Larry, borrowed it to go to a party. Gordon wrote down the mileage and gave him a strict limit on how many miles he could drive. As you would guess, Larry ran out of miles and had to back it all the way home, so as not to go over his limit on the speedometer. The following appeared in *Time* magazine, July 9, 1956: "In Coeur d'Alene, Idaho, after householders reported that a car was tearing around the neighborhood in reverse, assistant police chief Robert Schmidt investigated and found behind the wheel a teen-age girl who explained: 'My folks let me have the car, and I ran up too much mileage. I was just unwinding some of it.'"

Richard had a black 1946 or 1947 Ford coupe. When he took Zeta Beth to the Baptist Church on Sunday night, Jackie and I would go get it and drive it around until time for church to be over, and I did not even have a driver's license. I guess the Methodists got out earlier than the Baptists, allowing us this opportunity. Jackie's first ride over 100 miles per hour was in K.D.'s '50 Ford. I remember someone having relatives from Florida come visiting in their new '54 Mercury that would go 100 mph in second gear. Charles Fortune had a sharp-looking '55 Chevy two-door green and white hardtop. Jackie's first car was a '48 Dodge with a taxi tag that he bought for $80. Terral McKellips' old Buick had a leak in one of his dual carbs, and when he turned a corner too fast gas would spill out catching on fire. He and Karen Sweeney would have to quickly get out and throw dirt on it. Dad had a 1954 two-tone, four-door blue Plymouth Belvedere that I always used to cruise Main and go to the movies. I never owned a car in high school.

Charles Fortune was also one of our wild drivers. He was five years older than me, but would occasionally take me gallivanting on reckless speedy rides in his Jeep when he was tearing around the country just so he could scare the daylights out of me and laugh like crazy as he was doing it. I loved having my hair blowing in the wind and the air currents thrashing against my rippling shirt as Charles drove like a moonshiner. The worst ride was after he had put the pedal to the floor and started cranking down the road at the velocity of Niagara Falls, when he suddenly just pulled off into the bar ditch, attacking it like a stunt driver to show me some things a Jeep could do that cars couldn't. He had me sucking air and wishing I had not gotten in his Jeep on this day, but the train had already left the station on this ride. At these speeds, when the end came, as I was sure it would, there would be nothing left of the Jeep but buckets full of rusty dust, and the coons and squirrels would be picking us out of their fur for the next few days down in the creek. And remember, this was in the day when we had not even heard of antilock brakes, seatbelts, or air bags. Charles made a course correction, rocking like a washing machine when he fishtailed out of the ditch, but as steady as a locomotive on rails, or we would have been crashing in the creek or the bridge abutment. My heart did a painful contraction. I felt like *Charlie on the MTA*. I can't tell you how delighted I was to be in the land of the living when I exited that Jeep when the harrowing ride was over. I was ready to pop the champagne cork! I don't think Charles had had any beers, but it made no difference because he drove the same sober or tight. He was the Barney Oldfield of my teenage years. Oldfield was the first person to drive a car 60 miles per hour. Oldfield was the first famous race-car driver even though he never won the Indy 500. His accomplishments led to the expression about driving a car fast, "Who do you think you are? Barney Oldfield?"

Another crazy thing we would do for an evening's entertainment would be to go "spin a wheel" on roller-coaster road just north and east of the river bridge, trying to emulate Orville and Wilbur Wright. Our conversation would be momentarily interrupted as the car crested one of the hills, and for a second or two the car would be airborne. Certain mystic sects believe the gods are especially protective of small children and idiots. The same deities must also have been watching over us when we were doing these stupid car things. I leave it to you to decide under which category we fell.

Jackie, Junior Garner, and Larry Crowdis used to slightly deflate the tires on their cars and drive them on the railroad tracks. Another little trick some liked to do when things were slow was to shine a flashlight on the photoelectric cell to turn off the street lights, as mentioned above. Of course, when the lights went off, one would have to hightail it out of town so that the night watchman wouldn't catch you.

I don't know who the "Sherlock" was who discovered this interesting device.

One car and driver Thomas didn't have as far as I can recall was "a little old lady from Pasadena." This would be your little old woman no taller than a Pepsi can, barely able to see over the steering wheel complete with a pillbox hat, driving a little too fast, two white gloves gripping the steering wheel, like a life preserver, and not looking to the right or left. If one could have seen her legs, she would probably have been wearing brown stockings short of the knees. I guess the closest person we had to this would be Bob Ogden. He had a black '46 Chevy in which he would rev up the engine and pop the clutch. The revving of his engine would warn the innocent of this unpredictable operation and scatter them and any cars in the vicinity. Otherwise he drove well below the speed limit, unfazed by traffic signs, other cars, or anything else.

Tommy, from Fay, drove an old pale green 1951 Starlight Coupe Studebaker and came to Thomas frequently because he was dating a local girl. The Starlight coupe was of an unusual trunk design that produced the running joke that one could not tell if the car was coming or going. One day, the night watchman saw the Studebaker parked and thought it was backed illegally into a parking slot. It was not. He went looking for Tommy to issue him a ticket or to get him to repark the car. We still talk and laugh a lot about this car story. The Starlight coupe with that bullet nose was one of the most unusual American cars ever built.

The first ambulance Thomas ever had was an old two-door Chevy of some kind. The backseat and front passenger seat were removed to make room for a stretcher to fit.

An interesting phenomenon that one will notice in family photos taken during the 1940s and '50s is the frequency that the car appeared in the family photos. A family would drive hundreds of miles across this country to see national parks and natural wonders, then take a picture showing the car and three kids standing in front of it. "You can't see it here," they would tell their friends after returning home, "but that's the Meteor Crater behind the car and the kids." As I think back, it is also interesting to remember the familiar scene of two or more guys standing at the front of a car with the hood up talking about the specifics of the engine and everything else under the hood.

I would be remiss in writing about cars and living so close to the old Route 66, America's first national highway, to not say something about this old "Mother Road" of America as it was dubbed and romanticized by John Steinbeck in *The Grapes of Wrath*. Often referred to as "America's Main Street," this highway was a spine supporting the breadth of the West and Midwest of the United States. It still survives in the hearts and minds of thousands of Route 66 enthusiasts who yearly travel the old highway to experience the oft-forgotten persona of the heartland. This highway connected Chicago and Santa Monica, California — a distance of 2,400 miles. Oklahoma has played a large part in the history of this road, being centrally located along the route and holding the country's longest section. When traveling on this road as a youngster, I remember the unique old ubiquitous barn advertisements: pouch tobacco, caverns, Burma Shave signs, and art-deco diners. Many of the '40s and '50s gas stations often looked like cottages. One can still see a few of these empty deserted vintage "cottages" along some highways. Lucille's Service Station, which is one of the old landmarks on this nostalgic route, is one of only two gas stations of its kind left on Oklahoma's stretch of Route 66, just east of Weatherford, one of the best-preserved sections in the United States. While no longer in business, Lucille's is a tribute to a bygone era, restored to its original condition. The highway's mystique — captured in songs, on television, and in the movies — lures travelers from around the world. The Interstate Highway System was born in 1956, the largest public works program since the pyramids. There were no cars manufactured during the war years of 1942 to '45. Their factories were converted over to produce trucks, tanks, and airplanes for the war effort. The initial construction of Route 66 was in the 1920s. At its pinnacle, Route 66 was the romance of traveling the open highway. It seemed to me that Route 66 stood for everything good about

America, and there was just something about the look of that iconic Route 66 sign.

Hot-rodding was not real big in Thomas. It was largely a Los Angeles phenomenon. These Angeleno car fanatics that gave birth to the hot rods would turn their rusty heaps into dream machines which evolved into the illegal street races of the '40s. After 70 years they are more popular than ever. Largely because of the Beach Boys and Jan and Dean chronicling cars in song, we have another good addendum to the culture of cars. Some of the more popular songs were "409," "Hot Rod Lincoln," "Little Old Lady from Pasadena," "Little Deuce Coup," "Fun Fun, Fun," "Drag City," "Dead Man's Curve," "Surf City," "GTO," "Hey Little Cobra," "Little Honda," and "Tell Laura I Love Her."

There were even hot-rod movies, such as *Hot Rod Rumble, Hot Rod Girl, Hot Cars, Hot Rod Gang, Drag Strip Girl, The Fast and the Furious, Out of Sight,* etc. The movie *American Graffiti* tells all one needs to know about the relationship between teenagers and their cars in the 1950s.

So breathe in the smell of your new car's fresh aroma. Lift the hood and admire the new technology. As good as it is, it will never replace the car of your youth that created great memories and the genesis of car-swapping stories. Because of their connection with people, cars could become just like members of the family. If only we could roll the odometer back to Detroit's glory cars of the '50s.

CHAPTER 23

Watermelons

"The memory of all that—No, No! They can't take that away from me."
– Ira Gershwin

OH, THE SOUND of the crack of a watermelon splitting open. On rare occasions it was royal fun in the summertime to visit a watermelon patch and lift a few for a late-night snack. We would eat them until we were full as a tick on a hound's ear. The girls liked to occasionally go with us on these nocturnal excursions for a bit of rascality. One night, in the revelry of the evening, we boys cooked up a plot to scare the girls. Two guys went out to a patch early with a shotgun. The other boys would show up with the girls and quietly walk out into the field. At the appropriate time the shotgun guys would jump up and yell, "What are you kids doing trespassing in my field?" They would then fire a couple of rounds in the air scaring the daylights out of the girls, who would be retreating like Confederate soldiers and screaming like a banshee.

Another prank we played on unsuspecting people at times was the infamous snipe hunt. A snipe hunt is a type of practical joke that involves experienced people making fun of credulous newcomers by giving them an impossible or imaginary task. It is kind of like a "wild goose chase," where a person embarks on an impossible search. Where a wild good chase may be accidental, a snipe hunt is always initiated by other people as a prank. It usually started out by someone in the group saying, "Hey let's all go on a snipe hunt." The inexperienced person would be told about a bird or animal called the snipe as well as a usually preposterous method of catching, such as running around the woods or a creek carrying a bag or making strange noises such as banging rocks or cans together or shouting some silly phrase. Then the unsuspecting person would be sent to a destination, ostensibly to meet up with the rest of the group at an assigned place at a certain time. Of course, the group never showed up. Eventually, the unsuspecting person would show up back at the drugstore, pool hall, service station, or wherever, and say something like, "Where were you guys, I could never find you?"

One night we were in a watermelon patch in the Amish community, doing some nocturnal reconnoitering, when we alertly noticed Dave Miller driving down the road toward us on his little Ford tractor with the lights off, hoping to catch us in the act. It was quickly decided that I would run to the road to drive the car off so that he would think we were gone while the rest of the group, with catlike stealth, scattered like field mice, and like Brer Rabbit laid low in the tall cornstalks next to the watermelons, where they dug in like an Alabama tick. This scared the girls into blobs of quivering jelly. It was like a Gilbert and Sullivan operetta. I made it to K.D. Lapel's car in good time, but had never driven a car with an automatic transmission, and didn't know that it had to be in park before it would start. Where was the cavalry when I needed them? Dave collared me and I gallantly took the fall for everyone — playing the role of *Horatio at the Bridge* to protect the others. He took me into the field, cut a watermelon, and shared it with me while explaining why we shouldn't be in his patch at night tearing up his vines. We did try to be careful about this. At the Thomas vs. Cashion state football championship game in Enid on 12-13-14, I met David Yoder, Dave Miller's grandson, and told him about this story. He found it hilarious and enjoyed hearing about his granddad.

Richard and his buddies drove a vehicle into a patch one night, and the owner saw them go in. He shut the barbed-wire gate on them. When they drove out, Richard and someone else were riding on the front fenders and didn't notice the gate had been closed. The wire tore up their jeans and cut their legs. I guess they deserved that one. Larry Steward was the driver, and this is his account of the prank.

There were two car loads of us that decided to drive up to steal watermelons from a local farm. I was driving one of my dad's used cars that he had traded for — it was a two-toned green 1953 Chevy. We didn't want to drive two cars down to the patch, so we loaded everyone into my car, which was so full that Richard and the other person sat on the front fenders. We opened the farmer's gate, and with lights turned off drove down the narrow road, maybe a quarter of a mile to his melons. After loading the trunk with all we wanted, everyone loaded up and we started to back up to the main road. The farmer had heard us, and unknown to us, had shut the barbed-wire gate. We were driving very slow without our lights, and I, thinking the gate was still open, drove right on through. The gate wire cut Richard and the other person, pulling them off the fenders as the car went through. We were all scared and very lucky no one was cut more seriously than they were. The farmer, who was waiting for us, was very upset with himself for shutting the gate and apologized over and over for doing so.

Stealing watermelons was wrong and we should not have been doing it. However, there was no larcenous intent and it was so ingrained in the prevailing culture that it did not seem wrong to us. Or, as Huck Finn would say, "mainly wrong." There is even a song titled "The Watermelon Song" written about this very issue. It is about the thrill of eating watermelon teasingly hanging from someone else's vine. I have visited with friends from other communities who have told me that they did the same thing when they were in high school. Also, I have since learned that even some of the Amish boys engaged in the same activity.

In the same vein of "picking" watermelons, one's rite of passage into teenhood was not complete without a sneak or two into the drive-in movie via the trunk of a car. So, like the Greeks sneaking into Troy inside the Trojan Horse, we would put two or three guys or gals in the trunk, drive up to the ticket booth, and buy tickets for the car. This little trick enabled us to have more money for the concession stand. In the end, the owner ended getting our money, anyway. It seemed like we were always up to something. It was our job.

CHAPTER 24

Shivaree

"Home is where when you get there, they have to let you in."
– Robert Frost

TRADITIONALLY, A SHIVAREE was an invasive, noisy, clamorous, tumultuous celebration of friends and family that took place on the wedding night or after returning from the honeymoon. The whole idea was to irritate the couple by any kind of mischief. The general mayhem was usually headed up by brothers of the bride or another close male relative. These organizers who initiated the shivaree used word of mouth to gather the largest possible crowd to participate. Friends gathered at the couple's home, making concussive sounds banging on pots and pans, hooting and hollering and singing a song or two. It was loud, it was silly, and it was harmless. Someone would always manage to get into the couple's house to do mischief in the kitchen by tearing off all the labels on their canned goods and mixing cereal in their boxes. So, it was "potluck" every meal until all the new pantry items were consumed. Also, the bed was usually "short sheeted" to cause even more harassment for the new couple. Sometimes crackers or cereal were tossed in between the sheets to add to their "troubles." On one shivaree I remember seeing the groom being made to parade his bride down the streets in a wheelbarrow, and that usually ended with the groom being thrown in a tank of water. After all the fun, the new couple would often invite everyone in for refreshments or give everyone a candy bar. Your mother and I were never shivareed and I am quite thankful; however, the serenading might have had a certain appeal. I remember attending a few shivarees, but can only specifically recall one shivaree. That would be the one for Virgil and Judy Richardson, who were both classmates of mine. It is fun to know that I was part of something that's now largely passed into history.

CHAPTER 25

Wheat Harvest

"June is Bustin Out All Over." – Oscar Hammerstein

AS MY GOOD friend and classmate Karen McKellips once said, "The annual summer wheat harvest did more than any other one thing to prevent juvenile delinquency in our little community." When June arrived, the fields turned to amber and the wheat harvest filled the air with a golden haze of dust and tiny bits of threshed straw. When a boy turned fourteen, he was usually hired by one of the local custom harvest crews to drive a combine and begin this annual nomadic Bohemian rite of passage. I always worked for the Harley Hamar/ Kenneth Roof crew, and these men took their responsibilities *in loco parentis* seriously. There were several harvest crews from Thomas, and at the time I worked for a crew, there were probably over fifty combines owned by local cutters.

Harvest would begin in southern Oklahoma, usually the first week of June and end in Berea, Nebraska, the first week of August, with stops in between at Meade and Scott City, Kansas, and Julesburg, Colorado. It was like a working safari absent the elephants and lions. I was paid from $1 to $1.50 per hour plus room and board at a time when the minimum wage was 75 cents an hour. We normally worked 12- to 15-hour days. Most kids would come home with about $500 to get them through the school year. When I received my first big harvest check, it felt like Monopoly money. Of course, this was never enough so most of us would get a Saturday job working for a farmer or carrying groceries during the busy Saturday shopping day. I remember taking home $4.50 for a twelve-hour day toting groceries at the Farmers Union Grocery Store. This was more than enough, however, to fund a Saturday night date. One dollar for car gas, fifty cents apiece for a movie ticket, and ten cents each for a Coke. Frank Self was the manager and meat cutter of the Farmer's Union store and Billie Hawkins was the checker.

One night in Temple, at their teentown hangout, we were enduring some tribal abuse by some of the local yokels who were blowing smoke about their athletic prowess. They appeared to be tough, but we were no shrinking violets. One of our guys said, "I'll bet you 50 cents we have a guy who can outrun your fastest jock." When I was selected to race him, he looked at me and said, with not a little mockery in his voice, "A Thomas stud, huh?" But, I was ready to do battle with this ace and brave the bears in their own den. During the middle of the run, it was obvious to me that I could take this schmuck, so I let him barely beat me. I made the excuse that I had gotten a bad start and bet him $1 that I could beat him in a rematch. This alpha dog guy's eyes lit up like I had offered him the winning lottery ticket. He quickly took the bait and I took him without too much difficulty in the second race causing consternation among the gathered onlookers. With his neck veins sticking out, he looked at me like he had seen a new constellation in the cosmos and folded like a lawn chair. I got way too much pleasure out of that experience. I played that guy like a cheap guitar. I guess that made me a "ringer" or "hustler." However, it did not do much for the bonding of harvesters with the local teen crowd as things were deteriorating into an atmosphere of derisiveness. We were mostly thought of as the sweepings of barrooms, anyway. As I walked away from this scene, we were being serenaded with oral diarrhea mutterings of secular unpleasantries and vivid suggestions about what we could do with ourselves. To which I replied, "I never said that you would like the ending." This little event only heightened the animosity of the locals. To avoid further acrimony, I returned to our trailer and went to bed.

A not-too-funny practical joke was played once on one of the truck drivers by a combine driver. The perp placed a wedge of limburger cheese on the manifold of his truck. Much later when the engine was started and became hot, the smell of limburger cheese was just awful. This smell would knock a buzzard off a fence post 500 yards away. This cheese has an unmistakable pungent smell that is slightly fishy and difficult to get rid of. In a not too jovial mood, the driver set about cleaning up the mess, but it took several days for this smell to wear away.

Sometimes, when it was too wet to cut because of rains, we would look for some type of entertainment or local areas of interest to visit on these "off days." A couple of things I can recall were the driving of a truck from Scott City to Garden City, Kansas, to see the movie *Rock Around The Clock* and driving from Berea, Nebraska, to the Black Hills in South Dakota to see Mt. Rushmore. And there was the Dalton Gang Hideout Museum in Meade where we cut. They had a tunnel that ran from the house to the barn to aid them in escaping from the authorities. There was a time once, in this town, that Jackie and Richard Keller could have used this tunnel. They had been putting in long days without any breaks and no opportunities to go swimming. One night after getting in from cutting, and with the public pool closed, they just climbed over the fence and went swimming. The cops came by, caught them, and put them in jail for the night. The next day Harley Hamar, their boss, called the farmer they were cutting for and asked him to call the municipal judge, who was a friend of his, and got them released after they paid a fine of $10.

While cutting in the fields of gold, one had ample time to observe the afternoon sky and watch hawks circling lazily, hitching rides on thermals. Unlike Achilles petitioning Zeus for fair weather, we always prayed for rain, like aging ballplayers, so that we could get a couple of days off from working under the unforgiving hot prairie sun. Sometimes the skies obliged us, and we accepted the rain like grateful flowers. With the skies as blue as fairies' eyes, one would scan the heavens in big sky country for thunder clouds, and one would many times marvel at those huge silvery-tipped, fleecy, marshmallow thunderheads of a cumulus cloud bank as they drifted across an incredibly azure sky as though they were hung by God, suspended like feathers, thinking "that cloud looks like . . ." No artist could match this work of God. Neil Diamond's "Jonathan Livingston Seagull" claims "the clouds were hung for the poet's eye." These scenes gave the world a marvelously clean fresh laundered feel. It was easy to believe that the hot sun threw itself at you personally, as I always offered a *thank You* to God when an exceptionally large cotton-ball castle in the sky moved across the sun to somewhat temper the heat with a large shadow. This would provide a few minutes of shade as I remembered that the sun is a continuing nuclear cataclysm 93 million miles from earth. When these clouds providing moments of shade would pass overhead, it was like God was smiling down on me. Riding that John Deere combine, I became a connoisseur in the beauties of the sky, finding that the artistic patterns of the clouds were to me like the Sistine Chapel ceiling was to Michelangelo.

One of the most adventurous things to happen to me during the harvest run was in Julesburg, Colorado. After work one night, a couple of us were walking around town, and for reasons lost on me, found ourselves getting picked up by two local *femmes fatales* who were not ever going to be someone's third-grade teacher. One of their boyfriends, King Kong Junior, who sported a jaw that looked straight out of central casting, saw us getting in the car. He and his Minotaur buddy, with sinister notions and wanting to impress us with their rich vocabularies, started shouting some serious invectives as they got in their car and started chasing us. We took off like a lost soul fleeing from the devil. You know, vehicular Darwinism — survival of the quickest. The gal driving just happened to be a really good driver. She hung a U-turn heading out of town that would have made a NASCAR driver proud. She was driving like a racer in the Monaco Grand Prix, hugging the curves, bouncing like a boat in a stormy sea, never slowing for anything. She could make that car smoke. At one point in this chase, I was wishing that I had an adult diaper on because these guys were definitely on the lower end of the social and cultural "food chain." "Sorry to be taking you on the scenic route at night," our driver commented after several minutes. *Toto*, I've a feeling we aren't in Colorado anymore, let alone Kansas. After a long chase we ended somewhere in a salubrious part of southwest Nebraska where a GPS would have to think twice about pinpointing our location. Even though she managed to ditch them somewhere in Zululand, I felt like my fate was being held together with string and chewing gum because I think King Kong Jr. would have left us looking like casualties from a shipwreck. Although these girls were pleasing and comely, they would not fit into the category of *lilies of the valley*, but we never saw them in the light of day.

We cut for a family in Berea, Nebraska. They had a 16-year-old daughter who had a habit of spinning out when she drove her brother's 1951 Ford. This was the first time I had ever seen a girl really dig out like a demented rabbit in a car. I thought it was really cool.

Occasionally, we would cut a patch of barley or oats for a farmer. We didn't like having to work with these grains because they were itchy and easily clogged the straw walkers in the combines.

Most of our meals were eaten in cafes. Our boss would bring hamburgers to us in the field for lunch. When we cut in Thomas, his wife would bring a home-cooked meal to the field and we really looked forward to this food. Working in the harvest could really jack up your appetite to the point where eating takes on a kind of holiness. We bunked in an old trailer house that we pulled along with us most of the time. The trailer had all the comforts of a medieval castle, but offered no prospect of fresh-cut flowers, or the smell of fresh baked bread. Occasionally, we lodged in motels that had to have been built during the reign of Henry VIII, and located in a part of town that was neither chic nor quaint.

We occasionally received letters from girlfriends addressed to us general delivery. Although devoured and very welcomed, these epistolary exchanges were mostly prosaic, awkward, and not very affectionate — just chatty missives. We were just mostly exchanging agreeable nothings about things in general. There were no reminders of tender moments, no declarations of love — just mostly news from home. However, they did momentarily transport our imaginations to another more desirable world of swimming, going to movies, dragging Main, etc. We rarely had the opportunity to date any local girls, not even dowdy girls, because harvest hands were regarded as social pariahs just a notch above carnival workers, but we used deodorant and did not act like 18-year-old sailors on shore leave.

Joe (a pseudonym), a poor kid without a father, who worked on our crew one summer and managed to get home with $300. Instead of depositing this money in the bank, he cashed the check and got 300 one-dollar bills and went around to almost every store in town to buy some small item just so he could pull out that wad of cash to show people that he had money. We were servicing our combines and doing routine maintenance one morning, amid the smells of gasoline, grease, oil, and carbon monoxide, when our boss told Joe to go fuel one of the trucks. Joe tried backing the truck over to the pickup where the gas tank was kept. His executed maneuver managed to broad-side the pickup. Joe could take a simple task like turning a vehicle in a 160-acre field into a national disaster. After all, the nearest impediment was a six-inch gopher hole a mile away. I thought to myself, good grief, Joe, I am afraid that you have wandered off the reservation.

Once, old Billy "The Whangbangor" was smoking while driving his combine. Harley, our boss, climbed on the machine and asked Billy if he was being careful where he was putting his cigarette butts? Billy replied, "Yes, I am being careful. I am not throwing them over on this side where the wheat has not been cut." Duh! Logic and Billy are not two words with the congruence of, say, "love" and "marriage." Try "oil" and "water" or "Hatfield" and "McCoy." I will always remember Billy singing "On Wolverton Mountain" while plucking his guitar after work in the evenings.

Mary Lee (Norris) Sweet-Darter related the following neat harvest story.

My dad had a 1939 or earlier Ford truck with no lift. As a sixth-grader I was entrusted to drive that stupid thing to the elevator. My dad put blocks on the clutch, brake, and gas pedals so that I could reach them. They had to tip the front of the truck up in the air on a lift to let the wheat slide out. Of course, when the truck came down it was flooded and the nice men at the elevator had to push me off the grain dump down the ramp and I would double-clutch it and get it to start. This was all very embarrassing in front of all those nice new shiny trucks driven by handsome young men who worked for custom harvesting crews. They just looked at me like I was something out of The Grapes of Wrath.

Before becoming a wheat harvester, at the age of 14, I drove a little Ford tractor pulling either a planter or cultivator in the sweet-potato fields for Webb Barton. I worked from 7:00 to 7:00 for $3 a day. As a 12-year-old, I hardly knew what to do with my newfound wealth. During this era, a farm kid could drive a car, pickup, truck, tractor, combine, motorcycle, bulldozer, or steamroller before he had a driver's license. Before this, I toiled chopping and picking cotton and other serf-type jobs. I would surely eradicate cotton picking and extracting blackberries with my metacarpals from among the briars if I ever came to power. This was backbreaking labor, especially during the heat of the day. At least I never had a job where I had to deal with vomit or sewage. We moved slowly up and down the rows, bent over so we could reach the bottoms of the stalks to pick the bolls and cram them into long ten-foot sacks that dragged behind us on the ground, suspended by straps that cut into our shoulders. These sacks could hold up to 100 pounds when full. We wore those dark brown jersey gloves to aid somewhat in the picking process. When our sacks got too heavy to pull, we would drag them to the wagon where there was a balance scale to weigh our harvest. We would be paid two cents a pound, and if I really worked at it, I could make $2 a day. More often than not, however, I would waste time throwing green cotton balls at Jackie and Richard. Sometimes, I would be tortured by having to weed a garden for some of Mother's little old lady friends for 50 cents. I did not fancy this indentured-servant work. Did my mother have a wish for me to be a martyr? I bet Robin Hood and The Three Musketeers never had to weed a garden. Oh well, God put burdens for us to bear for His own reasons. Child labor laws did not cover the work of children on family farms, or any form of agricultural labor. At least not in Oklahoma. I guess in some states a teenager could not even serve a milkshake. I am glad we were not affected by any labor laws. How else would I have made any spending money?

CHAPTER 26

The Red Light

"Much Ado About Nothing" – Shakespeare

THIS IGNOBLE STORY is a part of my school history and I reluctantly record it. I will get it over with as swiftly as possible. Frankie
had recently bought a car trouble light that plugged into the cigarette lighter. It came with three supplemental lenses in the colors of
red, amber, and green. The actors in this drama without a script were
Frankie Bontrager, Rusty Kraybill, Sammie Harris, and me — mates
and mischief makers. One night we were flapping around town like a
loose roof shingle in a five-mile-an-hour breeze in Frankie's car with
nothing constructive to do — like an infection coming on. Rusty has
admitted that he was the culprit who had the bright idea of a little
nefarious activity by going out on the highway, driving up behind
cars, flashing the trouble light with the red lens, hoping they would
think we were the highway patrol, pull over, stop, and then we would
"23 skidoo" on around them. Sounded like a good idea to me. We
must have had visions of sugar plums dancing in our minds. How had
Gilbert and Sullivan put it? *Provide a little innocent merriment?* With
Rusty flashing the red light with the precision of a criminal dueling
with a combination lock on a bank vault, we were pleased as punch
that our scheme worked, not realizing that we were showing an early
aptitude for a life of crime. We successfully stopped two cars. We

were firing on all pistons, but as it turned out, we should have taken an "off ramp" before the third car.

As we quixotically encroached upon the third car, it turned out to be the final act of the evening play and with dire consequences. The woman in this car, in a state of agitation, turned us in to the town night watchman, who in turn called the highway patrol. What's that old saying about a woman scorned? As we were buzzing through town confidently laughing about our little "patrolling" stunt, we spotted a highway patrol car parked at the American State Bank in town center. This black-and-white car had a sobering effect on us as an awful epiphany seeped through us. Our evening had been suddenly thwarted. We weighed our options as the analytical part of our brains told us that we had been collared. Like cornered felons, we cowered, knowing the jig was up. We were crumbling like a stale cookie. We could have used a little dose of fairy dust. Realizing it wasn't coming, this little band of merry men immediately pulled in next to the patrol car, surrendered, and started singing like a nightengale. Our little escapade was as dead as a lawyer's conscience.

The highway patrolman, fighting a never-ending battle for truth and justice, took Frankie's spotlight as evidence, looking at it like it was the *True Cross* and made us feel like the guiltiest of villains — like we had committed some heinous crime. Our mantras of mercy were like King Canute trying to hold back the tide. This did not do one bit of good as he ordered us to report to the district attorney's office later that week at the county courthouse in Arapaho with our parents. I felt like I was slowly sinking in a vat of manure. I leave it to you to imagine my embarrassment. Man, we needed this like we needed a case of peritonitis. Bad news rides a fast horse, but contrary to the rumors that were spreading like a tumor to the Thomas guys at Southwestern State College, we were not arrested and taken away in handcuffs. Nor were we photographed, fingerprinted, asked a hundred questions for the record, relieved of all belongings, and given a change of jailbird scrubs. The plot of this story was moving way too fast. However, we penitents did spend Sunday in the Amen corner at church having a private word with God, seeking absolution for our ill-fated terrestrial actions. I feared extracting ourselves out of this mess was going to be more difficult than getting a piano out of the bathroom. Like Little Bo Peep's sheep, we had lost our way for one brief hour on this ill-fated night.

Stoically, like Shadrach, Meshach, and Abednego, we four perps reverentially and lamentably marched into the fiery furnace with as much aplomb as we could muster. With the trepidation of a snake charmer's audience, we arrived at the courthouse. Because a courthouse is for lawyers and the criminally inclined, we tried hard not think of all the unpleasant fates and doomsday scenarios that might be about to befall us — retribution involving a juvenile facility or a mental home. I was fully prepared to endure thirty-nine lashes in lieu of doing time, if allowed to do so. With an air of solemn intensity in our eyes, we were in a frozen state of anxiety. The room in which we were sequestered until our scheduled time with the DA was like the anteroom to Hades — and just as uncomfortably warm! The furniture looked like leftovers from the Roosevelt era and reminded me of every police drama I'd ever seen on television. The tension in the air seemed thick enough to cut with a knife. As the minute hand on the clock moved slowly towards the appointed hour, the DA called us in as we tried to look serious and committed. The DA explained the seriousness of what we had done and that the lady was bloody well upset about the whole thing. We conceded the point. He said that he realized we were just trying to have some fun, but that what we were doing was not safe and that we had stopped the wrong car. We had been spiraling into despair until we learned that the DA had talked to the woman — or should I say inquisitor? — into just giving us a stern talk and not filing charges. The skill of the DA was a miracle of strategic and diplomatic finesse that would have been the envy of the American ambassador to the Court of St. James as he unraveled this unfortunate affair. We readily accepted this absolution. The DA did not want us to do any "tap dancing," so he told us to maintain a neutral and sedate expression, to look her straight in the eyes, and to not crack a smile or smirk of any kind when she walked into his office, and warned us that her lecture to us would probably be somewhat evangelistic in nature. This was not a request. The lady had not *come to praise Caesar*. We were also instructed to not say anything unless asked, so we sat there in judicious silence with an air of fragility all around us. I was glad to hear this because my voice would have come out raspy and betrayed me like gargled vinegar, and I was afraid that I could not trust my voice to mask my anxiety. There was not an atom vibrating in my body. We robotically did exactly as instructed, and I can tell you that the look on our faces was not that of one expecting a bedtime story.

Madame Guillotine marched in giving us a withering glance like Caesar looking at Cassius. She lectured us like she had a religious calling from Mt. Sinai. She would make Machiavelli look like a Sunday school teacher. We sat as mutely as Harpo Marx, doing no eyebrow signaling, but did shift uncomfortably in our chairs occasionally. I had never known such throes. I did not roll my eyes, which I thought showed considerable restraint. However, it was not an allowable option anyway. If we four would have glanced at one another, we would have caught a look of shared common helplessness in the hands of this woman. As she conveyed her anger, she spoke with definite emphases as if she was underlining the words as she spoke. To her credit, I will admit, she wasted no words — no flowery quotes from the Bible or Shakespeare. Our repentant apology was camouflaged in a murmured tone and it was straight from the spleen, not the heart. In reality our feigned apology was more dutiful and automatic than sincere. It was also in a voice more of the DA's than ours, so it was more like ventriloquism than apology — remorseful without repentance. After all, this was not a capital crime, but one would have thought that our actions had signaled the end of the free world as we knew it. I don't think the lady felt very reassured by our *go and sin no more apology*, but at least she accepted, or pretended to accept, our apologies. I have to admit that what we had done was as wrong as wearing white socks to a funeral. I got through it by not looking at my amigos. By herniating most of my facial muscles, I managed to refrain from grinning during her speaking. Whew! Somehow we managed impeccable decorum all through this procedure, but my mind was swimming in syrup. That was a close one as I fought for what little oxygen was left in the room! The angels were on our side. Does "the lady doth protest too much, methinks" ring a bell?

The DA must have had a little sense of humor and remembrances of his boyhood pranks to conclude that this episode was probably garden-variety misbehaving. We later found out that Sammie's uncle, who was a county road foreman, had called the DA and explained that we were all good guys, from good families, had never been in trouble, went to church regularly, and made good grades in school. I think the old lawyers referred to this as "earwigging." This was probably the fulcrum which tilted the DA's position to our side of the equation. The DA understood the situation and was able to smooth things over with the lady. We really weren't bad guys. On the other hand, we were not candidates for *Sunnybrook Farm*. After the lady finished her oration and left the room, the DA gave us a few more words of advice and indicated that we were free to go. I'd had enough of this place and needed no encouragement to leave. I felt wilted after this ordeal, but what a relief it was to walk out of that office realizing the gulag was not in our future. After all, a courthouse is not exactly the place *where never is heard a discouraging word, and the deer and the antelope play*. We exited the building with a rapturous sigh and with a sort of malicious triumph. We were once again immersed in normalcy with this reprieve. Everything suddenly looked brighter and extravagantly beautiful. The air fresher, cleaner, and more balmy, and the landscapes more lovely — like looking at a rainbow after a rain. Everything, including life, had become more radiant and ginger-peachy. I felt like Dante. *I walk through hell, but I am not burning.* Our time in "Babylon" had been short. Our gratitude was measureless as I whispered a prayer of thanks. As I think back about this infamous episode in my youth, I have to think that the assistant Solomonic DA handled this matter of gravity and delicacy in a brilliant manner. He will be rewarded in heaven. The highway patrolman who stopped us would probably have just given us a warning if we had stopped anyone but the person we did. This story will not become a Disney movie, even though I felt like Tom Sawyer coming out of hot water grinning and winning in the end.

We arrived back in town just in time for football practice. The prodigal had returned. With looks of mirth on our faces, we triumphantly sauntered to the stadium dressing room. To say our arrival at the dressing room caused a bit of a stir would be an understatement. Our welcoming teammates were gathered at the door like a Greek chorus with all kinds of "artistic" kidding. "How many years did you get?" "Does your probation allow you to play this week?" Everyone was as festive as ocean liners in port. We expected this reception surer than gravity. Looking askance, Mr. Ross and Mr. Roof were not amused. I was tempted to embellish our little foray to my teammates to make it sound slightly glamorous, but couldn't muster the necessary deceit.

This was not one of our prouder moments. In fact, it was dumber than dirt and as stupid as dandelion fluff. This impulsive adventure embodied all the errors in judgment we had ever made, even if it had seemed so delightful when we had thought of it. I am surprised that no one put up a permanent monument to our imbecility. Like Icarus's perilous journey, *we flew too close to the sun* on this ill-conceived cowboy operation. What were our mercurial minds thinking? This little undertaking cast a pall on an otherwise happy beginning of our senior year. And yet, why do I continue to remember this night with fondness? Burr Morse, an acquaintance of mine, has said that his father-in-law used to say, "It takes a long time to go over fool's hill." Fortunately, my trip over this hill pretty much ended with this intellectually impaired event.

CHAPTER 27

Football

"Excuses only satisfy the people who make them." – Joe Ross

IF A THOMAS native were asked to name the Holy Trinity during the 1950s, they might have jokingly replied, "football . . . and Joe Ross and Kenneth Roof," two of the most vaunted gridiron mentors west of the Indian Meridian that really put our town on the map. I wouldn't say that 1950s Thomas High School football substituted for life's Holy Grail, even during those golden moments of THS football history, but it likely snuck in at number two on many locals' priority lists of the time. Young Thomas boys grew up in awe of the high school football players. At the time, I obviously would not have known how to describe how I perceived these guys, but today I would have recounted them as having the jaw, cheekbones, and torso that one usually finds sculpted in marble inside a Greek temple — a Greek Adonis. Come each autumn, football took its near sacred place as an annual tradition embedded deeply in the hearts of those young boys — and fixed firmly on the calendars of almost every Thomas household. For several consecutive weeks each fall, football owned the attention of each Thomas fan from morning till deep into the night. Football gave our school something to rally around, to boost the spirit of our community. It was a product of civic pride.

From those sultry stifling dog days of summer when we first put on our uniforms, endured the cauldron-like heat, the endless perennial penitential two-a-day August practices, the burning lungs, quivering quads, and the protesting of some previously undiscovered muscles in my complaining body — football passion was intense. The air was the consistency and temperature of a rabid dog's mouth. Football was a percussive tonic for aspiring young laddies like me. It was kind of like New Year's Eve every Thursday night. It was in our DNA. However, the beginning of every season was like seeing myself at the bottom of a mountain, looking up, and trying to decide if I was ready for the long hard climb. But we always tore into it with an aggressive dynamism even though it was difficult to haul myself out of bed each morning during those first two-a-days. Mr. Ross and Mr. Roof had always drilled into us that the road to success consisted of working hard, making sacrifices, and not taking shortcuts, and I think it must have been their voices that prodded me from beneath the sheets on the most difficult mornings.

The field on which I played, home of so many *battles royales*, was built in 1950 and runs east and west. The old field, a WPA flag-stone project, ran north and south. This new stadium did not rival the Circus Maximus, but it was probably the best stadium in the state in our class. THS held a rich tradition of winning state champion-ships during the 1950s, when only three classes of Oklahoma high school football existed: A, B, and C. By the time Richard, Jackie, and I had graduated, Thomas had secured six class C titles: 1947, '50, '51, '53 (runner-up), '55, '56, and '57. This period in the fifties was to become the apogee of Thomas football. During this period, Thomas was the reigning heavyweight champ of Oklahoma class C football. I was a varsity athlete on these last three and a starter on the last two teams. I started in the '55 championship game against Hennessey as a sophomore defensive back because some of the starters were sick with the flu. I was a starter! A word had never tasted so good in my mouth before; however, getting the call to start for the first time ever, and in a championship game, caused fear to accumulate in my blood like some kind of toxin, making it difficult for me even to tie my shoelaces. It was a lot to absorb. I struggled a bit as I tried to hide the tremors that were rippling through my body from my teammates. I had pre-traumatic stress disorder, or, I was scared — a persistent ache in my stomach, a common sensation called "butterflies." Adding to my anxiety was the fact that the weather was cold enough on this day to freeze the clappers off the Liberty Bell. As the Duke of Wellington wrote in his memoirs, "The worst moment of any campaign is waiting for the sun to rise on the morning of battle." This proved to be prophetic as my fear started ebbing away after the kickoff and I got a few plays under my belt.

We started this 1955 season coming off a 1954 record of 5–5. Thomas' equivalent of an *anni horribili*. We were up and down like the Tower Bridge in London. Burdened with the '54 season record that ended up like the *Andrea Doria*, we were almost ready to declare ourselves serial losers, but we had a pedigree, were not accustomed to defeat that brought a sense of doom and submission, and the '55 season lifted us from the depths of despair. We rose like the phoenix out of the ashes. During the middle of the '55 season we lost one of our best backs to a knee injury. One of our other good backs spent a lot of time on the sideline during the championship game with calf cramps. As I mentioned above, we also had some sick starters. Coupled with all this adversity was the fact the *Enid Morning News* had us pretty much beaten before the game even started. But the theory of *competition* says, "Just because they're strong doesn't mean they can't get their butts kicked." As the fourth quarter began, we put together our best drive of the afternoon, a gritty, clock-grinding, in-your-face testament to toughness and will. Here is how the *Enid Morning News* reported this last quarter drive: "While primarily concerned with keeping possession of the ball, the Terriers chopped off steady chunks of yardage with Christensen and Lapel doing most of the carrying. The longest gain was an 18-yarder by Lapel which gave the Rossmen their fourth first down in the series and placed the ball on the Hennessey 11. Christensen picked up 3 and Lapel went the last 8. McKellips passed to Jimmy Sweeney for the extra point and Thomas led 21–12 with 2:01 left." I would not say that we kicked their bottoms, but we showed up to play and won the game. Coaching, tradition, and passion made the difference. I discovered that I liked being in a drama worthy of Sophocles. 1955 turned out to be quite a reclamation project for Mr. Ross and Mr. Roof.

The 1951 championship against Davis was memorable for being won on first downs at Owen Field in Norman. There was no system in the fifties for continuing play when time ran out with a tie score. The game ended 25–25. Both teams were tied in penetrations (getting inside an opponent's 20 yard line) with five each. The game was ultimately decided on first downs. Thomas won in this department, 14–10.

We would play pickup-style football during every recess at school from grade one until we were issued uniforms to play organized ball in the seventh grade. There were no youth leagues at this time. The first would play the second grade, the third played the fourth, etc. On the first day of school every year, someone from each class would go to Mr. Ross and he would give each class an old football to play with at recess. It was always kind of a fight to determine who got to take the ball out. This was the most rough-and-tumble smash-mouth ball I ever played. Actually, it was more like semi-organized mayhem — rough as a night in the Waycross jail. We played tackle with no pads. When the recess bell rang to line up to go back to class, we always had to run a few more plays on a playground harder than Chinese arithmetic, and this frequently got us into hot water with the teachers for being late as we contrived excuses for our lateness. We always came back to class covered in dirt, and at least one person always had a button or two missing. School-yard football was its own culture where you were constantly being tested — a Darwinian struggle. We were drawn to football like a magnet. This was a time when mothers never complained to the school about torn clothes and skinned knees. It was just accepted as part of the rite of passage for Thomas boys.

The lawn between Ronnie Ogden's house and his granddad's was busier than Times Square during football season because we often gathered at Ronnie's house after school to play ragtag *kamikaze* football. We always played there because his yard had good grass and it was about the right size. When you were tackled, you fell into a soft claustrophobic scrum of bodies because there were always about a hundred and twenty kids. It was a game played somewhat according to the standard rules, but naturally some were improvised. The game played to its own cadence, and without a referee, could be brutally tough. At times it was like nineteenth-century warfare. There were no Marquis of Queensbury rules for us. Only three things ever stopped a game — darkness, a fight, or blood. Once someone banged his head on something with more molecular density than human flesh and cut his scalp, which immediately began bleeding like a water fountain. "Is he dead?" someone asked. One of the "doctors" who examined him said, "No, he is not dead, but he is gonna die if he doesn't run down to Dr. Ryan's office and get it sewed up." Another said, "Your nose is broken." One of the guys placed his used handkerchief on the wound. The blood slowly soaked through the handkerchief, crawling, as blood crawls. I can just see our injured friend walking in Dr. Ryan's waiting room filled with the weary, wilting, woeful, and walking wounded as they waited to be admitted into the doctor's *sanctum santorum*. On another occasion one of the guys hurt his shin and could not get to his feet. I hoisted him up, drew his arm around my shoulders, and took most of his weight. Hopping on one leg with me supporting the other, we managed to get to his house a couple of blocks away. My heroic efforts were rewarded with a tasty snack.

If someone was stupid enough to start a fight or cry like a sissy, Ronnie's mother would shoo us off as if we'd been a pack of runaway chickens. It was important not to cry, not to show that a particularly hard tackle hurt, although of course everyone knew that it hurt, could see that it hurt, even though you felt like your guts were going to spill out on the ground. Crying would only make things worse in the long run. How simple the world would be if left to children. To experience joy from something as simple as a ball, some boys, and a sunny day.

Nothing more is needed. It was a *Happy Days* experience. Playing football at recess time or at some kid's house made you feel safe. We blended into the tribe and were in our element when we all played together.

Playing football at home with Richard and Jackie, playing recess football at school, sandlot ball in different neighborhoods after school, and tagging along with Richard in the dressing room really helped prepare me, both mentally and physically, for just about anything I would face in the years to come in football, basketball, and track. Our joys knew no bounds as we donned our first uniforms and played organized ball in the seventh grade, our first year of junior high. We received old, ragged, hand-me-down uniforms, including leather helmets, remnants from another time, and, although we must have looked like poor, underprivileged schoolboys trying unsuccessfully to project the appearance of a respectable football squad, we were paradoxically the picture of true contentment — so pleased and excited to be wearing real uniforms after playing recess football for six years. This was a fitting overture for the day when we would put on a high school uniform and start playing big-boy football. I have a picture of me in this old hand-me-down ragged uniform. I looked like a Christmas ornament in that old, beat-up leather helmet.

The only football loss during my junior high years was at the hands of class "A" Clinton. The score was 7–20. The most significant accomplishment of my junior high was a 55-yard punt against Clinton. It didn't do much good because Billy Meacham ran it all the way back for a touchdown. I had an 86-yard punt in high school against Seiling that seemed driven by the Lord himself. Their receiver was playing up too close. He had no respect for my abilities, I guess. The ball went over his head and rolled forever on a very dry and hard field. "The second coming of Bill Lonebear," someone said. Stories of Bill Lonebear's kicking and punting feats were legion.

When we finally matriculated to high school and were admitted into the holy circle, our Spartan, unaesthetic, but functional dressing room was located under the stadium. It consisted of uniform hangers, dressing benches, a foot-powder box, showers, and a desk or table of some kind on which were analgesic balm, tape, salt pills, etc. A multi-sensory experience of sights, sounds, and smells pervaded the dressing room. And they were all intense. The cold bare concrete floors and walls were a dispiriting battleship gray. They held the cold with thermos-like efficiency, and smelled of sweaty practice uniforms. However, it was our humble sanctuary, a safe haven, our womb, our citadel, where we were understood, accepted, welcomed, and, when necessary, exonerated. It was a place of tension-breaking jocularity before practices and after games that we had won, a place of horseplay, raucous laughter, joking, general blarney, dissonant note singing, cheerful foolishness, — a language we could all understand. Good fun popped like soap bubbles. This jock culture of strict discipline, training, and play enforced community and camaraderie for a significant amount of time both in and out of season for most of us. Dressing-room banter is not like playing Mozart on the piano. It's a freestyle jam session. The rhythms are instinctual. There was something about it. It had a mood, an ambience. It was a comfortable place to be ensconced and had a self-nurturing attachment to it.

At 3:15 each day the dressing room would slowly come to life as the different team members drifted in from their last class of the day. As I would be undressing, I would always hear Jack Kippenberger throw self-consciousness to the wind as he less-than-tunefully bellowed out "The Book of Love" in that cracking, adolescent baritone voice between his daily jaunt from the school to the stadium dressing room. Even against tone-deaf ears, his song ricocheted annoyingly among us with unabashed abandon. This was one of my favorite musical memories as I remember Jack thinking he was Caruso singing "Nessun Dorma." The effect of this intoning was enough to dislocate the senses. Oh well, we all have our crosses to bear.

Playing and winning was fun, but dressing-room high jinks were also great fun. Fun, that is, if you were an upperclassman. Woe to a freshman who had any kind of a slight or perceived bodily anomaly. It was always duly noted and appropriate or inappropriate comments made, depending on if you were the recipient or commentator. It was great fun, if the opportunity presented itself, to catapult someone out of the dressing room when naked and hope that some girls were around. Today, such behavior would probably be grounds for us to be accused of being some kind of pervert. Some of the more prominent rabble-rousers that I remember during my time were Gordon Crowdis, K.D. Lapel, Jack Keller, Don Richardson, Charles Cleveland, and Virgil Talbot. They were the crown princes of dressing-room humor, and they milked the comedy for all it was worth.

Gordon started each season with a new "T-shirt" to wear under his shoulder pads and never washed it. When this shirt was dry and so saturated with salt, it would stand up as if made of corrugated cardboard. This shirt stank like a toxic waste dump and should have had a warning label: *Standing close to this shirt could be dangerous to your health.* About once a year, someone would covertly manage to put some red hot balm on someone's jockstrap. Not knowing it was imbedded in the material until one had worn it for a few minutes, one would not notice the burning until after hitting the practice field and then be in constant misery. Our stadium dressing room exuded a kind of precious talismanic power, not to mention the powerful smell alluded to above. This room was one of my best friends. The atmosphere was collegial. If only its walls could talk they'd tell us stories that could make this document explode. Such was the culture of the dressing room. The camaraderie, solidarity, and fun of the dressing room created a unique and lasting intimacy for many of us. I should mention that there was a sign above the dressing-room door that read, "Gentlemen need not use foul or profane language to express themselves." As far as Mr. Ross and Mr. Roof were concerned, the language they used could be used in Sunday school. Not that they did not raise their voices when correction or discipline was warranted.

A freshman always took much teasing before his first health physical to play football — all part of the local masculine protocol requirements. "The doctor is going to 'do this' and 'do that' to you naked in front of the nurse." As each exited the examination, the humiliation of our body and spirit was compounded by the upper classmen in the outer waiting room. The indignities suffered during the exam were not mitigated when an upperclassman would come out of the exam room. He would naturally exaggerate both orally and by indiscreet mimicry what the doctor had done to him. The check for a hernia was the worst part of the exam. I never knew anyone to flunk a physical. An occasional heart murmur, maybe, but of course, we were all teenagers. The trials and tribulations of being a freshman never seemed to end. The arrogance of entitlement was something we freshmen just had to endure. We were an oppressed minority. In general, when taking in all the hazing and tough practices as a freshman, we were more or less chewed up and swallowed in one gulp. We were at the bottom rung of the ladder and fully understood the pecking order. Sometimes I felt like we were being spent like pennies at an arcade. The end of the season was also an interesting part of being on the football team. When I was a freshman, the upper-class players made all freshmen stand nude on the dressing benches. While holding our dongs up, they would come by and paint our private parts black with bootblack. This was a polish and preservative that was used to treat our shoes once a week during the season. It took several days for this substance to wear off. The freshmen were required by the upper classmen to bootblack their shoes once a week, the day before a game as if we were scullery help, which we more or less were.

A tradition that knew no class bounds was the beltline that I remember the older guys employing, but had died out by the time of my high school years. Any team member who broke a training rule was required to run the gauntlet through a line of all team members equally arranged in two parallel lines. Each member of the line would take off their belt and give a good lick as the runner ran by their position. You never saw the coaches involved in this activity; however, it was carried out with their "unofficial" sanction. This activity took place on the lawn in front of the building during the noon hour. I guess today these silly rituals would be known as hazing.

Rah, Rah, *Siss Boom Bah!* On game days, the band twirlers would marshal all the high school girls and start a snake dance on the front steps of the building when the noon bell rang to come in. They would join hands and run through the halls and classrooms shouting cheers. Or, as Keren Payne Miller said, "We would whiz through the rooms and halls and at times it could get a little scary." Kay Halle Lancaster said, "It could get a little crazy at times." "Being on the tail end was wicked," Paulette Steward Kraybill told me. Part of the group would shout "Powder River" and the rest of them responded with "Pour it on." I think this comes from the Powder River Coal Company in Gillette, Wyoming, with the cheer referencing "pouring on the coal." I witnessed this activity from grade one on up, and it was kind of neat to experience this when I was finally a member of the team. It was a show worth watching.

We were to play Weatherford in the annual backyard-brawl opening game of the season one year, when some disaffected bottom-feeding riffraff from Weatherford came oozing into Thomas like termites from the woodwork looking for trouble like bad guys in a spaghetti western. They painted graffiti on the stadium, trying to make it look like an archeological ruin. During their brief incursion into enemy territory Mr. Ross, our coach, who had a nose for stinky cheese, and this was definitely stinky cheese, got wind of them and managed to catch them. He got a bucket of gasoline, made them take off their shirts and scrub the paint off the concrete, and it was clear that this was not community-outreach work. Working as hard as funeral-home fans, these low-rent, unsavory characters finally finished and there was nothing left of their shirts. This was poetic justice. *What fools these mortals be.* These guys needed an industrial enema. Of course, news of this event quickly spread and a bunch of us arrived on scene like we had been subpoenaed because people are always unusually drawn to spectacle. We watched the scrubbing and zeroed in to the scene like a hawk to a field mouse. However, our presence was more curious than hostile. I walked home from this incident with a feeling of ecstasy, delirious joy, and supreme satisfaction from having a free ticket to this unexpected event. There was always comfort in the misery of one's adversary. It was ignoble of me to enjoy these Weatherford characters' anger, but I could not help myself. I had to applaud Mr. Ross's sleuthing on this exciting event.

During my eighth-grade year, I was one of the water boys for the high school football team. About all this amounted to was carrying Coke bottles of water out to the players during a timeout. However, this job entitled me to free admission to all the games, and a hamburger after the away games while the players ate steaks. It also allowed me to hang around a group of great guys. Richard was a senior this season.

We always played our high school games on Thursday night, as opposed to the traditional Friday-night games for most schools, so that Mr. Roof could go scout future opponents. Mr. Roof was an excellent scout. He could spot and pick out things our next opponents were doing that "telegraphed" what they were going to do so early, and so obviously, they might as well have sent their intentions to us in a postcard three weeks ago. Mr. Roof's scouting skills gave us an incalculable advantage.

Frank Leahy, coach at Notre Dame, had a 15-minute college football prediction TV show at 10:15 every Thursday night during football season. After we played a home game, I would always rush home to see this show. He would show a few seconds of action film of each team that he was reporting on, then his football cartoon caricature named "Fumble" would bounce around to the tune of some college fight song and land on the team he picked to win. I loved this show.

Our practices were scheduled the last hour of the school day at 3:15, and we had to be on the field by 3:30. Our practices were disciplined, hard-hitting, and utterly exhausting with those oxygen-sucking drills that went by as slow as molasses. Additionally, the goathead patch in the northwest corner of the field that had never seen any 2,4-D and no water breaks during practice contributed to this endless misery. One might mitigate the thirst somewhat by managing to get tackled near or in a sprinkler puddle, where one might cup a handful of this murky water into one's mouth. Or, as some did, smuggle a lemon onto the field by hiding it somewhere in your uniform and take an occasional lick on it. I just learned to keep repeating the words: *It could be worse.* However, as a wise man once said, "The more you sweat in training, the less you'll bleed in war."

A symphony of whistles greeted us on Monday, the longest and toughest practice day of the week. After our warm-up exercises and various drills, we would line up in close-order combat and scrimmage for two hours as Mr. Ross and Mr. Roof choreographed practice as smoothly and effortlessly as a maestro does an orchestra. However, as difficult as practice was, it was somewhat cathartic. On Tuesday we would practice our plays with the defense holding blocking dummies. The freshmen and sophomores had to hold these dummies, and it wasn't fun. It was always tempting to let go of the dummy just as the upperclassmen would throw a block into it. However, at the threat of evisceration, we would not ever do this. Being at the bottom of the food chain, we neophytes got worked over like rented mules as we went ricocheting around the practice field in the manner of pinball machines. I always felt as if I had been put in a sack and kicked around the dressing room by the juniors and seniors. The first time the freshmen scrimmaged the upperclassmen, they learned the meaning of Newton's second law of motion — force equals mass times acceleration. Penetrating the first team line was like trying to pierce the Maginot Line. Many times after being knocked down, I would be waiting to be helped up by a mate or unconsciousness. Whichever came sooner. However, with hard-nosed tenacity, I would always pop back up, surfacing like a cork even though sometimes my vision was crowded with white floaters. In general, they went through us as though we were made of butter. As the old Timex watch commercial said, "could take a licking and keep on ticking." Other than holding the dummies that Mr. Ross had arrayed with an engineer's precision, the freshmen were forced to learn mostly by osmosis. But, as Milton has written, "They also serve who stand and wait." We were squires waiting to become knights. These big-as-a-Buick cousins of Genghis Khan upperclassmen towered over us like visitors to Lilliput.

Sometimes these guys gave me enough nightmares to make Edgar Allan Poe look like a beautiful dreamer. A freshman trying to block or tackle a grizzled upperclassman, as physics kicked in, was like the futile charge of the *Light Brigade* that Alfred Lord Tennyson immortalized: ". . . into the maw of death." Fearing physical retribution, we endured all this without complaining because as Jim Croce wrote in one of his songs, "You don't tug on Superman's cape."

It was on Monday or Tuesday, right before we ran wind sprints, when we practiced on the hanging tackling dummy. It was hung on a wood frame in a sand pit with a mechanical device that could be adjusted for degree of difficulty on knocking it down. If you hit it and it did not come loose and fall down, you had not hit it hard enough, which meant that you were given the luxury of hitting it again. Another drill that I really dreaded was the charging sled. This drill would rank near the top of most hated drills. Pushing that sled was punishing. When the sled drill was called for, we all ran to the sled in an attempt to get one of the prized interior positions. No one wanted to draw the "short straw" and be on the end because it required all the strength you could muster in a sustained manner, or you would quickly be exposed as a wimp because, if you couldn't push as strongly as the guy on the other end, the sled would veer off a straight path and start turning in your direction. It was like gravity pulling sideways. It was so difficult for all the guys to move in rhythm because not all were of equal physical ability. That sled and I were not on good terms. I abhorred that sled as much as nature abhors a vacuum. On Wednesday, we ran through our plays up and down the field with no contact of any kind. We would also practice our punting and kickoff procedures. By this time each week we were as precision-tuned as a Ferrari anticipating the Thursday night kickoff. We would take our game pants and jerseys to Murray's laundry or have our mothers wash them after Wednesday's practice. Thursday was game day. We did not suit up. We went home at 3:15 to eat an early dinner. Usually a piece of meat and cottage cheese was about all I ever ate before a game. On Friday we would suit up and do just enough drills to break a sweat. The blocking dummies, tackling dummy, and charging sled were hated drills, but did the job of honing our skills and whipping us into better physical conditioning. Winning was a strong elixir. It softened and neutralized all these "hardships" we endured in practice so that we could play on Thursday night. Someone has said, "Pain lasts a minute, glory lasts a lifetime." Like the French say, "By dint of hammering one becomes a blacksmith." This sort of training and practicing regimen was designed to try our souls as well as our bodies, and it did both. As Edgar Frost wrote in *Port Robertson: Behind the Scenes of Sooner Sports*, "Football is a tough sport, and people who do not relish physical contact should not be involved in it. One does not prepare to participate in football by playing hopscotch and having tea and crumpets."

When captains were selected by the team my senior year, I was among three elected. K.O. Kippenburger and Rusty Kraybill were the other two. About the only two functions of a captain were to make penalty decisions during a game and to crown the queen during half-time at the homecoming game. My queen was Glenda Reiswig. Paulette Steward was Rusty's queen and Joy Renfrow was K.O.'s. Joy was the first real standout girl basketball player in the infancy of renewed Thomas girls' basketball.

My junior year, Thomas played its first all black football team, Booker T. Washington from El Reno. Even though desegregation occurred in 1955, Oklahoma was not completely desegregated. Segregation had been doctrinally successful but not practically so. Over 90 years after the Civil War, black people more or less remained in social and economic serfdom. Whites lived in one part of town, blacks in the other. Separate schools, separate churches, separate restaurants, separate lives were still the norm in most places. It is interesting that the Boston, Massachusetts, schools were integrated in 1855. Of course, Boston was a hot bed in the abolitionist movement. We approached this game with trepidation because we just didn't know what to expect. I thought they just might be the Beowulf of football. They turned out to be a weak team, and I felt sorry for them. They had only eleven helmets. When they substituted, the player leaving the field had to give his helmet to his replacement. The first black player I ever played against was Pat Griffin from Weatherford. He was a good athlete and a prince of a guy. Although Thomas never had any blacks we had several Indians, and I am proud to say that Thomas probably had the best graduation rate for Indians of any public school in Oklahoma according to research done by Karen McKellips, a classmate who later taught at Cameron University. Thomas was overwhelmingly white, so we basically grew up without any sense of prejudice, firsthand or even in the abstract. I remember us boys associating with Indian boys outside of school activities more than the girls did.

For some reason, we always played our first round play-off games on Thanksgiving Day. I went three consecutive years without a Thanksgiving dinner. No complaints, however. At the end of the season, there were three important functions we eagerly anticipated: the all-school assembly where we were awarded our letter jackets and small medal-size gold footballs, the team party, and the Cotton Bowl trips to Dallas each New Year's Day, which were sponsored by the local booster club. On January 1, 1957, TCU beat Syracuse 28–27, and on January 1, 1958, it was Navy winning over Rice 20–7. An interesting story about one of these Cotton Bowl trips was related to me by Karen McKellips. A group of the girls, in an expansive mood, were having a slumber party with Ila Lee Inman, who lived in an apartment in the bank building, and climbed on top of the building to cheer us off by climbing out of an upper-story window. Other girls who were in attendance were Paulette Steward, Patty Talbott, and Elaine Huckins.

A football practice that we did not particularly enjoy was the infamous early morning meetings that all players were required to attend, which were called "skull practice." In this class session, the coaches worked on the Xs and Os. This meeting took place in the library an hour before the first morning class in an effort to further hone our knowledge of the game. The coaches would diagram and explain new plays, review old plays, go over rules, football theory, diagram the next opponent's offense and defense, and explain different situations that could develop during games. I will never forget having drilled into us that all decisions and play calling were dependent on time, down, distance, and score. The coaches rarely called any plays. One of the senior players was always selected to call plays regardless of the position he might have played. They would also review the previous week's game and never miss the opportunity to point out our mistakes. Mr. Ross could find mistakes like Joe McCarthy could find communists. On Monday morning instead of "skull" practice, the previous week's game film would be shown, and this was worse than "skull practice" when it came to pointing out our mistakes, because it was right there on film for all to see as Mr. Ross played our blunders over and over and over. Thomas was one of the first small schools to film their games with 16 mm movie film. After a game someone would take the film to Weatherford so that it could be put on a Greyhound bus to be delivered to a lab in Oklahoma City to be developed and returned by Saturday or Sunday. Even though I did not necessarily have an appreciation for having to go to school an hour early, I am sure all this contributed greatly to our success, as did our stoic suffering during those two-a-days.

We ran a variety of football formations. The "T" formation with an unbalanced line was our basic set. Other schemes that were mixed in from time to time were the old single-wing and what we called the "Y" formation, which was a variant of the single-wing. The single-wing offense was an old-fashioned, run-oriented formation that dates back to the early 1900s, popularized by Glenn "Pop" Warner at Carlisle Indian School when Jim Thorpe played there. In the single wing, everyone is lined up tight, the ball is snapped to the tailback, and he either runs, hands off, laterals, or passes the ball. It is as old-school as it gets. The tailback would be the equivalent to today's quarterback. About the only difference would be taking a direct snap of the ball instead of taking it from under the center.

If we were playing an out-of-town game we would usually travel by a private car "convoy" organized by Claude Johnson, who was the team statistician and a local businessman. For some reason I was usually assigned to ride with Mr. Ross and his wife installed in the backseat of his car. I was never too happy about this because everything was so serious in his presence — a solemn intensity. I preferred a little levity and jocular conversation and nonsense like most of the others were able to enjoy. He wanted us concentrating on the game, and he was correct in expecting this type of behavior.

Games are won by a good week of preparation. In high school that starts on Monday. Mr. Ross was a big believer in this and never did too much coaching during the game. At halftime he would admonish if we needed it and make minor adjustments. When one would go down the line and look at each Thomas player individually, we seemed to be just average athletes, but somehow Mr. Ross and Mr. Roof always managed to morph us into a cohesive unit capable of achieving above the ordinary.

We won many football games and we were allowed to celebrate only after we had played the game and won. There was always quiet seriousness in the dressing room prior to every game. The winning celebrations commenced on Thursday night after the game and lasted throughout the weekend. Playing and winning a game always left me feeling exhilarated, cleansed, exhausted, and energized, which was quite congruent with the post-game celebrating. When Monday rolled around it was all stoicism and a businesslike preparation for the next game. There was no freelancing or fanfare during our practices or games — we never punctuated a touchdown run with an end-zone tango or strutting like a peacock. Nor was there ever any hair coming out from under any helmets, tattoos, or feminine jewelry worn by anyone. It was burned into our collective memories that there was to be no self-aggrandizement of any kind. In Mr. Ross's view, bestowing praise simply for doing our work was as ludicrous as praising the horse for pulling a milk cart. I think he felt that too much praise contributed to a prideful attitude. Equally important, I do not remember any team discord during my four years of playing. Unlike today, Mr. Ross and Mr. Roof retained sovereignty.

Richard was four grade levels ahead of me and five ahead of Jackie, so we did not have the opportunity to play together. However, Jackie and I were both starters his junior year and my senior year. This was a real privilege. We fused, the two of us, like two sides of a mathematical equation. Jackie was mostly "Mr. Inside" and I was "Mr. Outside." However, Jackie, being faster than me, also ran some outside plays, punt returns, kickoff returns, some pass patterns, and was our kickoff man. He was as good or better than me (ahem). I was chosen second team All-State in 1957. Rusty Kraybill, our right end, was chosen for the first team. We lost only one football game in my three years of varsity playing. It was a 14–18 loss to class "B" Weatherford in the first game of my senior season, which broke a 25-game winning streak. As you might imagine, the dressing room was funeral — quiet as a tomb. The atmosphere was one of gloom and despair. I thought we played as well as we were capable, but can't deny that the weekend was as dark as a lawyer's soul. Also, I cannot deny that the sting of that defeat is not a distant memory. I think some of the fans were about ready to fly the flag at half-mast.

We went on to win our third consecutive state class "C" championship . . . the "Belmont Stakes." The third race in the Triple Crown, metaphorically speaking. *Gallant Fox* had nothing on us. We beat Hennessey, Morris, and Alex, respectively, in those championship games. Our *annus mirabilis* years. I can't remember what I had for dinner yesterday, but I vividly remember each of these championship games. It was like a high note you hit once in a lifetime. I remember the feeling of complete transported bliss. Was I really hearing seventy-six trombones leading a parade down Main Street? I know that these championships were not on any grand scale to anyone not living in Thomas, but to me it was like waltzing in Vienna. It was my *magnum opus*. This is the stuff that dreams are made of. These championships and the trips to the Cotton Bowl "atoned" for those awful hot August egg-frying-temperature two-a-days and the unremitting self-imposed pressure to win.

As that last championship game ended, a peculiar bolt of elation shot through me. After all the communal post-game jubilant celebrating, pennant waving, and rah-rah enthusiasm in the swirl of people of that last state title game in El Reno against Alex, I walked off the gridiron against the backdrop of a stadium slowly emptying into the hushed whispers of history in a near state of rapture. I looked up to survey the empty field. Just moments before there had been a rumble of expectation from the crowd as "The Star-Spangled Banner" finished playing just prior to the kickoff. The roar of the crowd and the adrenaline of youth had pulsated through this very stadium with a fervor unrivaled. Now, as I turned to make my own exit, the only sounds I could hear were the echoes of lifetime memories, though fresh in their infancy, fading quickly like the scoreboard lights into the solitude of evening and into the quiet recesses of long-sought contentment. I felt as if I'd been holding my breath for weeks — and now, finally, I could exhale. It was now possible to purge myself of a visceral intestinal churning that I had endured all season. It was all over. My mood alternated from suffocating to euphoria. The pressure was off. All season there was great expectation of winning another state championship, and with me being a halfback signal caller, this only increased the pressure. This journey could not have been scripted any better.

On the ride home, there was a welcoming placidity and peace about everything. When I awoke the next morning, yesterday grew clearer in my mind. I slowly pieced together the events, the game, the 34–0 scoreboard, the celebrations — feeling like I was walking in a dream, knowing that it was not a dream. We had won our third consecutive state championship. There was no brass band to herald our victory and no crowns of laurel to mark our achievement when we arrived home because the band and most of the town were on their way home from the game just as we were. I was in clover for several days. All of this exuberance was a prelude to several upcoming celebratory events that would be coming our way. I continued my decompression when arriving home by heading down to the drugstore and devouring a chocolate milkshake. It was nice to be a hot commodity, if only for a few days.

Richard, Jackie, and I were privileged to play on four state championship teams and one state runner-up team during those glorious years at THS. During each subsequent walk I have ever made down the hallowed halls of Thomas High, when I pass the trophy case and look at those reminders of championships gone by, I find myself somewhat entranced, as if staring at sacred chalices. Those venerable memories of yesteryear, now chronicled in the dusty annals of Thomas High School football history, remain unrivaled — both in the record books, and in the hearts of us who hold them most dear: those of us who were somehow blessed to be fatefully cast to play for Thomas during the 1950s. No mortal king can claim a throne more satisfying to remember and to reflect upon — a revered honor that humbles me in profound gratefulness to this day. Football was a pursuit that turned out to be one of my salvations and gave me entrées, which I would not have had otherwise. Mostly, we vanquished our opponents like Caesar conquered Gaul and marauded through our adversaries faster than a salami slicer, as we won district, regional, and state championships. Mr. Ross always said that spirit, speed, skill, savvy, and size were needed to be consistent winners. I don't know that we possessed all these attributes all the time, but I guess if we were lacking in one, we must have compensated in another or with good coaching.

If Thomas had a Mount Rushmore, Mr. Ross and Mr. Roof would be on it. These two guys knew more about football than Kellogg knows about cornflakes. Mr. Ross and Mr. Roof carried an aura about them, a sense of confidence and knowledge, a certain *savior faire*, like men who knew they were two moves ahead of everybody else. They instilled in me the belief that improvement and growth hinges on effort, attitude, and personal desire. It was indeed a five-star honor to be mentored by these two men.

Here are some additional thoughts about Mr. Ross. I greatly respected this man. He never came down hard on me, and I never felt like I was under the *Sword of Damocles* around him. The fear I had of Mr. Ross was that he might disapprove of me in some manner, and it was his validation that I wanted. On the football field Mr. Ross was an austere taskmaster and not given to flattery. He was an Old Testament coach. He was not a monster by any means, but a natural manifestation of what we expected of a coach. He did not like excuses and was intent on eradicating this trait in his athletes. He was not the kind of guy who drank his tea with his pinky finger sticking out. His presence could fill a room like aftershave, but he was a nice person under his outer crust and demanding demeanor. As I have gotten older, I have come to realize that his needling and stern voice were sort of a persona that most coaches adopted to motivate and simply to convey urgency or enthusiasm in an effort to encourage one to put forth more effort. Was Tolstoy thinking of Mr. Ross when writing in *The Sebastopol Sketches*, "A commander need not be sweet-tempered to be admired; rather, he had to be skilled, knowledgeable, fair, and preferably tough." And the old Machiavellian saying that it is nice to be admired, but far better to be feared might be at play here. At the time, on the surface, Mr. Ross seemed larger than life to me. He had an air of royalty about him that transcended football, and he carried himself with a quiet pride. Mr. Ross also had a humorous side. He used to kid his outside linebackers by saying, "I need you at this position because one can't fool a dumb guy." A good linebacker really needs to play his position and "stay home," meaning to not follow the ball, but stay at the assigned position in case the runner came his way. So, a dumb linebacker was needed instead of some smart guy who was always trying to figure things out and going for the ball. Actually, our linebackers were pretty smart guys, and they took this kidding in stride. It seemed that he always had an appropriate comment that was often a blend of warning, caution, instruction, and humor. And we listened! After all was said and done, we really did appreciate Mr. Ross's brand of coaching.

Years after my school days, Mr. Ross still had a lingering presence, like the ghost of Hamlet's father. One Memorial Day out at the cemetery, a bunch of us, as adults, were visiting and some were smoking. Someone jokingly said, "Here comes Mr. Ross." Those who were smoking quickly put out their cigarettes. Don McNeill, a 1969 THS graduate, named one of his race horses *Mr. Ross*. The horse won over $1,000,000 during his racing career and was inducted into the Oklahoma City Remington Park Hall of Fame in 2010.

Other stalwart coaches in western Oklahoma during this era with stellar reputations were: Earl Kilmer, Laverne; Steve Graham, Weatherford; Dean Wilde, Watonga; Otis Delaporte, Clinton; Jenks Simmons, El Reno; and George Ewbanks, Fairview.

A final thought about football. I have written quite a bit about Thomas football and rightly so. It had tradition and was a very large part of my boyhood and a positive influence that still resonates with me. It provided me with many good memories as I occasionally glance over my old photos, mementos, and framed accolades. However, I don't want my legacy to be thought of as only a "jock," having no pedagogical virtues. Granted, I was more interested in athletics than academics, but I like to think that there was some latent intellectual curiosity buried somewhere within me that caused me to have at least a small taste for the fruit of knowledge. I say this because a time came in adulthood when I actually started reading books because I wanted to, and the writing of this memoir is also an outgrowth of this matter. After all, the pen is mightier than the football, but I think the two have blended quite well as I have chronicled this document.

CHAPTER 28

Basketball

"Like everything else, Fletcher, practice." – from *Jonathan Livingston Seagull*

ATHLETICALLY SPEAKING, AFTER our last football game each season, a melancholy settled over everything like a cloud. It marked the beginning of the true winter, a dark stretch that did not end until March or April when track season began. We were just never very good at basketball. I really liked basketball, and Mr. Roof told me in junior high that it was going to be my best sport. However, except for my freshman year, when we won runner-up to Hammon in the Custer County Tournament, we never had much success. One night at this tournament in Hammon, I sashayed into the gym wearing blue suede shoes with the top of the sole edging trimmed in white, black pants, pink and black web belt, and a pink shirt. I walked all around the gym floor, ostensibly looking for a seat, just so everyone could see me. I was trying to look cool, but I was not cool.

It was good fun to slip in through an unlocked window at the HS gym or the Community Building to shoot baskets, play one-on-one, two-on-two, or whatever depending on how many kids eventually showed up. We would also show off trying to imitate the Harlem Globetrotters with fancy dribbling and trick shots that we never made. I don't remember anyone ever getting in trouble for these activities, so I think it was another one of those things where we had the tacit approval from those in authority.

Besides the school teams, the town had a team called Blackie's Clippers coached by Blackie Vaughn, the barber. Now, they were good. Moon Stinson, a member of that team, is legendary for his talents on the court. He was from Lone Wolf. He had a scholarship at Southwestern, but the coach wasn't playing him much so he came up with a couple of other SW players and played for the Clippers when Southwestern didn't have a game. Moon was 6'1" and could dunk from nearly the free-throw line. The Clippers had a good following with the seats frequently sold out. During their best year, they went 33–1. There were several town teams all over the country during the '50s.

CHAPTER 29

Track & Field

"Joy to you, we've won." – Pheidippides

AND NOW, I get to the third leg of my athletic holy trinity of football, basketball, and track. My interest in track began at an early age and like Pheidippides, I liked to run, although not as far as he ran from Marathon to Athens to deliver the message that the Greeks had defeated the Persians. Early in junior high, I learned that something was different about how I performed certain skills compared to Richard and Jackie. I threw right handed, ate left handed, punted right footed, batted right handed, but knocked flies with the bat left handed. Fortunately, this condition never seemed to bother me in my athletic endeavors.

In grade school, during track season, Haze Park and I would meet out behind his house after school to pole vault where we had built a pit and vaulting standards. We would go to Hockaday's Hardware Store to get discarded bamboo poles on which carpet and flooring had been rolled. We used these for a vaulting pole and crossbar. When we advanced to where we could vault higher than the last nail on the standards, we would stack bricks on top of the standards, on which to place the crossbar. However, when we failed to clear the bar, these bricks would fall, coming down just after our bodies hit the pit. I don't know how we managed never to be injured from these falling projectiles. I went on to establish the county junior high pole vault record of 10 feet. I wonder if Haze and I ever properly thanked Claude Johnson for keeping us stocked with these poles?

My first competitive track season was in the seventh grade. We did not compete by grade or age groups, but by weight. There were four classes: 85-pound class, 105-pound class, 120-pound class, and un-limited class. Most seventh-graders competed in the 85-pound class; however, I weighed more than 85 lbs. and had to compete in the 105-pound class with mostly eighth-graders. My very first track meet was the Custer County Meet, which included Clinton, Weatherford, and Thomas. Occasionally, there would be a few competitors from Custer or Butler. My first competitive event ever was the 75-yard dash. I had had butterflies in my stomach from school tryouts, but this was the worst case of butterflies I had experienced up to this point. My senses were tuned to such an excruciating state that they vibrated to every move around me. I was not expected to win the 75-yard dash and did place second in the morning qualifying heat. Eddie Berrong from Weatherford beat me. However, in the finals, as I stepped into the starting blocks, every neuron in my body was firing simultane-ously, and I surprised everyone, including myself, by winning. I felt like *Mercury*. I managed to get a really good start and felt as grace-ful as a deer as I ran eastward down the straightaway to the finish line, although I probably did not look like a deer. I thought God had realigned my atoms and formed a new me. After all, even my little brother could outrun me. I must have had a look on my face the like of which must have been there when Archimedes spilled his bathwa-ter. This first competitive athletic win was a eureka moment for me.

I went on to place second in the broad jump, getting beat by one-half inch and ran a leg on the winning 440-yard relay team. Receiving my medals after the track meet, while walking home — or should I say "gliding"? — I looked at my first track medals in a kind of ecstasy, like they were priceless objects of art. I would later come to under-stand that, like Dan Gable said, "Gold medals aren't really made of gold. They are made of sweat, determination, and a hard-to-find alloy called guts." I competed in the 120-pound class in the eighth grade and in the unlimited class my freshman year and had similar successes in those two years. We won the team championship all three years, and I was high-point man two of those years, which earned me an extra medal attached to a ribbon. Having a ribbon on it made it really special. In the eighth grade I set county records in the high jump and broad jump. In the ninth grade I set a record in the broad jump (19' 3.5"), but got beat a half inch by David Heathcoat from Weatherford on his last jump. Mr. Roof took me to the state junior high track meet at OBU my freshman season, where I tied for second in the pole vault with a vault of 10' 2." I can't decide which year was bigger for me, seventh or eighth. The seventh was big because I won my first track medal. Eighth was big because I started on the freshman football team and set my first county track records.

My high school track years were good ones. In most meets I ran the high and low hurdles, broad-jumped, and ran on either the 440 or 880 relay team. We won the county and regional meets all three years. I won four gold medals in my senior regional, but managed only a fourth place in the broad jump at the state meet with a leap of 21' .75." There were only two state classifications for track at this time compared to eight today. Probably my most valued track honor was the winning of the intramural Five Star award all three years in high school. This Five Star event was based on the old Olympic Pentathlon event where points were awarded based on performance. The event included the 100-yard dash, 880 run, broad jump, shot put, and high jump. Winning this as a sophomore against the juniors and seniors was a real high and marked a beacon for my high school track years. Being awarded a trophy instead of a medal was a new excitement for me, also. At one time or another, I held county and school records in the broad jump and 180-yard low hurdles. The annual intramural track meet was always the first meet of the season, where all four classes competed against one another. Only first-place medals were awarded, and Mr. Ross always displayed them in the trophy case for a couple of weeks before the meet. Every time I walked by I would get increasingly primed for the meet. Of course, seeing all of Richard's medals at home was even more of an incentive. I was never as fast as Richard, so I had to hone skills in several field events. He once ran a 100 in 9.9 seconds. 10.9 was my fastest time (freshman). He had made a plaque in shop class to hold his medals and made some more for me and Jackie on which to display our medals. I liked track and field a lot, so I did not need much motivation. However, if I had known that Shakespeare said, "Bid me run, and I will strive with things impossible," I might have trained even more intensely.

I should mention that Mr. Roof, my junior high and assistant high school coach, was instrumental in getting me started off in the right direction in track. A preternaturally gifted athlete, he was a living legend in Thomas, having been the last high school athlete to ever win four individual gold medals in the state track meet, and this was at a time when there were only two different levels of class competition. He was also a second-team All-Missouri Valley halfback at Oklahoma A&M and held some rushing records there for years. If an opportunity ever presented itself, even today, I would probably still "show off" for Mr. Roof, even though there is now more rust than iron in my joints. He was XXL in my world. I trusted him unquestionably. His charisma was palpable and he had that quiet humility that echoed. Like mothers who never stop kissing their children, do we never stop craving the approval of our teachers? One day at the noon recess while I was playing on the playground in upper elementary school, Mr. Roof came walking by on his way to the building having walked from his home for lunch. He came up to me, tousled my hair, and asked, "How are you doing?" This was like tapping my shoulders with *Excalibur*. Heady stuff for a kid. It seemed as if I were floating, carried along by the words he'd said. There was nothing anyone could have said that would have meant more to me than this brief gesture. This feeling was infectious and intoxicating. He was my main man, a perpetual inspiration, and helped keep me from floundering. What a blessing to be mentored by this gentle giant.

There is one humorous track story I must include. At the Fairview

Relays, they were building a new track. While it was being constructed, they had a substitute track which was just graded into a field. There was a horrible windstorm, and the dust was so thick you could hardly see. The mile relay team was composed of Melvin Bandy, Vernon Spencer, Terral McKellips, and Richard Tallbull. Terral was watching to see which lane to get in to get the baton from Vernon and was totally shocked to see him running in first place. He and Richard managed to hang on, and he thinks maybe win — at least place way ahead of where their talent should have placed them. Later, Vernon confessed that the dust was so thick that he just took a "shortcut" across the field before the turn, and no one saw him. Unbelievable! No, knowing Vernon, it is entirely believable.

One could say that I was totally absorbed in athletic endeavors. It was a rare day in the school year for six years that I did not have a practice or game. I would have played baseball if we would have had a team. I liked anything competitive. Football provided me more success, but being a thinclad was my favorite activity. One reason for this, I think, was the fact that one was immediately rewarded for one's performance with a medal and I measured myself by my medal count. My dream was to be a decathlon athlete like Bob Mathias, but the dream was an unattainable one. I might as well have wished to fly.

CHAPTER 30

Sports Notables

"Just play. Have fun. Enjoy the game." – Michael Jordan

HERE, BRIEFLY, I mention some of the big names in sports that I re-member as a kid and who we would try to emulate in our fantasies when playing whatever sport was in season. In baseball everyone wanted to play like he was Jackie Robinson; in football, it was Jim Thorpe or Red Grange, the "Galloping Ghost"; boxing, Joe "the Brown Bomber" Louis; basketball, Goose Tatum or Bevo Francis. I had bet-ter include Meadowlark Lemons, also. Is there a name more lovely? In track and field Jesse Owens. Jesse was faster than a telegram. Jesse gave Adolf Hitler — and America — a lesson in race when he won four gold medals at the 1936 Olympic Games right under Hitler's nose. Joe Louis did the same thing when he defeated Max Schmeling of Germany in 1938. This was a big deal — like Roosevelt defeating Hitler. It is interesting to note, I think, that all of the above mentioned athletes, with the exception of Red Grange, are minorities. In football, we sometimes substituted a local high school standout, Bill Lonebear, for Jim Thorpe. In the summer of 1947 Jackie Robinson, from the all-black Negro Leagues, had finally been accepted into major-league baseball. Rudyard Kipling wrote, "East is east and west is west." His meaning was that cultures don't easily mix. This was basically true in Thomas with the Cheyenne-Arapahoe Indians and the Caucasians.

They were accepted and played on the school's athletic teams, but I don't feel we really reached out to them the way we should have. They were stoic, never showing their feelings, and I just don't think we really understood their culture. As an interesting aside, several years later, I got to play in an alumni game with Bill Lonebear. Bill was an All-Stater in '47. By the way, I scored three touchdowns in that game, and Bill kicked the extra points.

CHAPTER 31

Flatulence

"Keep yourself to yourself." – Dickens

GEORGE FERGUSON, WHO always wore overalls and walked with a country swagger, was a big, tall, easygoing, good-natured, rough-hewn, but distinctly pleasing, member of my seventh-grade class who was always cutting the cheese. Having established himself as the wit and ringmaster of our assemblage, one day, George was nonchalantly holding court on the playground with a rapt audience of friends imparting intriguing tales with cleverly studded dialogue when he abruptly broke course with the words, "I can let a fart anytime I want to." I'll bet. One of the intellectual giants listening to George in rapt attention immediately said, "George, let a fart right now." "Don't want to," George grandly explained to the bastion of cerebral lighthouses surrounding him with his mocking smile and that deep voice of his. *Touché.* He Tom Sawyered us on that one — *fait accompli.* My eyes rolled back into my head as we all laughed, and I especially remember Butch's ever-present machine-gun laugh. What an unmoored imagination George had. George was always full of salty wisdom and taking every opportunity to spread the finest aspects of local culture to all his peers.

One day during seventh- or eighth-grade English class, things were ticking along nicely when, while allegedly preparing for our lessons, George, sitting sphinx-like, leaned to one side in his desk and ripped a ripe one with smooth familiarity, disrupting an element of calm in the classroom, louder than a snoring truck driver with a sinus infection on a descending scale: *phrrrrtttt* — a bravura performance. Yoiks! This gastronomical explosion could have killed a man. Not to mention that it smelled worse than a science experiment. A dozen heads rose like prairie dogs from their desks. Of course, it was impossible for us boys to mute our laughter. Faces in the classroom turned like sunflowers following the sun. Everyone, including the teacher, was now looking at George. With aplomb and never being at a loss for words, George, looking pontifically, hastily extemporized, "Why is everyone looking at me?" pretending it wasn't his. George was a real hoot, but was just a little short on decorum and manners. It hung in the air, and he acted like it was a bouquet of flowers. Fortunately, I had a ringside seat to see George because of a divine random arrangement of the desks. Mrs. Brown (a pseudonym), a Paleolithic teacher (a woman who was probably on the good side of 40) with a stern face and a gloomy demeanor, said in her usual frosty glare and permanent constipated scowl that I found unsettling, "Now, class, we have nice clean restrooms if you need to use them." The meaning eluded me. This made about as much sense to me as holding a séance. Perversely, this made the situation even funnier and we could not contain our case of the giggles as hard as we tried to stifle them. This statement of hers seemed like pretzel logic to me, I thought ungraciously. One does not go to the restroom just to let a windy. It is like a cardinal rule or something. I thought she was going to fall into a fit of vapors. Things now started going downhill pretty quickly as we boys continued our collective hysterics, making no attempt to keep things at room temperature. I wondered if all teachers were born so straitlaced or did it develop over the years. She was the least affable, metaphorically embraceable teacher I ever had.

I thought that we should have a laugh and move on, but Mrs. Brown had gotten her knickers in a knot, and promptly gave about six of us our sailing orders to the office in a somewhat urgent tone.

Okeydokey, if you insist, I thought. I guess she was afraid anarchy was about to break out. It seemed that she was always using us to sharpen her tongue, and smiling did not become her. However, in all honesty, I think her behavior could be labeled as justifiable rage toward our demeanor, and I am sure we exasperated our teachers to the nth degree at times. Anyway, we exited the room with our heads lowered like Judas in an effort to make Mrs. Brown think we were sorry as we headed to the office following one another like ducklings to tell the principal of the misdemeanor we had committed. I could tell that this little emergency meeting with the principal was not meant or going to be a happy chat or an uplifting emotional boost. We also expected that the principal's expression would hold about as much joy as Ebenezer Scrooge's. When we schoolboys were walking down the hall to the "torture chamber," I pretended to be remorseful, but thought instead about Brer Rabbit and being thrown into the briar patch, hoping that I could come up with some kind of a fabrication that would lead to clemency. But I was not able to muster my wits with a solution as clever as Brer Rabbit. I find it interesting that we were sent to the office without supervision. Wasn't our teacher afraid that we might escape?

When we arrived in the lion's lair, it was obvious the principal was not expecting the Prince of Wales as he acknowledged us with a wooden face. Things got worse. We were not even asked to sit down like normal human beings, so we just stood there at a ragged attention as principals do in order to raise the stress level of honest junior high boys. In our *tête-à-tête* with the principal (not Mr. Ross), we gave an oblique *Reader's Digest* version of why we were sent down, laying it on as thick as paste, exuding an aura of innocence as strong as a cheap drugstore perfume. In addition to giving the principal the runaround, we also had a little convenient collective amnesia set in. This amnesia was no doubt assisted by a previous visit to the office by one of our mates, who had told us about what had happened to him. The principal, looking at us like we were some sort of germ to be pasteurized, did not believe our hyperbole one bit, and dragged the whole story out of us one question at a time. His deportment would have one believing that this behavior of ours happened with startling frequency; however, this was my first visit ever to the office. In a somber voice, the principal told me that if I didn't straighten up that I would not ever amount to anything. I thought this was slightly outrageous and an unreasonable prediction. This situation was metastasizing in an increasingly poisonous atmosphere. As I was suffering the ignominy and humiliation of this lecture, I thought to myself, this latter-day Nostradamus is as wrong as Douglas "Wrong Way" Corrigan. One would have thought that I had violated some sacrosanct commandment. He just did not understand our schoolboy sense of humor. In my immature adolescent opinion, I thought the principal was being overly pious in his judgment and giving far too much of his life over to considering how bad we were. How could letting a fart turn into a tsunami of such biblical proportions?

Our chastened comedy club was sent back to the classroom without getting swats, but I thought the principal got a little too exercised with us. What did he expect from seventh-grade boys? Maybe it was because I was fiddling with my pocketknife (you could take pocketknives to school back in the day) as an aid to concentration as we were being addressed awaiting our sentence. We made a feeble attempt to perform in a fairly trouble-free manner for thirty minutes or so in class after visiting the principal. I did not know it at the time, but Voltaire had this guy pegged. "Sir, I may not agree with what you say, but I shall defend to the death your right to be a complete ass." It is okay to use the word *ass* because it is in the Bible. After this incident I developed a slight, quiet paranoia. I felt like my teacher was watching me more carefully — quizzically, as if I never listened. At the end of the day we had put our teacher and principal in a right old mood. Stay with me, I promise this story will not last out but a couple more paragraphs.

Ol' George, with that gentle bonhomie and humor, was pleasant, like fruit. He obviously heard a different drummer, and his bubble did not always stay plumb, but he was a source of sparkling wit and humor, a constant delight, an unforced rugged charm that radiated to all, and was as nice as a walk on the beach at twilight. I will never forget that Mona Lisa mystic smile of his. Good old George had my endorsement. He was a limited edition. George could warm your hands just being around him. He was a happy-go-lucky bloke and one of the human race's cheerier specimens. You need lads like that sometimes. These qualities of George go a long way to smooth over life's little irregularities. The thing that makes this country so wonderful is that God assigned so many guys like George to live in it.

The Boy Scouts were preparing to go to the scout cabin one Friday night for an overnight campout when someone suggested that we have a farting contest after our evening meal. I asked, "What is a farting contest?" One of the guys present opined that we would all eat a lot of beans for our evening meal and later gather in someone's tent and see who could let the most farts. This sounded pretty cool to everyone, so we all took a couple of cans of pork 'n' beans with us and stuffed ourselves at the appropriate time with our leguminous cuisine. I don't remember who won the contest, but most of us gave up pretty early and exited our gaseous environment lickety-split for precious oxygen not long after the first "vapors" started to saturate the atmosphere. Oh, what won't prepubescent boys think of!

CHAPTER **32**

The World Series

"When you come to a fork in the road, take it." – Yogi Berra

BASEBALL IN THE '50s was dominated by the Yankees, and this decade was considered the glory days when New York had three teams (Yankees, Giants, Dodgers) contending for championships, and even saw the Brooklyn Dodgers win in 1955. Many consider this the golden age of baseball — Micky Mantle, Willie Mays, and Duke Snyder — no other ten years like it. The Dodgers took game 7 in Yankee Stadium 2–0. This was the first time the World Series was broadcast in color. The corporate sponsor was Gillette and the announcer for the Dodgers was Vince Scully and Mel Allen for the Yankees. The Dodgers announced on October 8, 1957, that they were moving to Los Angeles — a sad day for Bum fans in Brooklyn. After this move had been announced, a couple of sports writers conducted independent surveys of the most evil people in history. Their top three were identical: Hitler, Stalin, and Walter O'Malley (owner of the Dodgers). Ebbets Field was but one of several historic major-league ball parks demolished in the 1960s, but more mythology and nostalgia surrounds the Ebbets Field stadium and its demise than possibly any other defunct ballpark. The Dodger fans were among the most loyal and devoted fans in the history of baseball. Because the Dodgers were perpetual underdogs, this caused Dodger fans to affectionately refer to their team as "dem Bums" in the local Brooklyn accent.

I have read that one could walk down any street in Brooklyn when the Dodgers were playing and never miss a play from all the radios playing in the stores and homes with their doors and windows open. Shortly after the seventh game victory in the '55 World Series ended, the phone system in New York went bonkers. It became next to impossible to get a call through into Brooklyn and Long Island from Manhattan. The phone company said that this jam-up was at least as bad as and probably worse than what had happened on V-J (Victory over Japan Day) ten years before. In these days the World Series games were played during the day, so we had to play hooky, fake an illness, or persuade our teachers to let us listen to the games on a little plastic, cutting-edge-technology, made-in-Japan transistor radio because this was an annual event understood to be more important than just about anything. The first transistor radio was produced in 1954. Baseball, in the '40s and '50s, dominated the American psyche in a way that can scarcely be imagined now. It was the nation's joy and obsession and called the National Game with capital letters.

There are many great World Series stories, but the National League play-off between the Brooklyn Dodgers and New York Giants in 1951 has frequently been voted the most iconic, heart-stopping and greatest moment in baseball history. The Dodgers appeared to recover their invincibility, taking a comfortable 4 to 1 lead into the ninth inning and needing just three outs to win in the last of a three-game series. The Giants scored a late run and put two more runners aboard when Bobby Thomson stepped to the plate. He swatted the second pitch over the left field wall for a game-winning home run so momentous that it was greeted with a moment's stunned silence, and then the fans at the Polo Grounds went wild. This home-run ball was never found. Even though the three major-league teams of the Yankees, Giants, and Dodgers were all located in New York City, it was reported that a Giant or Yankee fan in Brooklyn was as rare as a Republican in Brooklyn.

My favorite players were Mickey Mantle (when listening to a

Yankees game, I would always turn up the volume when Mantle was on deck), Yogi Berra, Phil "the Scooter" Rizzuto, Jackie Robinson, Roy Campanella, Gil Hodges, Whitey Ford, Allie Reynolds, Eddie Matthews, Hank Aaron, Don Drysdale, Robin Roberts, Don Newcomb, Joe "the Clipper" DiMaggio, Pee Wee Reese, Ted Williams, Duke Snider, and Willie Mays. Mickey was quite the phoneme when he first came up as a rookie. He was described as "Rookie of the Eons," "Magnificent Mantle," "Mighty Mickey," "Young Lochinvar," "Commerce Comet," "Oklahoma Kid," "Colossal Kid," "Wonder Boy," "One-Man Platoon," and "The Future of Baseball." Leo Durocher, Willie Mays' first manager with the Giants, said, "Willie could do everything but wipe off your seat and if Willie could cook, I'd marry him." I can't really list Lou Gehrig because he retired in 1939 before I was born; however, he is my favorite historical player. Late in his career, as he was suffering from Amyotrophic Lateral Sclerosis (ALS), now often referred to as Lou Gehrig's Disease, he delivered the greatest speech in sports history on July 4, 1939, in front of 62,000 fans in Yankee Stadium in a touching farewell to baseball. His famous phrase, "I am the luckiest man on the face of the earth," is often quoted today. This speech lionized Gehrig, and he died less than two years later. It has been said that this speech was baseball's "Gettysburg Address." He was the Mount Everest of baseball. In Kostya Kennedy's book *56* he wrote, "It was in the book *Cadillac Hotel* in Detroit when Gehrig walked into manager Joe McCarthy's room and took himself out of the lineup after 2,130 consecutive games. He told McCarthy that he could no longer play well enough to stay in the lineup. He did this for the good of the team. McCarthy said to him kindly and with love in his voice, "Lou, fellows like you come along once in a hundred years." Here is an excerpt from Jonathan Eig's biography on Lou Gehrig. "Gehrig stood still, his shoulders hung limp and heavy. At last, Joe McCarthy walked over and whispered in his ear. Gehrig nodded, ran his fingers through his hair, and stepped hesitantly toward home plate. The chanting stopped. Silence blanketed the stadium again. Ever so slowly, Gehrig leaned toward the microphones and drew a deep great . . ."

We never played much baseball when we were kids. We did play in a summer church softball league. During recess at school and in the summer in vacant lots, we would play a lot of work-up baseball. This was a game where there was only one team plus a batter(s). You worked up to batter through a series of advancements when an out was made. The progression was from the outfield to the infield, pitcher, and then batter. It took nine outs to get up to the much desired batter position. When you made an out as a batter, you went to right field and worked your way up by position to pitcher after each out. When a batter made an out, the pitcher went to the batting position. One could advance directly to batter if one were to catch a fly ball hit by the batter. There could be any number of batters who also had a pecking order to get their turn at the plate. One would play in this manner unless enough kids eventually showed up to form two whole teams. This was a really neat game when there were not enough players to field two complete teams.

CHAPTER 33

The Skunk

"It is a riddle wrapped in a mystery inside an enigma." – W. Churchill

HOLY COCKROACHES! THIS is the most fortuitous event and interesting story I remember about my eighth-grade year, and, thank goodness, I had nothing to do with it other than being in the classroom where this serendipitous incident occurred. As it turned out, this story could not have been more explosive had the desk drawer been filled with black powder and equipped with a fuse. Sometimes drama appears when you least expect it. Sometimes fascinating events, good and bad, appear out of nowhere. All was not well. Read on.

Late one night, some high school guys put a dead skunk in my English teacher's desk drawer. This reeking odor that had permeated the premises overnight was seeping out of the building as the bell rang, starting a rumble of conversation that built to a crescendo as we walked into our classroom. This volatilized smell produced fumes that fouled the air and sent chemical signals to my brain of a polluted atmosphere that was the Bermuda Triangle of stink. This fetid stench that seized and twisted our nostrils was worse than dead pigeons, stale sweat socks, and vomit all mixed together — a smell that all the Lysol in town could not mask. As one would imagine, the event produced noises and conversation like an out-of-tune orchestra warming up. This did not put Mrs. Brown in a chipper mood. It fact, she was incredulous and resigned on the same day, which was regrettable. But her replacement, Leona Woods Alexander, with an arresting beauty, was a breath of fresh spring air, and as pretty as Anna Maria Alberghetti. She was *très chic* and had an easy grace, an eloquence about her, a smile of exceptional warmth that exuded a patient kindness. Mrs. Brown and Mrs. Alexander were two teachers as different as Beethoven and Vivaldi.

Fifty years later, I still do not know who the culprits were — a mystery rivaling the *Mary Celeste*. Typically, rumors of anyone's prankish exploits of the previous night would spread like a brushfire the next day at school because to a teenager, information was currency, but not in this case. At every reunion, I would always ask the guys who I suspected if they did it, and, to this day, they only smile and say, "It wasn't me." The culprits were working on the principle of *omerta*: Do not say anything to anybody outside our group. Lloyd Ray and Millard Wright were the original prime suspects because they had stopped by Mr. Ross's house to get keys to play tennis in the gym the same night. If they hadn't done it, they were suspected of letting the ones who did do it into the building. They spent a lot of time in the office being rigorously interrogated and playing *Button, Button* with the administration. To add to the theater, Millard kept taking the *Fifth* just to make them think he knew something. I think they should have called in Boston Blackie or Sam Spade to get to the bottom of this! I suspected that it was someone in Richard's class, and a few years ago, I began hearing Jerry and Warnie's names pop up on a trip to Thomas, so I contacted Jerry and asked him the bluffing question of what his take on the story was. He took my bait, opened up, and, like Pheidippides, revealed news of a great victory. The following is the straight skinny from Jerry.

It all started when some of us were traveling back from Canton one night. I believe we had attended a Friday night football game there to see what our next week's competition would be like. Coming home, we ran across a couple of dead skunks and got to talking. We went to the grocery store and picked up a banana box from behind the store. We were going to go back and pick up a skunk for another teacher in the high school. Well, we picked up both of them and brought them in. We really liked Mrs. Brown, and the one that went into her room was a twisted way of showing attention to someone we really liked. We thought that after the smoke, maybe I should say "smell," cleared we would fess up, and everyone, including Mrs. Brown, would have a good laugh together. We really intended it to be great fun for all.

As you will remember, we had a resignation over it. In a called assembly, we were told by the principal that the perpetrators would be caught and punished, maybe even locked into the projection room at the back of the auditorium with live skunks. He even mentioned that the Oklahoma Bureau of Investigation would be called in if necessary. None of us were too worried about any of that until we realized that we would probably be kicked off the football team. Now, that thought scared the daylights out of us. All of us were on the football team, so, even though we were repentant, we absolutely could not run the risk of not being able to play football. We would have readily given ourselves up to help with the resignation problem if they would have offered some sort of punishment short of kicking us off the football team. Consequently, because of the football risk, we swore we would never give up our secret.

As a postscript here, one of the football players in our car that night opted out of the tomfoolery and went home before we entered the school building. He also kept the secret with us.

By now you know I was part of the group, although no more guilty than any of the rest of the bunch. And yes, Warnie was another good guess. In fact, he was the first to be called out of class to be questioned. We all about died because we felt that taking Warnie out of class first signaled that they already knew who was responsible for the dastardly deed of the "nigh of the skunk." We also thought he would cave in under pressure. Well, he turned out to be much braver than we thought. No bend in him.

Millard Wright was called down to the office pretty quickly after *that. His father was a member of the school board. Millard very firmly and adamantly pled the Fifth Amendment. That pretty well cinched it up from the administrator's point of view as we later learned from the custodian. The custodian told us that they knew it definitely was Millard. The rest of us were questioned, but mostly from the viewpoint that they wanted to catch Millard's accomplices and to get someone who would snitch on Millard so they could prove it was him. Well, ole Millard not only didn't do it, he wasn't even privy to information as to who did do it. He really saved our bacon, but, to my knowledge, he still doesn't know of his great service!*

The closest I came to telling anyone was one night when I was prowling around with Bill Ellis and he was speculating on who he thought might be guilty of the prank. He was wrong, and I was really tempted to fess up, but didn't. I may release some names later on but am somewhat reluctant to do that right now. Not that there would be any consequences, but we have kept it for so long, and I feel a bit like a traitor even admitting to Warnie's involvement. Oh, such deviltry.

This was some pretty clever sleuthing that these guys pulled off. Man, this story ranks right up there with the Constitution, pr^2, and the Mona Lisa. The best part of this story to me is Millard Wright's twinkling mischief in pleading the Fifth. Great stuff. However, over-all this was a bowl of cream gone rancid and these guys were on a listing ship in a stormy sea. A real lollapalooza. It played out like a Shakespearian play, each cast member making their exits and en-trances. We just weren't sure if it was a comedy or a tragedy.

CHAPTER **34**

Classmates

"A friend may well be reckoned the masterpiece of Nature." – Emerson

FROM FIRST TO grade twelve, our class size ranged from thirty to thirty-three. The class of '58 included Karen Sweeney, Billy Wilmeth, Dorothy Dean Hook, Mike Burnell, Marlane Cleveland, Bert Curell, R.L. Dalrymple, Virgil Richardson, Judy Robinson, Alberta Ryan, Sue Dunn, Louis Dunn, Emma Ruth Essex, Donald Schantz, Fred Self, Paulette Steward, Norma Jean Eyster, Ercel Tallbull, Sammy Harris, Ronnie Ogden, Haze Park, Stephen Rassmussen, Don Herring, Paul Huffman, Rodney Jump, K.O. Kippenberger, Rusty Kraybill, Charlotte McDaniel, Donnie Friesen, Larry McKellips, and Iola and Viola Miller.

Karen Sweeney, Paulette Steward, Claire Hooper ('57), and Jean D. ('57) wrote the lyrics to the school fight song. I think that this is neat even though one-third of the song consists of the word "fight." I'm glad that they all got an education and good jobs because they were no Cole Porter.

Bert Curell used an interesting ploy to save his Juicy Fruit gum when the teacher would catch him chewing it and order it disposed of in the trash can. He would walk to the can, simulate throwing the gum into the can while simultaneously kicking the can, making it sound like he had thrown the gum into the can. He would save the gum and start re-chewing it when safe, or as we sometimes said, "when the coast was clear." Old Bert could give a command performance when necessary.

These classmates with whom I went to school had dads who were farmers, laborers, clerks, delivery drivers, a doctor, plumber, mechanic — pretty much a blue-collar town of cultural stew. We all had English as first language at home and almost all had two parents except a couple who were deceased. Although Thomas High was a small school, it did provide a climate for opportunity. I do not recall very many friends and acquaintances who went sour in the end. Most turned out to be successes in whatever they set out to do. We were fortunate that few of our classmates and friends ever moved away. I am sure that this stability helped strengthen our growth and development in immeasurable ways as we grew and spread our wings.

CHAPTER 35

Nicknames

"The supreme happiness of life is the conviction that we are loved." – Victor Hugo

A NICKNAME IS usually given to someone by another. It is normally a familiar name that can be used in place of a real name without the need of explanation and can become more familiar than one's original name. These nicknames can sometimes be inelegant and irritating, but most like them and are not offended. It seems to me that small towns are pretty good at bestowing sobriquets. Some of the nicknames of guys that I remember were Dopey, Dynamite, The Coaster, Frosty, Frog, Opossum, Butch, Toothpick, Second Gear, Slick, Blackie, Tarzan, Peachy, Pee Wee, Bean Soup, Barney, Porthole, Hawkshaw, and The Whangbanger. Gale Smith bestowed one on me. He called me Fleet as in "fleetfoot." Sally McCall got his nickname when one of the Wilhites gave him a Sally Walker spinning top. He got to be good with it by spiking other tops, hence the name Sally. Not many people know this. How come girls never had nicknames? Lucille Southwell was one girl with a nickname — Cotton Top. Lucille was a tomboy in every sense of the word, holding her own with her brothers and schoolmates. Anyway, I have always regarded nicknames as names giving affection or flattery.

CHAPTER 36

The Water Tower

"Getting to the top is optional. Getting down is mandatory."
– Ed Viesturs, on climbing Mt. Everest

GRAIN ELEVATORS AND water towers were unquestionably the main small-town landmark in western Oklahoma. The iconic water tower in Thomas stood tall just off the school grounds on the southwest side of the school and recorded the climbing experiences and painting skills of past junior and senior classes. This black monolith was a four-sided tapering Eiffelized structure with a ladder attached to the southeast pillar. At the time, this monster reminded me of what Ptolemy's lighthouse, one of the seven wonders of the ancient world, must have looked like. Climbing the water tower was a rite of passage for most Thomas boys and even some gals. We would spider up the water tower late at night at least once a year to paint one's class identification on it when in high school. By the providence of God, no one ever fell. There were close calls and lucky breaks, but no accidents. Climbing the tower was a *clear and present danger*, but this never seemed to deter us from scrambling up, even if haltingly as I masqueraded my fears. We were young, strong, dumb, and thought we were as agile as a swashbuckler on a ship's rigging. What is that saying about fools rushing in? The initial part of the climb up the ladder is uneventful, but it was always with a flutter of apprehension that we began these climbs. The harrowing part that brought out our primordial anxiety, the real crux and most exposed part of the climb, was those last few feet of that perilous backward overhang just before getting on the catwalk. Negotiating this precarious pitch made me as taut as piano wire and was where our individual survival instincts kicked in. The only thing that stopped us from plummeting to the ground was the white-knuckle, tight-fisted hold we maintained and the powerful conviction that the journey of our lives was not yet over. On my first climb and attempt to negotiate this overhang, I was following the guy in front of me as faithfully as a pilgrim, when I wished there would have been a voice saying to me, "Donnie, you don't have to do this." Alas, no such advice was forthcoming. So, with adrenaline flowing, I pushed on and made it up to the catwalk. Once over this barrier, one had crossed the *Rubicon* and might as well go ahead and get the painting finished, enjoy the escapade, and a calm view of the town at nighttime — half terror, half ecstasy. That overhang was scary, but we led a Teflon life on that structure. However, every time I climbed this tower the whole business suddenly seemed crazy as we came to that overhang. There should have been a cylindrical lattice safety cage around that overhang section. But then again, we were not supposed to be climbing the thing.

During my senior year, Steve and I held Rodney Jump by his legs under the rail and over the catwalk to paint "SR '58" underneath the walkway to defend the honor of our class. We figured this was too dangerous an area for the juniors to ever paint over. But this was a major dumb thing to do. Even though it was 90 degrees this night, there was a chill in the air as we began this shinny up the tower. This climb had the makings of a disaster, but Rodney's words, "I am finished," rewarded our efforts as I waited for my heart to regain its normal rhythm as it vibrated somewhere in the vicinity of my back teeth. When we successfully pulled Rodney back up on the catwalk, I felt like I had dissolved into a puddle of jelly. After I shook off my paralysis, I started thinking about descending that wicked overhang. There are times I still lie in bed at night thinking about this alarming event.

While holding Rodney over the edge, I was making God a *quid pro quo* deal. Let us pull this off safely, and I will owe You one. I firmly believed that God saw everything and duly noted all transgressions, big and small. It was never my intention to do wrong, and so generally I thought I was in good stead with the Almighty and that it was my destiny to live a few more years. I was sure that I would not fall into the trap about which Euripides warned: "A man who has been in danger and comes out of it forgets his fears and sometimes forgets his promises." Not only could we have dropped Rodney, but also someone else could have fallen trying to paint over our masterpiece. I guess our minds had refused to consider what would have happened to us if we had lost our grip on Rodney.

However, after climbing and descending I always felt like I had conquered an insurmountable peak — elated, ecstatic, and unutterably free. This experience can only be described as the same feeling about which Churchill once spoke: "There is nothing so exhilarating as having been shot at without result." In all the years of different classes climbing this structure, and having no accidents, this has to be classified as a latter-day miracle. One night a group of us, while in junior high, were climbing the tower just for the fun of it. Along comes some kid who starts shooting BBs at us, not letting us down. Mercifully, someone's older brother came along and ran him off so that we were able to continue our descent. I always acted like climbing the tower never bothered me, but after a climb I always had this tidal wave of relief and exhilaration, but was thankful to be back on *terra firma* and safely away from the gates of eternity. The *terra* seeming more *firma*. Churchill told the generals, when planning for the landings at Anzio, "Without risk there could be no honor, no glory, no adventure."

As far as anyone can determine, Jackie, Junior Garner, and Larry Crowdis were the only guys to ever climb the tower in daylight. They had "borrowed" a ladder from the school the night before, climbed the tower with the ladder so that they could paint their class name higher up than anyone else's, and left the ladder up there. When Mr.

Sweeney discovered that a ladder had been left up on the tower, he knew that it had not been put there by Santa Claus's elves. He somehow found out who had done this and made these miscreants leave class to retrieve the ladder. Did these guys really know words with more than one syllable? Jackie says that they had to have help getting a very frightened Fay Comer Powers off the tower one night after she exhibited a paralyzing fear up on the catwalk. Alarmingly, her fear caused her to stay as firmly put as King Arthurs's *Excalibur* in the famous stone. This fear of heights is called "acrophobia." That comes from an old Latin word, I suppose, which means you have a phobia against becoming an acrobat. Just kidding. Usually one who had this fear would realize what a perilous position they were in after the first few rungs on the way up and carefully back down the ladder. This is what Fay's twin sister, Kay, did. Someone went to get a rope and an older "sherpa," Jerry Vickers, to help ease her down the ladder. When Fay arrived home, her mother told her that she had better get that smeared paint off her before her dad saw it. Jackie and his friends, which also included some girls, once climbed and painted the Custer City water tower. This is the only story I know about someone climbing the Custer water tower, and I only heard this story many years after the fact.

A really funny water-tower story related to me by some older guys involved an all-girl caper from the class of 1949. A group of girls climbed to the top of the town water tower to paint their mark upon Thomas history, only to discover that they had forgotten to bring a single paintbrush. "Not to worry," said one of the girls in her manifest charm. She then, unceremoniously, took off her panties and used them to daub on the paint, after which she tossed them over the catwalk rail. Predictably, there were by this time a group of boys who had migrated to the base of the tower like seagulls to a spilled order of French fries. Later, the panties "trophy" ended up hanging on one of the guys' car radio antennae. The next day, the only thing the kids wanted to talk about was the girls painting the water tower with one of the girl's undies. The story is also told about a girl peeing on Jack

Keller ('56) when they were climbing the tower one night. She was just above him on the ladder when she lost her nerve. Jimmy Ames ('46) tells about climbing the water tower one night when, just as he was starting to negotiate the overhang at the top, he heard a loud thrumming sound of wings as a bunch of pigeons exploded from their roost and swooped out from under the catwalk and scared him to death. It's a wonder he managed to hold his grip on the rungs and not fall. Ray Cain told me what might be the funniest "tower of courage," as he called it, story of all. It happened in the spring of 1965.

It was on a Sunday afternoon for the express purpose of testing a cat parachute. Three of us climbed up and attached a well-engineered parachute to a feral cat we found and launched from the catwalk. It did not succeed on the first try. It was like trying to throw Velcro. We questioned our engineering abilities when the chute didn't open until about halfway down. On opening it relocated around the cat's hindquarters, but worked fine. The cat made it to the ground and Rusty Loudenslager, feeling bad for the cat, rushed over to check on it. It about shredded him and took flight. Carrying the cat in an old pair of warm-up bottoms and attaching the parachute are stories in themselves. But the best/worst part of the daylight raid was the great view, and it was really easy to see Mr. Ross come out and get in that old black Chevy and head our way! We just knew he was aware of us and was coming to kill us on the spot. The cat's descent was only a little bit quicker than ours and by the time we three reached the ground we were afoot. Everyone else had bugged out so I headed downtown running full blast. Mr. Ross went on to the shop. He hadn't any idea we were in town, much less up on the tower. I never once considered the cat wouldn't make it down safely.

Man, this cat would make a banshee blanch. Thankfully, our water-tower glory days, without loss of life or limb, are past and not particularly glorious. All the painting and over-painting on this structure eventually came to resemble a pictograph that looked like the backside of a tapestry. Watermelons — the red light — the water tower. Were we not content with the world around us? Gertrude Stein once asked the question, "Is it worse to be scared than to be bored, that is the question." I guess we thought it was worse to be bored.

CHAPTER 37

'50s Fads/Slang/Fashions

"The Life—feeling—The Life—the late 1940s and 1950s, American Teenage Drive-In Life"

– Thomas Wolfe

THE DECADE OF the 1950s was a time of great change in American life. In 1945, a victorious United States had emerged from WWII and entered a period of growth and prosperity that would last throughout the 1950s. Jobs were plentiful. More Americans could realize the American dream — a home of their own, perhaps in one of the new suburbs springing up all over the country.

People will remember the '50s as the time of hula hoops, Frisbees, Slinkies, 3-D movies, coonskin caps, bubblegum, candy cigarettes, candy jawbreakers, water balloons, jukeboxes, 45 RPM records, wax Coke-shaped bottles filled with some kind of sugared water that tasted like cough syrup, Brylcreem hair "grease" — a little dab'll do ya, Dippity-do setting gel for your hair, pea shooters, and telephone booth cramming. As well as the slang terms of backseat bingo, blast, cat, cool, daddy-o, dig, drag, duck butt, flick, greaser, grody, haul ass, peel out, lay rubber, hip, make out, pad, passion pit, ragtop, raunchy, split, submarine races, threads, and wheelie to name a few. It was a time when doors were never locked and keys were left in cars.

Fashion of the '50s was composed of turned-up collars, white tee shirts with rolled-up sleeves, rolled-up jeans, bobby socks, can-can slips, full skirts, poodle skirts (they looked like parachutes), pedal pushers, tight sweaters, bikinis, saddle loafers, and ducktail haircuts, but no ponytail haircuts for guys. If someone would have worn his hair in a ponytail they would have been given electroshock therapy. The new look that popped up in the '50s for the guys was a style called the Ivy League look. This look originated on the campuses of Harvard, Princeton, and Yale as a forerunner to the preppie look — a style characterized by shirts with button-down collars with a button on the back of the collar, cuffed pants with no pleats, and with a small metal buckle in the back. The buckles on the back of the trousers were excellent for wrecking your car seats. In high school I wore mainly penny loafers with white socks because of seeing Gene Kelly wear them in *An American in Paris*. With this footwear combo, I wore jeans or Ivy League trousers and button-down shirts — very modish and up-to-date. Thomas did not have a bowling alley, so I don't remember anyone ever wearing a bowling shirt with their name embroidered over the pocket, nor any zoot-suiters, and thankfully, distressed clothing was not chic in the '50s.

Bobby soxer is a sociological coinage, denoting the fans of swing music and 1950s rock and roll. Fashionable adolescent girls wore poodle skirts and bobby socks. In high schools, the gymnasium often was used as a dance floor; however, since street shoes might damage the polished wood finish on the floors, the students were required to remove their shoes and dance in their bobby socks — thus the phrase "sock hop." The poodle skirt remains one of the most memorable symbols of 1950s Americana and is frequently worn as a novelty retro item, part of a nostalgic outfit. Pedal pushers are calf-length trousers that were popular during the 1950s. They are related in style to Capri pants and are sometimes referred to as "clam diggers."

In elementary school I once had an aviator's cap with earflaps and a chinstrap. They used to be considered standard equipment for a boy. Some came with goggles. I don't think kids are forced to wear these anymore. In fact, I don't believe aviators wear them anymore. However; at the time, I thought they were the essence of cool. In one '50s memoir I read, a kid would get beat up for wearing a nerdy cap like this. I don't remember anyone ever getting beat up because of what he wore, but I would guess that if a boy had ever worn sandals, he might have. I had one of those wool coats called a Mackinaw. It was a red and black plaid. Our jeans were always about two feet too long in the legs so we would cuff them up two or three rolls. *Store-bought* was a phrase I heard all the time in my youth. Of course, just about everything is store-bought these days. Once, it was bragging material to have a store-bought dress or a store-bought bag of candy.

Perhaps nothing changed and sculpted daily life more than the new-fangled invention, the television, which introduced a daydream world through *Leave It to Beaver*, *Dragnet*, *Lassie*, *Howdy Doody*, *I Love Lucy*, *The Dinah Shore Show*, *The Jackie Gleason Show*, *Dragnet*, *Father Knows Best*, *The Honeymooners*, *The Mickey Mouse Club (Mouseketeers)*, *Gunsmoke*, *Wagon Train*, *American Bandstand*, *The Rifleman*, *77 Sunset Strip*, *Rawhide*, *The Colgate Comedy Hour*, *G.E. Theater*, *Gillete Cavalcade of Sports*, *Playhouse 90*, *Route 66*, *The Millionaire*, *I've Got a Secret*, and many more. The 1950s was known as the Golden Age of Television by many.

The decade of the Fifties gave birth to rock-and-roll music. When Bill Haley's "Rock Around the Clock" became popular in 1955, the nation learned to swing to a whole new sound that easily came in on our wavelength.

Gums and candies of the '40s and '50s were: Bazooka Bubble, Double Bubble, Juicy Fruit, and Spearmint gums; Bit-O-Honey, Baby Ruth, Cherry Mash, Fifth Avenue, Mounds, Almond Joy, Three Musketeers, Hershey Bars, Milky Way, Peanut Patties, Payday, Jaw Breakers, Milk Duds, Moon Pie, Oh Henry, Red Hots, Safe-T-Pop Suckers, Slo Poke suckers that we polished with our tongues all day, Sen Sen breath fresheners, and Zero candy.

Such was the defining spirit and mood of the '50s, and we soaked up this culture like a sponge.

CHAPTER 38

Saturdays

"Who could ask for anything more?" – Gershwin

WHEN WE LIVED on the farm, drives into town were infrequent and didn't always involve paved roads. There were many times, especially after a rain, that we had to drive in badly rutted tire tracks that caused the car to wobble all over the road. It was easy to forget from one rain to the next just how quickly packed earth can turn to mud, and how completely and utterly debilitating this can be. However, we always went to town on Saturday to buy provisions and other necessities. Saturday was the most delicious and festive day of the week. As Betty Smith says in *A Tree Grows in Brooklyn*, "People were paid on Saturday and it was a holiday without the rigidness of a Sunday." Dad would always drop off our eggs and cream at the Caulkins Produce, or sometimes called "the creamery." Cream, whole milk, and eggs were still a readily accepted form of currency at this time. The produce would hold every egg they purchased up to a light to check to determine whether or not an egg was fertile. This was called "candling." The term must have come from medieval times when candles were the only source of light. I do not know what they did with the eggs they found that were fertile. Occasionally, we would have a hide to sell if we had butchered a steer. This was cash we used to buy a week's worth of groceries. Shopping day meant bananas and a new comic book bought at the drugstore. It also meant a 15-cent allowance. Ten cents for a movie and a nickel for either a Coke, peanuts, or popcorn. This was always a painfully tough decision. Going to town on Saturday to sell your produce and buy needed goods goes all the way back to medieval times. Only then, people had to go to specific market towns. A *market town* or *market right* was a legal term originating in the medieval period for a European settlement that had the right to host markets, distinguishing it from a village and city. In our time, all towns would be considered market towns because they all had the same basic services and, of course, different laws than those in force during the Middle Ages.

Grandpa McCracken was a horse trader. When someone wanted to buy a pony for a kid, he would always have me or Jackie ride it to show the prospective buyers that any kid could ride this "gentle" horse. What the prospective buyers did not know was that my brothers and I were practically raised on a horse and could ride like a Comanche. If he made the sale, he would give us a dollar. Additionally, he always saw to it that we boys had a horse to ride. Jackie and I used to go over to Grandpa's to play checkers and to occasionally write a letter for him. He would frequently want us to stay and eat with him. He would cook up a pound of bacon, fry a batch of eggs in the fat, and get upset if we didn't eat at least three or four of them.

Here is a bit of information about Grandpa McCracken as related to me by Mary Lee Norris Darter ('60), who lived just across the alley from him in Thomas.

He was my hero. I am afraid I was born with my Great-grandfather Herring's love of horses and your Grandfather McCracken was my connection to that world. He lived behind us for a long time and had a corral next to the alley and he traded many horses. He was very patient with me as I was probably in grade school and would appear on his corral fence on a daily basis, waiting for permission to pet or ride or groom one of his latest acquisitions. He taught me to use a curry comb, how to brush and thin a mane and tail, and how to use a hackamore and transition a colt to a bridle. He showed me how to clean hooves, use brown paper bags and vinegar to treat swollen horse ankles, and how to neck rein. My parents did not approve for two reasons: 1) was probably being a pest and they told me to quit bothering him, and 2) didn't like the idea that he encouraged me in my love of horses. When I got my first horse, he gave me a leg up and slapped the horse on the rear and off we went. The horse didn't stop until I got to the high school and I finally had enough room to make him run in circles. I rode the horse back down the alley and Doc was waiting for me with a big grin on his face. My father did not think it was funny but I learned my lesson: always be ready. He was very kind and I thought he was like a bigger celebrity than Roy Rogers or Hopalong Cassidy — and I thought they were big.

Before I had jobs, and after moving to town, Saturday mornings were frequently spent playing and exploring in one of two canyons one mile northeast of town center, the closest being called First Canyon. We would hike, climb the craggy canyon walls, and generally goof off exploring every nook and cranny. Some of the walls were quite precipitous, and occasionally our climbing activities would get a little too adventurous and the girls would freeze up and refuse to go up or down, and we would have to improvise with our belts, or a rope, if we had one, to help lower them to better handholds. Our childhood, in terms of entertainment, was austere in comparison with that of children today — a time when a simple pleasure could be an event. The farm north of town where my friend Maynard Book lived had some good canyon walls and trails. I remember one really good trail that descended and ascended a canyon wall where we would run and chase one another singing "She'll be Coming Round the Mountain."

The chief entertainment available to young people in Thomas was the movies. Aristophanes once said, "A town without a theater is like a party without conversation." Well, Thomas had a movie theater, not like Aristophanes' theater, but on Saturday afternoons, we would usually go to the matinee movie at our one-screen theater, which usually consisted of a cartoon, a Three Stooges short, Movietone News, March of Time or Pathé newsreel narrated by someone like Lowell Thomas, and a serial episode of Boston Blackie, Buck Rogers, Flash Gordon, Zorro, or Tarzan. A chapter from a serial always ended with a cliff-hanger that ensured you would come back the following Saturday with the ominous words: *To Be Continued*. During a suspenseful part of the serial, someone would sometimes blow up a popcorn sack and pop it just to hear the girls scream. The serial was a bigger attraction than the main feature. The feature was usually a grade-B western where I discovered the American West, vistas of beauty, of deserts and mesas and mountains. Sitting in the dark I could almost smell those beans cooking on the sagebrush fires, breathe the dust from stampeding cattle, and feel the pain of bad cowboys being hurled through saloon windows to the accompaniment of shattering glass. My favorite good cowboy heroes were Roy Rogers with his wife and sidekick, Dale Evans, the *grande dame* of movie cowgirls, Gene Autry and his horse Champion, The Lone Ranger, Red Rider with Little Beaver (Robert Blake played this role as a little boy), Hopalong Cassidy, Tom Mix and his horse Tony, Lash LaRue, The Durango Kid, Tex Ritter, and Tim Holt. It matters not that these movies were devoid of substance. It was the thrill of the galloping horses, the runaway stagecoach, arrows whizzing by, the fights, chases, and stunts. It was exciting to watch the good guys who were always clean-living, strong, decisive, clever, possessing no faults, having all the virtues to always win, defeating the Indians and the black-hatted rustlers and desperadoes. Basically, the cowboys protected the weaker people and beat up the bullies. I loved the Tarzan movies, with their scenes of jungles, tree houses, and Johnny "The Human Fish" Weissmuller, former Olympic swimmer, swinging on vines in his loincloth and bellowing his great triumphant calls. Tarzan's jungle upbringing gave him abilities far beyond those of ordinary humans. These include climbing, swimming in crocodile-infested waters, clinging, and leaping as well as any great ape, or better. He used branches and hanging vines to swing at great speeds — a skill acquired among the apes. During the glory days of my youth I also loved those Warner Bros. cartoons of Bugs Bunny, Elmer Fudd, The Tasmanian Devil, Porky Pig, Wile E. Coyote, and Yosemite Sam. We always got laughs from the unfortunate and uncontrollable speech impediments of Elmer Fudd and Porky Pig. Maybe the best, however, was Wile E. Coyote getting demolished by numerous anvils, blown up by dynamite, and burnt to a crisp by the cunning plots of the Roadrunner, who got his demolition supplies from the Acme company. These brave cartoon heroes provided us with lots of pleasure and entertainment.

Going to the movies was a moment of freedom when one could lose oneself in the magic of Hollywood and be oblivious to the world around them. Thanks to videos, cable TV, and DVDs, the B western of our innocent past can still remind us of how much fun we had at those Saturday matinees watching the heroes riding off into the sunset, the valor of knights in shining armor, and warriors riding upon white horses. Never again will children know the beauty of going to the movies every week to watch a simple morality playing — where good triumphed, evil was punished, and the world was safe. Once a year, a moment of silence should be observed for Thomas Edison for inventing the movie projector. It was a blessed childhood in an idyllic setting that many of us took for granted. These Saturdays of the '40s and '50s may be difficult for people today to understand, but somehow, it worked.

Alberta worked the popcorn machine at the LYNN Theater on Saturday nights and was paid the grand sum of 50 cents for the entire night. Prisscilla Self (Jackie's class) followed Alberta in this job. Alberta relates that watching moviegoers in Thomas was very different from the theater audiences today. It was interesting to see the couples come in. Teens hoping to sit on the back row or in the balcony for a little canoodling, young marrieds on their "date night," and younguns dashing for the front-row seats. The pop that was sold came in bottles and people would sometimes roll a bottle on the floor and it would make it almost to the front of the theater. Other distractions that we inflicted on the adults were booing the villains, cheering the heroes, and making rude noises when people kissed. The owner of the theater would make periodic trips down the aisle monitoring any misbehavior, and on occasion would have to escort a misbehaving youngster out of the building. Another annoyance was certain characters who just had to give a running commentary to the soundtrack, along with loud laughing. Fred Conkling is one I remember and Alberta remembers Bob Bates as another. If you ended up between these two it was like being in the middle of the choir. It was just their way of enjoying the movie. The theater was also owned at one time by Mel Danner and called the MEL. The LYNN was owned by Dick Frans, and Dr. Young owned the Young Theater. It cost 10 cents up to 12 years of age and then the price went up to 35 cents. Kids who were small in stature always tried to continue to pass for the 10-cent admission price after they turned 12, and some got away with it for a long time.

As we got older, we went to more Saturday night movies. During the movie, everyone's parents would be finishing up their shopping. When finished, the women would sit in the car and visit, discussing illnesses, deaths, new babies, etc. The men, dressed in their newest overalls, would lean on car fenders talking about the weather, the price of wheat, rain, and football. Some people drove their cars downtown early to get a good parking space to use later at night. This was quite a weekly cultural and social event. A place locked in a dream. Thomas, like most small towns, vibrated on Saturday with the energy of all the people who came to town, on what for all practical purposes was market day. As I look down the relatively sleepy main streets of Thomas today, it is difficult for me to remember how the streets swarmed with shoppers and the street sounds of cars, horns, balls ricocheting off the croquet court curbing, conversations, little kids running on the sidewalks, and other sounds on a Saturday back in the '50s.

Occasionally, we would go to Fay to see movies shown on an outdoor makeshift screen. The peak year for real drive-in movies was 1958, with over 4,000 outdoor screens showing movies. The first drive-in was built in 1933 in Ohio and boomed with suburbia after

WWII. Other sources say that the first drive-in was opened in Camden, New Jersey. At one time the drive-in was a piece of Americana. It was red, white, and blue. Some say that it was not as much about watching a film as it was about another excuse to drive, and this played to the American public's fascination with automobiles. Lily Rothman described the drive-in "As a summer evening, the white of the screen against the rose of the sky, the incandescent glow from the concession stand, kids tossing a football as they wait for the show to begin, the smell of bug spray, the rows of cars with patrons draped across the car roofs. There's the warmth, the sunset, the popcorn, the families, and the cars prowling for an open spot." At this writing there are only six drive-ins left in Oklahoma.

Movies were also referred to as moving picture shows, cinemas, films, and flicks. "Going to the flick" is an old term. It originated back when the silent movie cameras were cranked by hand. When the machine-driven projectors came along the old silent movies tended to flicker, hence the term "going to the flicks." When we were in high school we occasionally would go to a movie in Oklahoma City. These theaters were like palatial ornate opera houses and quite impressive to us small-town teenagers.

We never went to any dances unless it was at someone's house. In the seventh grade, someone's mother organized a dancing class that was held in Clinton for a group of us. We learned — or should I say were exposed to? — the fox-trot, waltz, cha-cha, and jitterbug. The class ended each week with the hokey-pokey, a non-couple dance. Most of us had a poor sense of rhythm, not to mention grace and our caveman charm. We boys were like a bloke with the feet of an ox and the gait of a pig. We just never got the hang of foot-flogging. My brain just never seemed to issue the correct preparatory commands necessary for rhythmic locomotion as I made futile dummy motions with my feet. The first time I took a girl's hand, I did it as though I were handling a stick of dynamite. However, these lessons managed to get me through some parties and two proms. Someone was always hosting New Year's Eve parties throughout high school, and I will always remember watching Guy Lombardo on TV with his Royal Canadians at the Waldorf Astoria playing the nostalgic "Auld Lang Syne."

One time when a small circus came to town, an interesting event was staged to promote ticket sales by the circus management. The circus brought one of their elephants to town center to see if it could out-pull a U model M&M tractor. It couldn't. The tractor won.

A traveling carnival would usually come through town once a year with its festive amusement rides, attractions, ballyhoo, and the colorful razzle-dazzle lighting to put people in a celebratory mood. The music and gaiety of the carousel and the bright lights of the carnival-arcade were a powerful gravitational attraction to this summertime ritual that allowed us to be relieved of a few coins while playing the ring toss, dart throwing, and having our picture taken in a photo booth where you would get four poses for a quarter. I probably spent a week's worth of earnings from odd jobs to play these games and to ride the carousel, tilt-a-whirl, and Ferris wheel. Of course, there were always the food items of buttered popcorn, cotton candy, snow cones, and a few sideshows. This carnival did not have a live fortune teller dispensing predictions, nor did they have a tattooed strong man. Lloyd Ray always had a lot of free carnival ride tickets because his dad would weld and repair their equipment when they came to town.

In an age when parents seem to plot their children's every waking hour, the childhood of my time stands out in contrast. We survived and succeeded for the most part without much guidance from parents at all. Once out of sight of our parents, kids of our generation were out of mind. Parents had almost no idea what we were up to. It's all there in *The Little Rascals*, that wondrous sequestered world of boys on their own, figuring out life for themselves. Life in our world was relatively unsupervised, unregulated, and physical, and yet it was a remarkably peaceable place. Happily, we were indestructible. Granted, there was polio and lockjaw, but we didn't need seatbelts, airbags, smoke detectors, or bottled water. We didn't need helmets when we rode our bikes or pads on our knees when we went skating. We have largely forgotten how much good can come from an unstructured childhood, enjoying the everyday treasures before us. However, there was also much unrealized support that was working in our early years. It reminds me of what Malcolm Gladwell wrote in his book *Outliers*: "The tallest oak in the forest is not tall just because it grew from the hardiest acorn; it is the tallest also because no other trees blocked its sunlight, the soil around it was deep and rich, no rabbit chewed through its bark as a sapling, and no lumberjack cut it down before it matured." I do, however, worry about the education kids are getting today; you see, book learning is important but that's only half of an education. The other half comes from the "knocks" of life, some hard, some soft. For that, a more unstructured, can-kicking, and stone-throwing childhood is a great classroom.

CHAPTER 39

Sundays

"Wagner is better than it sounds." – Mark Twain

SUNDAY WAS RESERVED for church and rest and almost all businesses were closed. On Sunday morning, everyone is in church as if summoned by Joshua's trumpets, contemplating their sinful unworthiness. The Catholics contemplating the unworthiness of the Baptists, the Baptists contemplating the unworthiness of the Methodists, the Methodists contemplating the unworthiness of the Pentecostals. But never mind.

Lloyd Ray did not like Baptists, but not because he was a Methodist. He did not like Baptists because their bonging church bells rang out every Sunday morning right next door to his home, as they attempted to cast an ecclesiastical spell over the neighborhood. The Clanging reverberated off his bedroom windows waking him long before he normally rolled out of bed.

One of the main things I remember about Sunday was polishing my Sunday Buster Brown shoes Saturday night with Shinola liquid shoe polish so that they would be spanking clean. This was a Saturday night ritual, along with the bath. It seemed that polishing shoes and cleanliness were next to godliness in our house. I wasted a lot of time just getting my laces right before polishing. I never could understand how one side could get four feet longer than the other from being left under the bed from the previous Saturday night. We also always wore our best clothes to church, often referred to as Sunday-go-to-meeting clothes, Sunday best, or just plain old church clothes. Some people called them "going-out clothes." In the '50s, when traveling by air, people still dressed as though they were attending a theatrical event. In college, we wore suits and ties to football and basketball games. Your mother wore dress gloves to church when she was in high school and wore them to my college graduation. A far dismal cry from the nonexistent dress codes we see today. On Sunday morning Mother would fuss over us getting freshly scrubbed and ready for church in a maternal fashion that made us squirm. As we rushed around getting ready to leave for church, we would give our memory verse a last run-through.

We went to the Evangelical United Brethren church two times every Sunday so that our parents could rat us out to the Lord to get us fixed for another week. This denomination later merged with the Methodists. Mrs. Brownlaw Cook was our primary Sunday school teacher who taught us about Noah, Abraham, Moses, the Ark of the Covenant, David and Goliath, and the birth of Jesus. Jackie and I liked Sunday school, but found church services boring and an agony. This frequently got us into trouble because we would get to giggling about some nonsense or other as the adults were theeing and thouing. So much for our spiritual pursuits. The only prayers I remember are those for rain as the church always followed the plough very closely. When one had a birthday, that person would go up to the front of the church and put into a birthday offering plate one penny for each birthday as the congregation sang "Happy Birthday." We always bought a paper and a package of Juicy Fruit chewing gum every Sunday before church. We were allowed to chew a stick of gum until we entered the building. At that point we had to dispose of it. We would, on rare occasions, leave church after Sunday school if we had an invite to Sunday dinner at the Kraybills or Clines because they lived several miles northwest of town in the Parallel community. Speaking of eating, I always looked forward to church potluck dinners when everyone brought their favorite casseroles and fresh harvestings from garden and orchard. These events were planned on a tribal scale with huge amounts of food. We went swimming most Sunday afternoons in the summertime. Sunday was also a time that aunts, uncles, and cousins would frequently get together for homemade ice cream or watermelon.

Mrs. Granville (Mabel) Green, the church pianist, really attacked those ivories, as I remember it. I will never forget her aggressive playing style. We always had a traditional church Christmas program with a manger scene along with the appropriate scriptures being read. The singing of "Silver Bells" by Maynard Book in one program is indelibly imprinted in my mind because he did not want to sing this solo, but his mother, the program director, made him. I felt it a blessing that I could not sing on pitch — no solos for me. Buddy Taylor remembers Harold Lancet, the high school band director, playing a solo on the trumpet at a Christmas program.

Our Sunday school class took a field trip out in the country to a home to view our first TV show in the early '50s. This had to be the only TV set in private ownership, which made it quite a novelty. I remember viewing *Wiley and Gene,* a country western music show. Their theme song was "When My Blue Moon Turns to Gold Again." Jackie remembers the second time he got to watch TV. He was out trick-or-treating one Halloween when the people in a home on School Street where he knocked on the door for a treat invited him in to watch the *Gene Autry Show* on TV. An unusual treat, to say the least. The first TV show that I can remember watching regularly was *Victory at Sea* with its beautiful soundtrack by Richard Rodgers. I used to go over to Bill Wilson's every Tuesday at 7:30 PM to watch this show before we had a TV. We got our first TV when I was in the eighth grade in 1953. It took five minutes to warm up because of the vacuum tubes.

There were a couple of businesses that had a TV sitting in their window. People would take their chairs from home and go downtown and watch TV. Harry Crites's Appliance Store had a TV in the window and people would sit out on the sidewalk to view it. One could go inside and watch TV at Hockaday's Hardware Store. Some would take colored cellophane paper and tape it over the screen, making it appear to be a colored TV.

Another Sunday school field trip enabled me to take my first airplane ride. Our class went out to Leonard Hutchison's farm south of town to take a short ride in his two-seated Piper Cub airplane. For two dollars he gave us a ten- to fifteen-minute spin around his farm south of town and the surrounding area. We were small enough for him to put two of us in the backseat. This was one of the most exciting events of my early boyhood. The Cub's simplicity, affordability, and popularity invoked comparisons to the Ford Model T automobile.

CHAPTER 40

The Standley Players

"All the world is a stage." – Shakespeare

ABOUT ONCE A year, a traveling theater troupe called the Standley Players came to town. They would set up residence with their tent on a vacant lot just south of the Ford dealership on the south side of town. They used their truck beds with other props to make their own stage. Their theatrical shows were skillfully done with surprisingly good acting. This type of entertainment was quite welcome in small towns that had no playhouses. The Standley Players brought a talented mixture of comedy, dance, and music to the family performances. One of the family's most popular skits involved what they called a "Toby character" — a simple country boy who always outwitted the city slicker. Right before the show began, they sold boxes of a kind of taffy candy wrapped in waxed paper that would pull your fillings out if you tried to chew it. There were prizes in the boxes, and they would show the audience some great things that were in some of the boxes. One of the things that they always showed as a possible prize was a pair of ladies' nylon hose. This would have been soon enough after WWII when women couldn't get such an item, and people still thought these were great prizes. One time Lloyd Ray won a pretty nice Indian blanket. Their plays were three acts and at intermission they read short commercials for local businesses, performed comedy and songs. Johnny Standley was an Oklahoma musician and comedian who told his fans, "It's in the Book." In the late 1950s, Standley sold more than 1 million copies of his record *It's in the Book*, a song that included imitations of a country preacher. He used this evangelistic style of acting to pretend to be serious about simple subjects, according to classmate Bill Wilmeth's memory. The recording was a live performance of Standley accompanied by his Musical Knights. Standley also recorded *Grandma's Lye Soap* and gained some minor fame from it. Standley, from Oklahoma City, began his career touring with his family. He also toured with Red Skelton during World War II. Jack Standley was an uncle to Larry and Paulette Steward.

CHAPTER 41

Jabbok School and Dairy

"To be happy at home," said Johnson, *"is the end of all human endeavor."*

THE BRETHREN IN Christ Church ran a boarding school about a mile southwest of town. The main building was three stories, with the top floor being the girls' dorm. The other two floors were classrooms. The boys had their dormitory in a separate building next to the main school. To help support the school, they operated a dairy and delivered milk in glass bottles with cardboard stoppers to patrons in town. The students did most of the work to help pay their tuition. Once a month, they came to school and presented an assembly program of gospel singing. Jabbok is a Biblical name for a river in Israel. My Great Uncle Pete Friesen owned a farm south of town, one mile east of the Brethren in Christ Church. He also preached for them. Engle, Switzer, Frymirer, Deck, and Eyster were prominent names in this community. This community of religious people were also known as the River Brethren because they baptized by immersion in creeks and rivers. They were more liberal in their approach to the world than the Amish. The River Brethren were unique in that the men did not wear neckties to church as was the practice of the Amish. The men did not grow beards after marriage as did the Amish; however, the women did wear prayer caps like the Amish women.

The Jabbok School was originally founded as an orphanage and school by President Eisenhower's uncle. When Abe Eisenhower came to Oklahoma as a missionary for their church, he sold his house in Abilene, Kansas, to his brother, President Eisenhower's father. After a while, the school began serving whites instead of Indians.

There was an Amish community southeast of town. Principal Amish names were Bontrager, Miller, Stutzman, Yoder, Mast, Wingard, Schrock, and Beachy. These people drove wagons and buggies pulled by horses. They had no electricity, telephones, or cars. Their tractors did not have rubber tires. They wanted to live out of the modern world as much as possible. They gradually eased into more worldly possessions as time went along for economic reasons. Mother used to take them to the doctor, and they would use our telephone occasionally.

CHAPTER **42**

Dating

"They say for every boy and girl there's just one love in this whole world."
– Sonny James ("Young Love")

"BOY MEETS GIRL" is a theme that is timeless — Helen and Paris, Heloise and Abelard, Romeo and Juliet. Love is the oldest story in the world. We were no different in Thomas as we were occasionally pierced by the arrow of Cupid, as well as experiencing the normal periods of teenage angst, as we began moving on to girls and dating and fitting in with the mores and restrictions of being in our mid-teens. It has been said that one is only really alive, in the fullest sense, when you're in love. Young love, puppy love, a crush, infatuation, or whatever one wants to call it probably started in late elementary or early junior high. If word ever got around that you were "sweet" on someone, you risked the shame of having someone chalk things like "Jimmy Loves Janice" on the sidewalk in front of the school. All you could do was pray for rain. A more permanent way to show affection when one was a little older was to carve hearts and initials on trees.

A Saturday night date in Thomas consisted of a young swain picking up his girlfriend around 7:15 p.m. for a 7:30 moving picture show, not wanting to spend too much time having to make small talk with your date's parents. We were always courtly in opening and closing the car door for our date. We would use a quart of drugstore aftershave so that we would smell like fresh air. I alternated between Yardley's and Old Spice — the height of sophistication. I think the girls wore Evening in Paris perfume that came in those little blue bottles. After the movie, you would go to the drugstore for the obligatory stiff Cherry Coke. The drugstore was the national park of Thomas teenage bliss. After the drugstore, one would cruise Main a few times listening to rock 'n' roll on the radio as we circumnavigated town and then on to your favorite lover's lane parking place out in the country. As one song says, "On soft summer nights we'd hide from the lights." One would smooch or neck (hugging and kissing were the main pursuit of our passionate endeavors) while listening to "Your Hit Parade." "Indian Hill" was a popular parking place and a major player in the lives of many people, our version of "Inspiration Point." Many car windows were fogged up on that hill. Karen Sweeney and Terral McKellips always parked on a hill because Terral's old Buick frequently wouldn't start. The rather draconian curfew rules imposed on us by most of our parents required the girls to be home by 10:00. I had to be home by 10:30. Our amorous pursuits were relatively innocent and in comparison with the modern generations, ours was an innocence which bordered on arrested development. Most of the girls were maidenly scrupulous. Our Saturday nights were void of any abandon and excesses. Most of us were in constant year-round training because of football, basketball, and track anyway. In addition to going to the movies, other activities that presented opportunities for dates would be after ball games, church, class parties, carnivals, skating, walking-around dates where we simply walked around town and met up with others as if there were no tomorrows. Also, swimming dates at Roman Nose, Auld Lang Syne parties on New Year's Eve each year, other soirees and the proms were fun times. Some parlor games we played at parties would have been post office, spin the bottle, drop-the-handkerchief, musical chairs, and gossip. Sometimes, we would park downtown in the center median to simply watch who would be out and about and for us to be seen. You had to be seen. I guess this was our way of making an entrance. We would also drag

Main Street so that the people on the sidewalks and those leaning on car fenders visiting would have some entertainment. Also, everyone did a fair amount of double dating. Thank the Lord for the nighttime. Or, as Lord Byron so eloquently put it:

She walks in beauty, like the night
Of cloudless climes and starry skies;
And all that's best of dark and bright
Meet in her aspect and her eyes;
Thus mellowed to that tender light
Which heaven to gaudy day denies.

We would go to Springlake Amusement Park in Oklahoma City a couple of times each summer. In addition to the Tunnel of Love, they had a fun house, the Big Dipper roller coaster, a very large swimming pool, the mirror walk, the air-jets blowing girls' skirts up à la Marilyn Monroe — the man in the booth controlling everything. Also, they had the barrel roll, the wooden slide waxed slick, and the burlap bags you rode down on like flying carpets, the merry-go-round, the mechanical fortuneteller in the turban with hands full of cards and arms moving up and down when you put your nickel in, and an outdoor amphitheater where concerts were held. We once attended a Johnny Cash concert in this theater. It cost $1. They had bumper cars with their electrical smell and sparks as you tried to ram and slam your buddies."

Going steady" was a popular dating practice. The announcement that a boy and girl were going steady meant that the two had agreed to an exclusive relationship but were not serious enough to continue with formal engagement and marriage. Wearing your boyfriend's class ring with a wad of tape wrapped around it so that it would fit, wearing it around your neck as a necklace, wearing a gold state champion football medal or track medals as a necklace were the main means of showing everyone that you were going steady. Some girls wore little dog collars on their left foot to tell they had a boyfriend and on their right foot if they did not, indicating they were available. And who could ever forget those ubiquitous cherry chocolates everyone always gave their girlfriend for Valentine's Day?

Those lazy summer nights were always fun, but harvest would always interrupt this. It was kind of sad having to leave the girls behind every year as we headed north to cut wheat. *Parting is such sweet sorrow . . .* I guess the old maxim that *absence makes the heart grow fonder* is true because both the boys and girls always looked forward to the harvest being over. We boys thought we were cooler than moonbeams coming home with our really swarthy suntans having gotten rid of that pasty white winter look. This brief two- to three-week period between getting home from harvest and the beginning of school just might have been my favorite time of the year. It made me feel like a school boy on Sunday, not wanting it to end. There was a lightness of heart I hadn't experienced since winning our last state championship. Hammerstein had it right, "There Is Nothing Like a Dame," or Irving Berlin's "A Pretty Girl Is Like a Melody." And I can document this. Chaucer wrote in *The Canterbury Tales*, "What is better than jasper? Gold. What is better than gold? Wisdom. What is better than wisdom? Woman. What is better than a good woman? Nothing." This is from the *Tale of Melibeus*, the most boring of all the tales, some would say.

CHAPTER 43

The Prom

"A White Sport Coat and a Pink Carnation." – Marty Robbins

PROM IS SHORT for *promenade* — a dance or gathering of high school students. It figured greatly in our school culture and was a major event among the high school students. In some schools the juniors called it the Junior Prom and the seniors called it the Senior Prom. Most, however, called it the Junior-Senior Prom. For most of us it was our first big social event, our first real dress-up occasion, and for some the first time to use the family car after dark.

A tradition at Thomas with proms was the selection of sophomores to be servers for the juniors and seniors. I was one of those chosen my sophomore year to serve at the "Hawaiian Cruise" in the decorated high school gym. The male servers wore white trousers and Hawaiian shirts. The girls wore sarongs.

When I was a junior, our prom theme was "Moonlight and Roses" held at the Roman Nose Lodge. In the crowded banquet room the odors of perfume and cologne created a jungle of smells. As class president, I adjusted the microphone to give a short speech called "Remembrances in Roses." I don't remember anything about this speech because I didn't write it. It came in the theme package deal with the decorations. I think I did okay in delivering this homily, but I doubt it would have impressed Daniel Webster. We did not have a tradition at Thomas to elect the honorary Prom King and Queen. My date was Glenda Reiswig, and I wore a light-colored suit thinking I looked quite svelte for my first big social event, but it did somehow give me a feeling of empowerment. The carnations in her corsage looked a little wilted as I helped her pin it on, but she politely said nothing. It was a magical night as we slow-danced cheek to cheek to the mellow and cheerful rhythms of the jukebox music. We had not yet advanced to the hip-swaying and shimmying of true rock-'n'-roll dances such as the bop, jitterbug, and twist. It was obvious that we would never dance for the Bolshoi.

Our senior prom was also held at Roman Nose with a theme of "Stairways to the Stars," but I stupidly didn't have a date. A group of us got all dressed up like pallbearers and went as a posse, thinking we might get lucky and get sprinkled with a touch of stardust, I guess. Other than the teachers lending a bit of gravitas, I remember the event as an evening of light hearts and bubbling laughter. I wore a dark suit this year with my shoes shining like a mirror. I don't remember if Hoagy Carmichael's "Stardust" was played that night, but this is a good place to mention that I think "Stardust" just might be the loveliest melody I have ever heard. I didn't date too much my senior year because I spent too many Saturday nights at Southwestern watching Richard play football. Southwestern basketball was also a big draw for me. Richard worked in the concession stand at the basketball games and gave me all the popcorn and soda I wanted. From about the seventh grade through grade twelve, he was the wind beneath my wings. And he taught me and Jackie how to not throw like a girl.

CHAPTER 44

Senior Trip

"You can't go home again." – Thomas Wolfe

IT WAS A tradition at THS for the seniors to take an out-of-state trip at the end of school. It was a time to have one last adventure with classmates, create lasting memories, and to celebrate the impending end of school. Usually, the THS seniors went to Galveston, Texas. For some reason, we decided to go to a dude ranch in Bandera, Texas, a place that billed itself as the Cowboy Capital of the World. I think the sponsors thought that this would be the easiest and safest way to control and keep all of us out of trouble and make life easier for them. I barely made it back in time from the state track meet before the bus left. I don't really remember this trip being remarkable. I couldn't believe we covered more territory than Lewis and Clark just to get to this place where there really wasn't much to do except eat, swim, and ride horses. Some of us had some wild, quixotic notions, but I don't think we were successful in pulling any of them off. We did manage to sneak up to the windows of the girl cabins and at least visit with some of the girls late at night. The most daring thing to happen on this trip was the smuggling of *Peyton Place* on the bus before leaving by one of the girls. This book was about the social and sexual hypocrisy of a small New England town. I haven't been able to nail down who did this. These shenanigans were reasonable predictions, I think, for a senior trip. Some of the girls once had a slumber party devoted entirely to the reading of this book from cover to cover. One of the girls worked at the drugstore, and at closing time sold herself a copy when the boss was occupied in another part of the store. Camden, Maine, is the town that was the inspiration for the setting of *Peyton Place*.

There was a sense of melancholy when we arrived back home for graduation week. The senior trip had been like *two ships passing in the night*. It was a time when life was so tender, very much like the Beach Boys song "Graduation Day" says: "It's a time for joy, a time for tears, a time we'll treasure through the years." It was a time before the tumult of the '60s, before Kent State, the anti-war protests, and other utopian movements, before the race riots of Atlanta, Chicago, Detroit, and Watts. Life as we knew it, however, would change forever. That world of my innocence was coming to an end. Our high school days were over. It was time to cut the umbilical cord. The "carnival" was over. These were unrecoverable moments. There would never be another time like the graduation and senior trip days had been. We didn't know what the future held or if we would ever be together again. Yet, I don't recall any of us ever mourning our carefree childhood. I would go back and visit from time to time, but it was never the same. Passing through town and visiting the old farm felt nothing like the country paradise I remembered. Nothing is ever the same. Once you change something, you can never go back to the way it was before. However, even if things and people change, memories do not. Thomas Wolfe says, "You can't go home again." Chris Hillman was saying the same thing when he said, "You can go home again, but you can't go back." What they are all saying is, you can go home again but don't expect it to look like the home you left. The past is something you were once, but can never be again. All the things you thought were permanent do change. Even though things have changed remarkably, Thomas is still an inseparable part of me, and I enjoy going back periodically to visit old friends. Wasn't this the theme of *The Iliad* and *Odyssey* — longing for home? Perhaps the truth, often as tangled and murky as our memories, is that a boy's innocence and a town's charm both fade with time? Ritu Ghatourey has written, "I've learned that things change, people change, and it doesn't mean you forget the past or try to cover it up. It simply means that you move on and treasure the memories."

As an adult, I have often known that peculiar feeling that time occasionally brings. A yearning for something that's lost. The longing to seek out a place a second time, to find what we stumbled on once before, to recapture the feeling of discovery. It can be an unremarkable place — a place we look for simply because we remember it. If we do find it, of course, everything is different. The old building, door, alley, or sign is still there, but it's much smaller. The hill is not nearly so steep or the road winding. Some of the old fences are sagging and uneven, there are weed-choked trails, a broken windmill, a crooked old barn, etc. Stanley Cohen seems to have captured the feeling. "It seems now as if it were all part of another lifetime. As the years pile up and fold into decades, and what once burned bright in memory recedes into the more remote pockets of hazy recollection, we treat the past as if it were a vault in which events can be stored and preserved against the incursions of time. Time stakes its claim. Memory is an untrustworthy guide. It can be elusive and tricky. The tale, cast anew each time, becomes transformed in the telling. The facts, of course, are always the same; it is the way we see them and feel about them that changes." Perhaps A.E. Housman can shed some further understanding:

Into my heart an air that kills
From yon far country blows:
What are those blue remembered hills,
What spires, what farms are those?
That is the land of lost content,
I see it shining plain,
The happy highways where I went And cannot come again.

CHAPTER 45

Afterword

"Nostalgia is like a grammar lesson . . . you find the present tense, and the past perfect."

– *Reminisce* Magazine

SO, AS THE swell of "Pomp and Circumstance" set us marching like grand peacocks, or at least shuffling, we proceeded down the aisle in our unaccustomed, unflattering rented white gowns and feeling faintly ridiculous in our mortarboards. For a brief moment it was difficult to find an answering emotion in myself, but as we continued the march I would swear that I heard Handel's "Hallelujah Chorus" playing in my head. We flipped the tassels from one side to the other as the vestiges of time slipped through the hourglass, and I received my diploma, filling in one more piece of my jigsaw puzzle. This was our ultimate moment — graduation — at Thomas High. What did the valedictorian say? As I glanced at my new Wittnauer wristwatch given to me by my parents as a graduation gift, I thought, does anyone really care or remember? The outside world was beckoning. I was eighteen years old, still soft at the edges, but confident good things would come my way.

Our carefree cocoon days into which we were immersed came to an end on May 22, 1958 — salad days that I could not have enjoyed more. Time that we savored and soaked up like a sponge. We were young, rash, joyful, energized, expectant, and the future seemed a distant rumor. *The world was our oyster.* Fitzgerald wrote, "There went my old safe secure world," but we did not yet know that. At our young and tender age, we did not know that the world could be dingy and flawed and that most of our innocence would fall away. We had the sense of invulnerability as did all boys of this age. Future probabilities or possibilities were not allowed to interfere with the pleasures of the present. It was a halcyon time in an era that roared. We felt the planet turn. The anesthetized 1950s were an era of conformity, prosperity, and rock 'n' roll. Most of the stuff written about the '50s is good enough in which to grow roses. It's written down somewhere. It's got to be. Man, we probably blew through more good times in these fleeting school years than most people do in a lifetime. As Jaques Brel wrote, "We had joy, we had fun. We had seasons in the sun." Cloaked in these vivid memories were my childhood, my adolescence, and the world that I left behind to embrace and discover a new world and bold course. We were uninhibited, naive, untested, often unwise, and our days were filled with adventure. Our heads were not filled with grand and noble ideas, and we did not fully appreciate the everyday complexities of our lives. My memories stand strong, stretched like an elastic band even though I am sure they are colored by the tricks that the passage of time and old age play on memory. One thing is for sure. We did not live a cloistered life. My life was a documentary to adventure, fun, and achievement. It was kind of like what Sherlock Holmes said: "Life is infinitely stranger than anything which the mind of man could invent." Even though high school graduation closed a part of my life, I did not make a valedictory tour of the school and town because I knew I would be coming back like salmon from time to time. I was excited about the independence of leaving home and going to college, but knew I had far to go. However, I don't think it ever occurred to me that others had done this before me.

At times it seemed we had more end-arounds than Mr. Ross's playbook, and they say that sap runs in the spring, but with my friends and me it seemed to run all year and we weren't able to sidestep all the potholes with our overactive imaginations. We seethed with youthful exuberance, energy, creativity, and passion, but it was all somehow manageable and the world continued to spin on its axis. We were the Barnum and Bailey of bold adventures. At times we were stirred with excesses and sailed a little too close to the wind. Some of the ornery contrivances in which we indulged might have seemed a little over the line, but our misdeeds paled in comparison to kids in the big cities. Even students of an earlier time, it appears, were more daring than THS students in the twentieth century. David McCullough, writing in *The Greater Journey — Americans in Paris*, tells about James Fenimore Cooper getting expelled from Yale for "locking a donkey in a recitation room and setting off a homemade bomb under a door in a dormitory," among other things. I have also read in other memoirs in which recorded events were far worse than anything my friends and I ever did. We never organized any panty raids, never ran naked as jaybirds around the school circle and through the goldfish pond on May Day, and never tore down any goal posts. What most torments me about the foolishness of my youth is not the crazy things I have done, but the fact that I can't go back and do them again. Robin Williams once said, "You are only given a little spark of madness once. Don't lose it." I read once that we really never grow up, we only learn how to act in public. But then, I have never tried to extinguish the child in myself and Gertrude Stein has said, "We are always the same age inside." In spite of all the trouble that found us, I wonder in retrospect why we didn't bring even more calamity down upon us. If everything had played out in a more normal manner without the unexpected twists and turns of the plot, our performance would not have been as memorable. So, I guess that maybe it was best that our frontal lobes had not yet fully developed. Considering how we all turned out, I would say it is a great tribute to redemption. A lot of the stories written in this memoir are funny because we lived them, and survived them. If I had not dared to do a lot of these adventures I might never, later on, have dared to do anything. We were fortunate to not live in a litigious society like the one that exists today. We would not have had nearly as much fun. Emerson must have been thinking of us when he said, "Congratulate yourself if you have done something strange and extravagant and broken the monotony of a decorous age." Those were happy days in so many, many ways.

1950s rural Oklahoma was an insulated, unshackled time of innocence for teenagers. We had no taxes to pay and no big responsibilities. We were not yet jumbled by the obligations of being a grown-up. We sensed that this was probably the last time in our lives that would be relatively unpressured. We were indeed nurtured, wet nursed, and shepherded in one end of childhood and out the other in relative safety by the unremitting labors of our parents, relatives, teachers, and neighbors with a minimum of broken bones, no head trauma, and no time in juvenile hall. Perhaps Wordsworth's lines commemorating the French Revolution resonated with us: "Bliss was it in that dawn to be alive, but to be young was very heaven!"

Eisenhower was president, *Gigi* won the best movie award, David Niven the best actor in *Separate Tables*, best actress was Susan Hayward in *I Want to Live*, Tim Tam won the Kentucky Derby, the Nobel Prize for literature was won by Boris Pasternak for *Dr. Zhivago*, the World Series was won by the New York Yankees over the Milwaukee Braves 4–3, the NFL champs were the Baltimore Colts, LSU was the AP national NCAA football champs, the Heisman Trophy was awarded to Pete Dawkins of Army, the National Basketball Association champs were the St. Louis Hawks, and the Explorer I satellite first orbited the earth in 1958.

The 1950s spawned its fair share of movie classics: *Ten Commandments, Sunset Boulevard, A Streetcar Named Desire, Some Like It Hot, Singing in the Rain, Roman Holiday, Rebel Without a Cause, On the Waterfront, From Here to Eternity, Ben Hur, Giant, and On the Beach*.

Notable musicals that were popular in the '50s would include *Peter Pan, Brigadoon, Carousel, Guys and Dolls, The King and I, A Tree Grows in Brooklyn, Oklahoma, Kiss Me Kate, Porgy and Bess, Can-Can, South Pacific, Damn Yankees, My Fair Lady, The Music*

Man, *West Side Story*, and *The Sound of Music*.

It has been said that music is what feelings sound like. Nietzsche said, "Without music life would be a mistake." I have read that of the nicer things in life, music was the most missed by the pioneers who settled the Western frontier. Music can probably evoke memories and emote the soul as much as anything, especially all the doo-wop crooning, melodies, and soulful love songs of the 1950s. This is when music first started mattering to me and *will linger in my ears for years to come*. A sampling of music from what I think was the golden age of American pop music would be: "At the Hop," "Sugar-time," "Catch a Falling Star," "Bird Dog," "Young Love," "Twelfth of Never," "Party Doll," "Little Darlin," "Marianne," "A White Sport Coat," "Old Cape Cod," "Tammy," "Honeycomb," "Chances Are," "Unchained Melody," "Three Coins in the Fountain," "Love Is a Many Splendored Thing," "Autumn Leaves," "The Wayward Wind," "April Love," and "Peggy Sue." "Peggy Sue" might just be the greatest piece of music ever written. LOL! Buddy Holly should be *beatified*. The Coaster's "Yakety Yak" (1958) was the first stereo recording to make it into the top ten. Many of these tunes are obviously musically sophomoric and the lyrics a bit maudlin, but they reflected the era perfectly and could make the air sparkle for me. I loved listening to them on the radio, the TV show *Your Hit Parade*, and on Wurlitzer jukeboxes with those bubbly, colorful lights. Jukeboxes were sometimes called nickelodeons because one had to plug them with nickels. The melodious pop music of the '50s has been replaced by something that brings to my mind dueling leaf blowers and lyrics written for juvenile delinquents.

As I reflect on what was almost *Camelot*, I feel like doing what Arturo Toscanini did when he first viewed the Grand Canyon. He said nothing and after a few minutes he simply applauded. My path was relatively smooth, predictable, and has been decked with more roses than thorns, more mountaintops than valleys, much sunshine, many rainbows, and many Good Samaritans in my foxhole who lit me up, cheered me on, made me laugh, contributed largesse to my life, and made most of my life's memories so sweet. I can never repay the no-strings attached love of these charitable people. What is it about high school that made you friends for life, regardless of the time that had passed? Why did those few years create this strange bond? Why have these relationships been so sustainable? I clearly won the lottery with all my pals and Richard and Jackie as we shouldered one another through the years. My brothers were unflaggingly generous, magnanimous, and unselfish to me. Thanking them is hardly sufficient, but I thank you in spades for helping give me one of the best childhoods a kid could have ever wanted. I have many cherished memories of the Friesen brothers, and we are fortunate that Mother managed to take an abundance of photos, thoughtfully preserving moments of yesteryear for subsequent days of happy recollection and poignant reflection. These photos help substantiate what I have written in this document and bring to life much more. While authors throughout time have penned humble words in valiant efforts to describe the bond between brothers, perhaps my favorite of all those words remains these precious few: "He ain't heavy; he's my brother." Though strikingly simple, they herald a relationship more complex, intricately woven throughout shared lifetimes — a relationship at once intangible, and embraceable — a brotherhood the three of us were divinely blessed to hold. This was a brotherhood by blood and choice.

I will always feel a comforting rush of gratitude for everything I'm leaving behind. I have never been the eternal optimist that *Candide's* Dr. Pangloss was, but I have been blessed and as Douglas Adams said, "I may not have gone where I intended to go, but I think I have ended up where I needed to be." With my limited time on this planet, I think I have lived my life in a way that mattered. Even in charmed lives a little rain must fall, and there were times when I had to run against the wind when life would throw a curveball, but I always seemed to somehow find a firm stepping stone, I never felt weirdly unanchored or adrift, and no one has ever attempted to amputate my spirit. No one ever tried to snuff out my passion for life. At least my life would never become a country music song. If you would have told me at the age of 15 that my life would have turned out the way it has, I would have said, "Give me a pen so I can sign off on it." Or, as Thoreau wrote, "My life has been the poem I would have writ." I am probably recalling those days with more fondness than they deserve; I may have embellished those times a little and we all have a tendency to see the past through rose-colored glasses. I suppose that I have been impeded, somewhat, by the mellowing effect that the erosion of time has, particularly on painful memories. That is the game memory plays, but I wouldn't trade it for *Aladdin's Lamp*. It was a time for *joie de vivre* to blossom all around us. I have had a front-row seat to "Masterpiece Theater."

I hope this little trip down memory lane hasn't come across as sentimental hooey, even though there does seem to be something genetically encoded into the aging process that makes one lament that nothing was as good as in one's youth and the magnetic pull of the meandering road of nostalgia. I hope I have offered some sentiment without sentimentality, and it has not been my intent to make myself the valorous hero of my story. Also, I have not been searching for youth and laughter left in Thomas — just indelible memories. Don Larson, a columnist, has said, "Nostalgia is a file that removes the rough edges from the good old days." Maybe so. Then there is this from *The Book of Counted Sorrows*: "In the real world as in dreams, nothing is quite what it seems." I have focused this writing almost exclusively on the distant past, beginning sixty years ago, in an attempt to explain myself, to recount interesting experiences, and maybe bring some perspective to our changing circumstances as we enter the twenty-first century. I have attempted to write true accounts that have, hopefully, conveyed the very fabric and essence of life in the '40s and '50s. Another reason for writing these reminiscences is that anytime I might want to be transported back to this mosaic memory, I only have to pick up this manuscript, read it again, and experience the richness of memory. If that is not magic, what is? Somehow youth remains with us. As William Faulkner once wrote, "The past is never dead, it is not even past." Kierkegaard has written, "Life can only be understood backwards, but it must be lived forwards."

I left Thomas several years ago and parts of the town have worn away like a bar of soap. It is also gently crumbling around the edges with only remnants of many of the old buildings left, but I'm making sure that it will never leave me. I ponder how lucky I was growing up in a town like Thomas in an era like the '40s and '50s. The town on the surface might have seemed poor, but was in so many important ways not poor. I realize that when I passed through I did not understand that I had been remarkably privileged. We never had to worry about a Bhopal, Three Mile Island, or Love Canal. It is almost like we were all from the same gene pool. The small-town way of life no longer exists as it once did. The small-town paradise was a cherished reality for my generation, and I feel like I really "struck ore" there. But, Main Street isn't the Main Street I once knew and the lights don't shine as when I was a boy. However, a part of this writing is an attempt to feed its soul. We still have small towns, but with TV and the Internet they're not the isolated front-porch-culture places that they once were. The world was just different back in my childhood. Time goes by and time brings changes. People change too and process the past in different ways. Come what may it is still our town, but faded in grandeur. There's no getting it back, but I can still dream of Thomas green as Dorothy did of the Emerald City as I dredge up buried memories I hadn't visited in years. I will remember the old familiar storefronts of Thomas like old friends. As Nelson DeMille wrote in *The Gate House*, "In some ways, we have come to the end of an era, but these old dramas do not really end, because as someone wisely said, the past is prologue to the future, and short of a meteor strike and mass extinction, the dramas of each generation roll on into the next." However, I still feel a part of the vanished world because of the strong emotional association I still have with my early impressionable years. I am grateful for having gone down the paths that I have, for having this access to enchantment, this way of remembering that stories count, memories matter. I guess we never exactly ever leave Thomas. Thomas was not exotic. It was just special and home.

Dickens has written, "How many friends who have been dispersed and scattered far and wide, in the restless struggles of life, are then reunited, and meet again in the happy state of companionship, which is a source of such pure delight. How many old recollections, and how many dormant sympathies, does a school reunion awaken."

We all leave a trail of little pebbles scattered on the forest floor. So, think about the legacy that you are going to be leaving behind. Sometime, read Rudyard Kipling's poem, "If." "If you can keep your head when all about you are losing theirs and blaming it on you, If you can trust yourself when all men doubt you . . ." Also, remember how lucky you are to live under the protective glow of the *Magna Carta*, the Great Charter of English liberties and the human rights that grew from it, which was signed in 1215 at Runnymede, a hallowed site in the annals of English history. The *Magna Carta* is the foundation of English law — bulwark against tyranny.

Oscar Wilde said, "At times you may find yourself in the gutter, just be sure that you are looking at the stars." Keep your dreams close to your pillow, hold them tight, and remember that the horizon is not that far away. Occasionally, as Stephen Foster wrote, "Sup sorrow with the poor." Remember what Victor Hugo wrote in *Les Misérables*: "What is said about men often has as much influence upon their lives, and especially upon their destinies, as what they do." Live a good honorable life and enjoy whatever is going on now. Then when you get older and think back, you'll enjoy it a second time. Keep a song in your heart, and try to contribute joy to the world; be kind, be polite, be appreciative, be content, do good things, be kind to yourself, leave a path, grow flowers, look for the goodness in people, remember the good times, live through the bad times, love always, give thanks to God often, listen to love's melody, and your soul will have wings. Be aware of the fragility and preciousness of time. May you be worthy of your mother — a rose folded with all of God's sweet chosen words. Remember that Sophocles said, "All men make mistakes, but a good man yields when he knows his course is wrong, and repairs the evil . . ." Whitman wrote, "The powerful play goes on, and you will contribute a verse." Frequently read Romans 12:9–21 and remember that half of beauty is attitude.

When you girls were growing up, your mother and I made every conscious effort to give you good advice and to put you on the right paths. However, the final forming of your character lies in your own hands. As of this writing you have done well in this regard and have made us proud. Keep soldiering on and make your own children as proud of you as your mother and I are of you.

So, it was there, as a boy, where this great receptacle of visual images and memories formed in my mind like photographs. And now, until the fat lady sings — *Carpe diem*.

Acknowledgments

"God gave us memory so that we could have roses in December."
– J.M. Barrie

THIS MEMOIR WAS begun after I retired from being an elementary school teacher and principal for 37 years. I was sitting around, allegedly working in a part-time job, when I had the thought of writing about my childhood and adolescent experiences — the most frightening terrain imaginable. Hopefully, I have made a bit of a contribution to the literary canon of boyhood, adolescence, and high school. Below are listed the people who helped me gather information when needed and helped make this document better than it would have otherwise been.

It would have been nice to have had an agent, editor, and publicist; but, alas, I didn't have the luxury of these services. Nor did I have an attorney to vet and provide me with clarity on any possible legal issues, but I think I am on pretty solid ground with most of what has been written, even though there has been a certain amount of embellishment that I hope will not damage or taint my self-portrait. I do apologize if I have attached levity in places where some might consider it inappropriate. I also apologize to those who have read this document and wished they had not. Further, if you are bothered by the idea of this being real, you are invited to pretend that it is fiction, or make up your own version.

The process of transforming an idea into a memoir was not a long and complicated one for me. It was a labor of love. To a degree, this memoir is a collaboration between me and the people who populate its pages. First and foremost, I wish to acknowledge the generosity of those who have allowed their real names and actions to appear in this memoir.

My accolades are bequeathed doubly to my two brothers for their help when my memory became fuzzy about a story or memory. At those times I depended on Jackie or Richard, whose memories were many times more vivid than mine — ultimate friends and champions on my behalf. Bring up the trumpets and drums for their help. Also, I sometimes relied on classmates or friends to confirm, correct, and assist in general ways. Thanks to the charter members of the Compassionate Classmates and Friends Society — Dr. Karen Sweeney McKellips, Lloyd Ray, Jerry Vickers, Larry Steward, Maynard Book, Eddie Beck, Jim Ames, David Stratton, Ross Pickens, Keren Payne Miller, Kenny Jones, Gary Helzer, Gene "Sally" McCall, Ray Cain, Kay Comer Horn, Fay Comer Powers, Billy Wilmeth, Alberta Ryan, Larry Foster, Fred "Butch" Self, Kay Halle Lancaster, Buddy Taylor, Gary Jones, and Paulette Steward Kraybill. I hear their voices as I write. I am deeply indebted to Karen, classmate extraordinaire, who has been especially encouraging and helpful. Her literary gifts, memory, friendship, love of books, and trenchant analysis of various topics are a blessing. Also, I must thank a few strangers who might have unknowingly contributed to any thoughts I have included. I want to state that all of the above mentioned individuals are free from any degree of ignorance on display here. I would like to acknowledge and plead guilty to this memoir's flaws, shortcomings, and errors, whatever you consider them to be. They remain mine alone.

I thank all of you who have made it this far in your reading, because I have put more fluff in this manuscript than anyone's patience should allow.

And last, but not least, I would like to thank my daughter Kara for her writing acumen and help with some of the grammar editing which makes me sound smarter than I really am, the copy editor at Outskirts Press, and my daughter Kela for her help in getting this project started and putting together the original document with photos for the family. I swoon with gratefulness before my wife Nancy for her tolerance, simple kindness, forbearance, and her heartened patience of my not being able to put this silly thing to rest. Nancy, Kara, and

Kela shine a beautiful light on the universe — a gentle splendor —infusing my life with sunshine. To paraphrase a popular football cliché, I definitely out-kicked my punt coverage when Nancy joined me on this life journey. My cup runneth over.

Looking back over the meandering route that brought me to this writing, I find that I owe an enormous debt of gratitude to so many good, kind, and compassionate people whose friendship has warmed me all my life. This is a small hymn to a veneration of wonderful family, friends, teachers, and a unique village of long ago — a community really — whom I have valued and appreciated over these many years. I am perpetually amazed at how this community helped to choreograph my life and expose me to the cultural substance that is so much a part of me today.

CPSIA information can be obtained
at www.ICGtesting.com
Printed in the USA
BVHW081139130620
581307BV00002B/62